RELIGION

RELIGION

An Introduction

T. William Hall
Richard B. Pilgrim
Ronald R. Cavanagh

1817

Harper & Row, Publishers, San Francisco

Cambridge, Hagerstown, New York, Philadelphia
London, Mexico City, São Paulo, Singapore, Sydney

RELIGION: *An Introduction.* Copyright © 1985 by T. William Hall, Richard B. Pilgrim, and Ronald R. Cavanagh. All rights reserved. Printed in the United States of America. No part of this book may be used or reproduced in any manner whatsoever without written permission except in the case of brief quotations embodied in critical articles and reviews. For information address Harper & Row, Publishers, Inc., 10 East 53rd Street, New York, NY 10022. Published simultaneously in Canada by Fitzhenry & Whiteside, Limited, Toronto.

FIRST EDITION

Library of Congress Cataloging-in-Publication Data

Hall, T. William (Thomas William).
  Religion: an introduction.

  Includes index.
  1. Religion. 2. Religions. I. Pilgrim, Richard B.
II. Cavanagh, Ronald R.   III. Title.
BL48.H297 1985   200   85-42777
ISBN 0-06-063573-8 (pbk.)

85 86 87 88 89 HC 10 9 8 7 6 5 4 3 2 1

Contents

Preface

Why study religion? There are at least two related answers. First, because it is out there. Religion is an aspect of human life and culture expressed in beliefs, rituals, scriptures, the arts and morality. To neglect such a study is to be cut off from understanding a major aspect of human existence. Second, religion is a dynamic dimension within every individual. Persons inevitably search for the meaning of birth, love, pain, death—all of life. This quest may be carried out while one is a devout participant in some religious tradition or by one who does not affirm any corporate expression of religion. In either case, the desire to grapple with the fundamental issues of life is ignored at our own impoverishment.

The study of religion, then, will constantly focus both outwardly and inwardly. The study demands rigorous investigation of characteristic expressions of religion wherever they are found in order to understand what is out there—to discover how religion functions and in what way it relates to the whole of culture. At the same time, religious studies demand reflective thought about one's own values, varied symbolic expressions having power for the self, and awareness of one's own response to what is affirmed as ultimate. It is no wonder that the study of religion has become so important for students and has been accepted as part of most liberal arts curricula!

As the study of religion has expanded within colleges and universities in recent years, it has also matured. No longer do scholars and teachers advocate one kind of religion or suppose that existential questions have but one answer. Rather, we have concluded that the study of religion can and must be as academically responsible—neither proselytizing nor debunking—as any other branch of the human sciences, while addressing issues that lie at the heart of culture and every person's search for value and meaning.

Moreover, within a contemporary world perspective, we find data about religions from every continent. Thus in a thorough study we encounter religious expressions in the Middle East, Africa, East Asia, South Asia, as well as in Europe and the Americas. While no single course can deal in depth with all religious data, we can no longer ignore examination of what religion is and what it means for persons all over the world.

All persons, of course, bring to this study their own personal information and attitudes about religion. Yet a formal study needs an orderly plan to prevent us from merely rehashing present opinions or becoming lost in the miscellaneous information we may already have about religion. That orderly plan is provided in this introductory text.

Part I of this book is an invitation to the reader to participate in defining religion as something we can study as well as an invitation to explore how and why religion might be studied. The major section, part II, examines eight universal expressions of religion, drawing upon illustrations from many religions and cultures throughout the world. These chapters focus on individual and community religious expressions we have called the holy, sacred story, ritual, the arts, belief, scripture, and morality. Following the examination of this variety of religious expressions—an examination that may be augmented by films, novels, works of art, or other resources—we look back over these many expressions in part III to see how they function within particular religions. We then explore important methods for the study of religion and conclude by looking ahead into the future of religion.

While most of the content of this book has not previously been published, the entire volume has evolved from an earlier book, *Introduction to the Study of Religion.** Suggestions from readers of that book, along with continued teaching of an introductory course in religion at Syracuse University, resulted in something new—a book more accessible to students and more comprehensive in presenting the many important expressions of religion throughout the world. Eight chapters are totally new; the remaining four are recast from the earlier volume to become a coherent part of this new text.

We, the three authors are members of the faculty in the Department of Religion at Syracuse University. All of us have been active in teaching the basic introductory course out of which this book grew. T. William Hall, a former chairman of the department, holds a Ph.D. from Boston University and specializes in modern religious thought. Richard B. Pilgrim holds a Ph.D. from the University of Chicago, and he specializes in the phenomenology of religion as well as the religions of the Far East and Japan. Ronald R. Cavanagh is a former chairman of the department and currently is interim Dean in the College of Arts and Sciences. With a Ph.D. from the Graduate Theological Union in Berkeley, California, he specializes in philosophical theology.

The material and structure of this book, as well as the course that formed its base, have proven to be exciting and rewarding for many students over the past several years. We appreciate the thousands of students in our course who entered enthusiastically into the study of

---

*Hall, ed. (New York: Harper & Row, 1978).

religion. Their participation, questions, and critique significantly shaped the course and this book.

We offer special thanks to the office of the Dean of the College of Arts and Sciences at Syracuse University for providing typing services. Mrs. Marilyn Bergett, with skill, patience, and good humor, helped see this project to its conclusion. We also thank our departmental colleagues and our current chairman, James B. Wiggins, for their interest in and support of the project. It is within such collegial contexts that research, thinking, writing, and teaching best take place.

T. William Hall
Richard B. Pilgrim
Ronald R. Cavanagh

Part 1

RELIGION AS A FIELD OF STUDY

CHAPTER 1

Religion as a Field of Study

Your introduction to religion as a field of study begins with an invitation that is both fundamental and crucial. When you understand the importance of this invitation you will have learned a basic fact about any field of study.

AN INVITATION

The invitation to participate in a field of study is fundamental because your contribution as a student is critical to the field. Apart from the responsible involvement of students, their personal attention and inquiring minds, no field of study could be constituted or sustained. Students supply the energy and imagination, the questions and the persistence to pursue them, that determine and maintain a field of study. A field of study is a sphere of intellectual activity produced through student involvement. Thus any effective introduction to a field of study, to its dynamics, its data, its questions and issues will require your sympathetic participation as a fellow student. You are of fundamental import to religion as a field of study.

Your response to this invitation is crucial because the quality of study within the field is at issue. That you participate is fundamental. How you participate affects the character of the understanding produced in the field. The intensity of the student's commitment to study, the breadth of a student's concern, and the focus of a student's attention directly affect for better or worse the results of a field of study. Where students are not prepared to raise new or radical questions, a field of study will produce at best the expected results. Where students of energy and imagination contribute demanding standards of inquiry, however, the products of the field may be genuinely exciting and fruitful.

If you accept our invitation, you will join a historical community of students whose desire to understand more critically the various phenomena of religion has given rise to and sustained the field of the study of religion.

A Starting Point

An appropriate starting point for our study of religion is to examine the method we will use. You might respond to our invitation with a comment and a variety of questions. Consider the following statement from a young sophomore. "I'm ready for a challenge. Sure, I have some anxiety about entering a new field, especially that of religion. People seem to be very sensitive about their religion, and I do not want to step on anyone's toes. However, I think that I could overcome my inhibitions if I better understood 'what' would be studied; 'how' it would be studied; 'why' it was being studied; and what kind of people or 'who' studies religion. At least I would be able to make a more intelligent response to your invitation."

This is a very interesting comment for a number of reasons. First, because this person speaks candidly about her own feelings, she identifies questions many people have at the beginning of a study, especially that of religion. She reminds us that at the outset of any study we might reflect on the attitudes, dispositions, feelings, or prejudices that we bring to it. Since these factors may influence the nature and results of our study, or themselves change within the context of the study, it is important that we attempt to be aware of them and their impact on our work. Therefore, we recommend that you and your fellow students discuss your attitudes about the study of religion at its outset.

Second, the student's comment is interesting because the questions it poses (what, how, why, who) press directly upon the formal structure of any field of study. They ask about the data (the "what") to be studied, the methods (the "how") to be employed, the goals (the "why") to be sought, and the background and intentions of people who study (the "who") in the field. These questions are fundamental, for a field of study is an identifiable sphere of intellectual activity with specifiable subject matters, specific methods of interrogation and interpretation, and students concerned with particular kinds of questions for which they seek appropriate and critical answers. When these questions are answered with respect to the study of religion we will have established a basic overview of the field.

How might you respond to these questions? One student responded in the following way. "Let's not complicate things. It's simple enough to understand that you study religious data in the field of religion. Therefore, let's begin our study by looking at some of these. Data have always helped me think of questions and methods. Once we know what we are dealing with, the rest of the field will fall into shape."

This comment is sound and perceptive in certain respects. Certainly data do provoke questions and, in turn, tend to suggest appropriate methods for developing responses. However, from the perspective of an academic study, it contains one major flaw. This student has assumed that religious data are clearly recognizable and obvious to everyone, and that what constitutes "religion" is commonly understood by all. We want you to challenge this assumption, for it obscures the nature of data and its creation within a field of study. Why? Consider the following question: How would a student within the field of religion recognize, identify, or locate religious data?

If we mean by the term data, "things that can be denoted or specified by some perspective of thought or speech" then data are religious to the extent that they can be thought or spoken of from the perspective of religion. All data are in part human artifacts, products of human judgment, meaning, or signification. This is true of the data of physics, chemistry, religion, or political science. Data are phenomena appearing to particular human perceivers. Data are never simply "out there" apart from human judgment. It would, therefore, be misleading to overlook the role of the student in "creating," through judgment, the data of a field of study. Students are responsible for the data included or excluded from a field of study. This much is relatively clear. What is not so clear is what is meant by the term religion and how its perspective is defined. Is there a common idea about what the term religion means? Do people mean the same thing when they talk about religion?

We think that the answer to these questions is no. The term religion means many things to many people. It is in fact highly ambiguous; it means a variety of things to different people. It is important that you come to recognize the nature of this ambiguity and the effects it could have upon an academic study. In the section to follow we will discuss some of the definitions of religion that have been used by others. In the process, we want to assist you in recognizing some of the key characteristics that distinguish the emphasis of one definition from another.

CHARACTERISTIC EMPHASES OF DEFINITIONS OF RELIGION

To help you become more sensitive to the differences in emphasis within definitions, we are going to look at eight characteristic emphases that appear in various definitions of the term *religion*. The number eight is not important; we could certainly have chosen more. These particular characteristic emphases, however, will help you to understand some of the issues that must be considered in developing our own definition of religion appropriate to an academic study.

Feeling

The first characteristic of definitions of religion is feeling. Friedrich Schleiermacher, an important nineteenth-century German theologian and philosopher, defined religion as "the feeling of absolute dependence." Notice the emphasis on feeling or emotion rather than on knowing or doing. Here the definition of religion is based on the person's feeling and intuition that he or she is completely dependent on God, the Infinite, or the Eternal. In this approach any beliefs and practices of religion must be understood as expressions of this unique feeling of absolute dependence. Schleiermacher also said that "true religion is sense and taste for the Infinite."

Ritual Activity

Ritual activity is another emphasis in some definitions of religion. Contemporary anthropologist Anthony Wallace defines religion as "a set of rituals, rationalized by myth, which mobilizes supernatural powers for the purpose of achieving or preventing transformations of state in man or nature." Notice the emphasis on organizing, doing, or acting —"achieving or preventing transformations." This definition emphasizes the performance of specific acts that are established by the religious community.

Belief

Definitions of religion commonly emphasize belief. The *Universal Dictionary of the English Language* defines religion as a "specific system of belief in God, including a group of doctrines concerning Him, and His relations to man and the universe." Notice the stress on the intellectual act of affirming doctrines rather than on the performance of any actions. In this approach all activities and feelings that are part of the religion support a belief rather than, as in the previous example, the other way around. For example, consent to such dogmas as the Nicene Creed (ca. 325 C.E.) has long been important in the Christian Church. The candidate for confirmation is asked to say, "I believe in God, the Father Almighty . . . and . . . in one Lord Jesus Christ . . . and I believe in the Holy Spirit, the Lord and Giver of Life . . ." to indicate that she or he affirms the universal truth of the Christian message.

Monotheism

The fourth distinguishing characteristic of some definitions of religion is monotheism, a term that emphasizes the important relationship between humanity and the one God. St. Thomas Aquinas (1225–1274), one of the most important theologians in the history of Roman Catholic thought, said that the term religion "denotes properly a relation to God." His definition excludes any other object except the one God as appropriate for religious relations. Judaism expresses this notion in its great creed, called the Shema: "Hear O Israel, the Lord our God, the Lord is One." Islamic scripture (the Qur'an) states, "Your God is one God. . . . There is no God but He—the living, the Eternal." Thus the faithful are called to prayer five times a day by the *muezzin*, who cries out, "There is no God but God!" In the monotheistic view neither humanism, nor communism, nor any feeling, ritual activity, or belief that does not express a relationship to this monotheistic God is properly religious because religion is essentially a relationship to one God who is conceived of as the only divine being.

The Solitary Individual

Some definitions of religion emphasize the solitary individual. Alfred North Whitehead, a prominent English-American philosopher of this century, defined religion this way: "Religion is what the individual does with his own solitariness; and if you were never solitary, you were never religious." This definition emphasizes the individual involved in an intimate personal dialogue with himself or herself. For Whitehead, the essence of religion lay in humanity's confrontation with "the awful ultimate fact, which is the human being, consciously alone with itself, for its own sake." We need to keep in mind, however, that it is possible for a person to be solitary in this sense while she or he is actually with other people; the solitariness is an inward state, not a public one.

Social Valuation

Emphasis on social valuation may appear in definitions of religion. Two anthropologists, William Lessa and Evon Vogt, state the following in a recent work on comparative religion: Religion is "a system of beliefs and prctices directed toward the 'ultimate concern' of a society." It is important to recognize that in this definition society and not the individual provides the center for religious valuation. Religious beliefs, practices, and attitudes are directed toward the expression of what a society of people holds to be of central importance. Contrast this with Whitehead's definition, which stresses the solitary individual as the center of religious valuation.

Illusion

A seventh characteristic sometimes emphasized in defining religion is illusion. Karl Marx, a nineteenth-century social philosopher whom you have probably heard of as the father of communism, defined religion this way: "Religion is the sigh of the oppressed creature. . . . It is the opium of the people. . . . Religion is only the illusory sun which revolves around man as long as he does not revolve around himself."[1] Marx's definition describes religion as primarily something that misinterprets reality. According to this definition all the beliefs, practices, and attitudes of religion reflect a distorted and essentially immature response to the universe as it actually is.

Ultimate Reality and Value

The eighth characteristic emphasis considers religion as the true focus on ultimate reality and value. John B. Magee, the author of *Reli-*

gion and the Modern Man, offers the following definition: "Religion is the realm of the ultimately real and ultimately valuable." Here religion is defined as the true and ultimate measure of people's existence, the final test of life's meaning. This is in direct contrast to Marx's view of religion as an illusion. Notice that this definition of religion as concerned with ultimate reality does not tell us whether the religious experience is monotheistic, solitary, or social; or whether it is best characterized by belief, ritual activity, or feeling. It does, however, emphasize that religion deals with ultimate reality and value.

DEFINING THE TERM RELIGION

Having considered the eight distinguishing characteristics of the various definitions of religion provided above, you should now be able to see that the term *religion* is in fact ambiguous to the extent that (1) it is actually defined in a number of ways; (2) these definitions emphasize several different distinguishing characteristics; and (3) some of them are in conflict with some others. Recognizing that the term *religion* has been defined in a number of different ways and is therefore ambiguous, we still need a specific definition of religion as a starting point for our study. Without a specific definition to clarify and stabilize the meaning of religion, it will be impossible to know precisely what we intend to study. In other words, our definition must help us answer the question, "What are the data to be analyzed and interpreted in this field of study?" When this question is answered, you may then move on to ask what methods or means are best suited for the study of these data. In short, an overview of the field of the study of religion can be developed from the perspective of our definition.

Let us consider the nature and purpose of a definition. All definitions are products of human decision; they are rules laid down by people for the purpose of establishing clear and precise meaning. When a term is clarified by definition the possibility of communicating it successfully increases. Thus a definition is a rule set down for the purpose of fostering clear communication. A definition is judged by the criteria of clarity and utility. In choosing or developing a definition, we must answer the following questions: Is it clear or is it confusing? Is it helpful or is it useless?

It is important to remember that we do not choose or construct a definition in a vacuum. We will have some purpose in mind, and we may—as we do in the case of religion—have examples of previous usage. The objectives of this chapter and the actual definitions of religion that we have already presented will influence our final decision on a specific definition.

In response to the question, "How shall we define the term *religion?*" one student made the following comment: "We do not have many alternatives. Either we are going to choose a definition already in use or develop one ourselves. I think that we should do what is in our best interest. However, what definition is in the best interest of understanding religion as a field of study? There must be some standards of judgment by which we come to prefer one definition over another. Let's identify them, build our own definition, and then see if it works."

Students often get right to the point, and this comment from one young freshman does just that. Whether we choose or develop a definition of religion, our definition should help us discuss religion as a critical academic field of study. Further, we should consider what criteria we will use in constructing, preferring, and rejecting definitions. We will call these criteria "predefinitional priorities."

PREDEFINITIONAL PRIORITIES[2]

In order to construct a definition of religion that is both clear and useful, we are setting certain predefinitional priorities. We must avoid the following features: vagueness, narrowness, compartmentalization, prejudice. We must achieve the following features: specificity, inclusiveness.

In the following pages we will identify and give examples of each of these features.

DEFINITIONAL FEATURES TO BE AVOIDED

Vagueness

The definition "religion is the quest for true knowledge" is certainly a possible one, but it is not very useful because it fails to differentiate religion from the pursuit of truth in the arts, sciences, or philosophy. A definition is vague when it does not clearly distinguish its subject matter from other subject matters; a responsible definition must avoid such vagueness.

Narrowness

We have already considered Aquinas's definition that religion "denotes properly a relation to God." Although this definition is broadly monotheistic (since it names the Western deity) and may seem quite liberal to Westerners, its scope is not adequate for our study because it excludes both nontheistic religious forms, such as some forms of Buddhism, and certain polytheistic forms.

If vagueness must be avoided because it is overly inclusive and does not clearly discrimiante its subject matter from others, a narrow definition must be avoided for the opposite reason: it is overly exclusive and does not allow consideration of the entire subject. For example, a definition such as "religion consists of the institutionalized thoughts and practices that relate humanity to a god or gods" excludes consideration of all forms of noninstitutionalized phenomena and does not allow us to consider such questions as, "Is there a religious dimension to a rock music festival?" or, "Might there be a religious dimension to some drug experiences?" This narrowness is inadequate since our definition must serve as the basis for a comprehensive study of religion.

Compartmentalization

Although it is very similar to narrowness, compartmentalization in a definition suggests an even greater limitation in the interests or concerns that can be addressed. Compartmentalization must be avoided because it signifies a reductionist view of the religious person. Definitions with this feature reduce religion, or the religious dimension of human experience, to one single, special aspect of the human self such as emotion, thought, or action. Some examples exhibiting compartmentalization are the following: "Religion is the feeling of absolute dependence" (emotion); "Religion is a specific system of belief in God" (thought); "Religion is a set of rituals" (prescribed action).

The chapters in this book provide a study of religion in relation to the whole of human experience. Therefore a definition of religion in this context must avoid any compartmentalization that would limit our view of religion to one aspect of human experience.

Prejudice

Prejudice severely limits our ability to consider religious experience fairly. Blanket evaluations of religion as "true" or "false," "good" or "bad," "relevant" or "irrelevant" are not helpful for the purposes of a critical course of study. Defining religion at the outset as either "a set of false beliefs constructed by a neurotic mind suffering infantile delusions" or "humanity's encounter with and response to that which is ultimately real and valuable" does not permit open, critical consideration of religious experience and beliefs. An inquiry like ours must avoid dogmatic or prejudiced definitions, either negative or positive. Our definition of religion, although specific and inclusive, must be as unprejudiced as possible in order to allow us to critically examine all phenomena.

DEFINITIONAL FEATURES TO BE ACHIEVED

Specificity

Specificity includes the feature of clarity as well as distinctiveness. Our definition of the term religion must indicate clearly what religion is and how it is to be differentiated from the nonreligious things to which it is most closely related. It is crucial that we avoid both vagueness and overinclusiveness that would blur the differences between, for example, religion and history, psychology, or ethics.

Inclusiveness

The criterion of inclusiveness does not contradict the criterion of specificity. On the contrary, inclusiveness requires that a definition clearly state the scope or the limitations of its use in such a way that narrowness, compartmentalization, prejudice, and vagueness are avoided.

To apply the criterion of inclusiveness to our definition of religion we should answer the following questions: Does it include the whole of human life, or is it restricted to one aspect of it such as thinking or feeling, or old age or adolescence? Does it apply equally to all people, ancient and contemporary, individual and institutional? Does it include that which may be true or false, helpful or harmful, of great or little social consequence?

Although we could ask other questions, it is important that we recognize that as definition makers we must consciously think about this criterion in order to avoid vagueness, narrowness, compartmentalization, and prejudice.

OUR DEFINITION OF RELIGION

Let us now consider a specific definition of religion. We will state it, examine its crucial terms, and then test it against our established criteria. Then, if it appears useful to our study, we will utilize it in the development of our overview of the field of religion studies. We proceed in this matter knowing full well that ours will not be the only definition of religion possible and that a new definition is always open to consideration as a result of further study. Our definition is as follows:

Religion is the varied, symbolic expression of, and appropriate response to that which people deliberately affirm as being of unrestricted value for them.

There are four crucial terms or distinguishing characteristics in this definition that require further examination and elaboration. They are "symbolic expression," "people," "deliberately affirm," and "unrestricted value." Let us consider each of them in more detail.

SYMBOLIC EXPRESSION

"Symbolic expression" is the first important characteristic of religion in our definition. Religion is a human or cultural artifact. Apart from humanity's capacity to symbolize, there could be no religion. Religion, as here defined, is the public or cultural product of the dynamic process of human or symbolic expression; the symbolic result of people's attempt to "ex-press" or "press out"—that is, communicate through language, art, social organization, technology, and other expressions their judgments about and experiences of the deepest meanings or fundamental significances of human life. If the term culture signifies the process by which human beings, over time, attempt to order and thereby transform the experiences of life, then religion is one of the basic manifestations of human culture. It is the external expression of a dynamic internal process of symbolizing what is perceived to be of unrestricted value for a human subject.

To define religion as varied symbolic expression is to anticipate that the manifestations of religion will not be limited to any one type or set of symbols. For example, the symbolic expressions of religion are not restricted to the symbols employed in art, music, or dance; they do not exclude symbolic expression in the poem or the narrative; they can include the ritually symbolic or the symbolic form of a moral code. Nor is the symbolic expression of religion limited to the expression of any one symbol set, be it European or Asian, Jewish or Buddhist, medieval or modern. Our definition anticipates and allows for a diversity of symbolic expressions.

To define religion in terms of appropriate response is to acknowledge that human action or intentional behavior is an essential element in the manifestation of religion. Behaviors are symbolic when they are informed or directed by human meaning or significance. To act intentionally in order to maintain or transform a state of affairs is an essentially human phenomenon. The human is revealed, disclosed, or made manifest in action. To act under the influence of a religious symbol or symbol system is to act religiously. An appropriate response is an action that intentionally expresses a religious meaning or significance. Our definition legitimates the study of human action as a potential source of the expression of religion. Once again, variety and diversity are anticipated and allowed by our definition. An act may be part of a ritual or a spontaneous undertaking in a political environment; it might be a response to moral principles or to an ethical command. The act of healing, as well as that of taking a life, may be understood as a religious act given the appropriate symbolic environments.

PEOPLE

According to our definition, religion requires "people" or human beings; apart from people there is no religion. While one may be a human being without being religious, all religious expressions have their origin in the human.

How is "human being" or "person" to be understood in this context? We will define the human being as the member of the animal kingdom whose symbolic self-consciousness differentiates him or her as an individual within a temporal and spatial environment perceived as a "world" (that is, a whole, a cosmos, a spatio-temporal continuum with a past, present, and a future) requiring intentional response. Symbolic self-consciousness centers the self as a locus of feeling, thought, and action; a focus of concern to live, to live well, and then to live better. The human self, as an individual, is aware of finitude and the questions it raises. (These questions include, for example, Who am I? Where did I come from? What will be my final end?) This human self in his or her world has been given the possibility of religious expression and, in a variety of ways, has actualized it.

Human beings experience themselves as beings in question, in development, or in the process of becoming. When, in the process of becoming, humans experience the holy, the sacred, the ultimate, or the unrestricted in value, they have, from the perspective of our definition, encountered the religious dimension within the self-world relation. We will call the reality of such an experience for the self "faith": that is, the individual's acknowledgement of the reality of an ultimate or unrestricted dimension to the experience of self and world, and the entrusting of the self to that. This experience of faith is not compartmentalized. It involves the whole self, the centered self, the integration of emotion, mind, and will. It is an existential recognition in that it affects the very being, existence, or constitution of the self, and it demands meaningful expression. As the self yields or surrenders to this demand or urge, the expressions of religion are born. The symbolic expressions of religion such as myth, ritual, or belief represent the self to give particular, specific, distinguishble expression to the experience of faith.

The self, which is the source of religious expression, is always an individual and a social or communal being at the same time. To the extent that symbolic expression requires language or a symbol system, religious expression is related to and dependent on a community or a cultural tradition. In addition, while faith is always the experience of an individual, the expression of such in symbols allows for the possibility of a public consensus—freely shared affirmation.

DELIBERATELY AFFIRM

A third characteristic of religion in our definition is deliberate affirmation. Religion is not an accident, but a human act. Our definition asserts that religion necessarily involves people in the self-conscious and voluntary expression of meaning. The phrase "deliberately affirm" points to an act of reflective self-determination; a behavior that is intentional, discriminating, and culminates in judgment. Thus, merely being born into a religious community does not make one religious. Association, apart from deliberate affirmation, does not make one religious. In our definition, a person must intentionally embrace, accept, or affirm for him or herself the unrestricted value before that person can be recognized as religious.

The phrase "deliberate affirmation" means an act of the human self, a "faithing," or act of faith that expresses the whole self. It is not simply an expression of reason or emotion or the will. Rather, it connotes an existential decision, a judgment that gives expression to human commitment, a trust in the risky act of self-definition. The human subject as a totality participates in the act of deliberate affirmation.

Religion may not be imposed. From the perspective of our definition no individual or community can be forced to be religious or make religious affirmation. To be sure, history has recorded the attempts of various rulers to extract religious affirmation from a people. Our definition regards such attempts, and any concession to them, as perversions of the religious. The human self must freely participate in a process of symbolic discrimination and judgment in keeping with the meaning of a free human act.

Religion need not be recognized as such by its subjects. This is often thought to be a controversial point, but it should not be so in the context of our definition. While the phrase "deliberately affirm" is understood to require a self-conscious and voluntary affirmation, it does not require that the people making such affirmations must acknowledge them as religious. Since our definition is but one perspective on the phenomenon of religion, we might legitimately regard the deliberate affirmations of a self-declared, antireligious Marxist as religious, while he or she, from a radically different perspective, would vigorously reject such a judgment. To be religious, a person must affirm that which is of unrestricted value, but they need not recognize such an affirmation as "religious" in order to be identified by our definition.

Religion makes a difference. Whether for good or ill, the act of deliberate affirmation transforms the very subject of this act as well as the subject's environment. The human is both producer and product of the symbolic expression of religion. Religion involves a radical self-interpretation; at the same time it orients the self to all others and helps provide the world and life with meaning and power. It is the means or mode of dynamic self and world transformation. In some instances the transforming power of the sacred, the holy, or the unrestricted will be symbolized as a "gift" (grace), while in others, it will be represented as the "release" of power from within the self. However, whether through the ritual sacrament or yoga, hearing the word or sitting in silent meditation, religious symbols effect the transformation of the human. Religion defines what a person ideally is and ought to be through his or her actions in the world. Deliberate affirmation, in the symbolic expression of religion, directly affects both human self-understanding and behavior. To act religiously is to affirm a transformation from what is to what ought to be, from the problematic to the ideal.

UNRESTRICTED VALUE

The fourth distinguishing characteristic of religion concerns what is of unrestricted value. Religion is the human attempt to represent, signify, or give meaningful expression to what is perceived to be of the greatest conceivable value for humankind and the world. The human subject gives symbolic expression to what is perceived or experienced as the object or locus of unrestricted worth, ultimate importance, or unconditioned value. Thus religion is the attempt, from within a human culture, to give expression to a perception and experience of value that at once surpasses, orders, and criticizes all other penultimate values expressed by that culture. Religion is the individual's and culture's attempt to transcend itself, to move beyond the conditions and limits defining it. If individuals and cultures essentially try to give symbolic expression to the real, the true, the beautiful, and the good, then religion tries to give symbolic expression to ultimate reality, truth itself, the beatific vision, and the holy. In its attempt to do so, through the relative symbols of culture, religion presses the limits of meaning in quest of an "understanding that passes all understanding."

In our definition of religion, the phrase "unrestricted value" intends both a *process* of valuing or "faithing," culminating in a deliberate affirmation, and a *product* or the symbolic expression of what has been so affirmed. It is most important to recognize that the object of unrestricted value so symbolized and affirmed is *not* the symbol itself. Religious symbols are understood to represent or signify without being themselves the unrestricted value. Failure to recognize this point can lead to gross misjudgments such as claiming people are worshiping sticks and stones. Thus, while a crucifix may be a powerful symbol in Roman Catholic worship, it itself is not being worshiped. Rather, the divine love symbolized in the sacrifice of Christ upon the cross is the object of unrestricted value for the Roman Catholic. Nor must the "object," or holy reality symbolized, be conceived as a "thing" or "person" among others. For example, the specific symbol of the "empty," so crucial to Buddhism, is hardly a thing among others or the simple absence of such things. Again, the symbol "God" for the Muslim is not appropriately understood to be a person among persons, but it must be understood as at least personal, that is, not subpersonal, but more than a person. Religion seeks to express within the limits, restrictions, or relativity of symbols that which is perceived or experienced to be of unrestricted value. Thus religious symbols continuously struggle on the borderline of meaning between their human authors and the ultimate reality that finally abides no restriction.

Similarly, while the human act of symbolic expression may be said to create or establish the symbol for unrestricted value, it should not, out of hand, be assumed thereby to have created its object or that which is symbolized. For example, to assert that the symbol "God" is exclusively a human projection, as German philosopher Feuerbach did, or an illusion that has captured the weak-willed among humankind, as did Freud, is to make an assertion that ends any study of religion before it can begin! Our definition rejects this prejudice and urges that such issues be addressed within the study of religion itself.

The term *value* implies a subject that estimates importance, assigns worth, or is involved in a process of valuation. Any symbolic expression of "that which is of unrestricted value" will convey an interpretive judgment on the various relations constituting human experience or reality. "Unrestricted value" represents a judgment of importance that includes and surpasses every restricted, temporary, local, or conditional value recognized in the relations constituting human experience.

TESTING THE DEFINITION

Now let us examine our definition first in terms of the features we have already said need to be achieved in definitions (specificity, inclusiveness), and then in terms of the features to be avoided (vagueness, narrowness, compartmentalization, prejudice).

Is This Definition Inclusive?

The answer is yes. Why? Because the definition opens religion to all humans regardless of gender, age, education, politics, economic status, and geographic or cultural location. The definition includes the possibility of both institutional and noninstitutional symbolic expression and response. By identifying religion as "the varied, symbolic expression of, and appropriate response to . . .," the definition assures us that religious phenomena must show or reveal themselves as conveyers of human significance. These phenomena may be critically assessed in several ways: as to their truth or falsity, their helpfulness or harmfulness to humanity, or their great or little historical, cultural, or social consequence. The definition is appropriate for our purposes, using the criterion of inclusiveness, because it allows us to consider the broad scope of religious phenomena in terms appropriate to the study of religion as an academic field.

Is This Definition Sufficiently Specific?

The definition we offer meets our criterion of specificity if it indicates clearly what religion is and how it is distinct from everything else. Human beings alone, through the use of symbol, deliberately discriminate and choose their own values, for example good/bad, beautiful/ugly, significant/insignificant, purposeful/purposeless. When such human judgment is further specified to be of ultimate and unrestricted (supreme, unconditioned, unqualified) value, it enters the domain of the religious. What distinguishes unrestricted valuation from all other forms of valuing is that its object is valued equally in all situations and is not restricted by the specific conditions of any situations. Therefore, it can be applied comprehensively. It is also the last value that would be sacrificed or given up by an individual because it is regarded as being of primary importance to the whole of human life. Thus a religious obligation takes precedence over all other obligations, or in other words, a religious good ranked as a highest good would not ideally be given up in favor of any nonreligious good.

By the criterion of specificity, then, our definition is appropriate because it discriminates the religious from the nonreligious by indicating precisely the difference between the two.

Does the Definition Avoid Vagueness?

Yes, our definition avoids vagueness. This does not mean that no one will have questions about the precise meaning of some of the terms in the definition. Words such as "unrestricted," "value," "symbolic," and "expression" may have to be further qualified and exemplified, but this is a standard expectation in any definition. However, the issue under this criterion is whether or not the definition has the power to discriminate religion from other forms of human valuation. We believe that it does differentiate and that this definition is appropriate.

Does the Definition Avoid Narrowness?

Yes, our definition avoids overexclusiveness or narrowness in its scope. For example, it does not limit religious valuation to monotheism or Christianity or institutionalized forms. It is conceivable under the present definition that certain atheistic phenomena could be considered religious if they reveal, at their base, an unrestricted valuation. Thus under certain circumstances communism could be viewed as a religious alternative; under other circumstances democracy could also be so considered. Certainly no particular religious tradition serves as the sole source of our definition.

Does This Definition Avoid Compartmentalization?

Our definition, by stressing unrestricted valuation, avoids compartmentalization. It allows us to consider any or all of the aspects of a person's being—for example, thinking, feelings, actions—as potential sources of religious data. It not only avoids compartmentalization but is defined in direct contrast to it. Since the process of human valuation is the most basic or generalized of human processes, our definition requires us to study the expression and response of human thought as well as emotion and action.

Does the Definition Avoid Prejudice?

Yes, our definition rejects prejudice. This does not mean that there is no value judgment involved in the construction of this definition; every definition involves value judgments in the selection of defining characteristics that will best explain the term. In this case we began, through our predefinitional priorities, with the conscious intent of constructing a definition that would serve the purpose of admitting a wide range of religious phenomena to be critically studied. We believe that we have successfully achieved an unprejudiced definition because we have avoided the kinds of judgments that would more appropriately follow rather than precede the study of religion.

RELIGION AS A FIELD OF STUDY

Armed with our definition of the term *religion*, we are now prepared to develop an overview of the field of religion. The phrase "a field of study" denotes an identifiable sphere of intellectual activity. Any field of study implies specialized subject matters, specific methods for interpreting them, and individuals who are concerned with particular kinds of questions for which they seek appropriate and critical answers. The task before us now is to ask and answer the question, "What is the field of the study of religion?" by providing a response to four more specific questions:

1. *What* is being studied?
2. *Who* is studying it?
3. *How* is it being studied?
4. *Why* is it being studied?

When we answer these specific questions in terms of the field of religion, we will have answered our larger question.

WHAT IS BEING STUDIED?

First Order Data

In many fields, when we ask what is being studied we are asking, "What are the generally accepted data of the field?" By "data" we mean the things that can be denoted or specified by some perspective of thought or speech. Data can include such things as ideas, ideals, individuals, feelings, human-made objects, natural and social phenomena. *Data will be classified as religious if they symbolically express what people deliberately affirm as being of unrestricted value to them.*

Religious data appear in a variety of forms and types of expressions. For example, in this book you will consider religious data that have appeared in the forms of myth, belief, ritual, scripture, and art. This is not to say that all myths or beliefs are religious, or that all religious expressions will appear in these forms. It does indicate, however, that religious data appear in a variety of forms and that the application of our definition of religion is the key criterion for judging whether or not a datum is or is not religious. Similarly, the form called "belief" may be expressed orally as a credo or personal confession, in an edited or nonedited text, or in song or literature. Religious data appear also in many kinds of media. As new media are introduced—for example, film or television—it should not be surprising if they now become religious data. Two specific examples will test our definition.

Consider a cross. Is a cross a religious datum? From what you have already learned about religious data, you would have to say that we do not yet have enough information to answer yes or no. To a Roman Catholic a cross might represent the crucifix, symbolizing the redemptive sacrifice of Jesus. To a truck driver on some highway the cross may symbolize nothing more than the crossroads soon to appear. To a black person a burning cross might represent hated intimidation by the Ku Klux Klan. Is a cross a religious datum? In the first instance your answer would be yes, for Roman Catholics ideally regard the crucifix as one symbolic expression of what is of unrestricted value for them. In the second instance the answer is no, for the crossroads indicator is no more than a functional sign, not a religious symbol. In the third instance the datam is ambiguous. If it can be determined that, for the KKK cross burner, the cross was an expression of what was valued unrestrictedly, then the burning of the cross would be a religious act or datum.

Now let us consider humanism. This interpretation of human existence dispenses with belief in the supernatural, considers the good of humanity on earth the supreme ethical goal, and applies the methods of reason and science to solve human problems. Let us try to decide whether or not this humanism, exemplified by the two individuals described in the following passage, can be considered a religious datum. Joe and Barbara, college students majoring in political science, do not regard themselves as religious. They refer to themselves as humanists. Joe considers himself a humanist because he feels that humanism is of practical value at this stage of history; he values it because he believes that societies under its influence are induced to increase their standard of living. Barbara on the other hand, thinks that humanism best expresses the highest possibilities for humanity's final destiny. She constantly criticizes the other worldly emphasis of religion and tries to make clear in her own actions that the final hope for humanity and for the world rests in people's reasonable and just dealings with other people. Is such humanism a religious datum?

In terms of our functional definition of religion, the best response would be as follows. Humanism in Barbara's case may be considered a religious datum because she states that it best expresses the highest values that humanity can attain. In this case humanism is a religious datum because it is an expression of what Barbara affirms to be of unrestricted value for her. Although Joe values humanism, he does not value it unrestrictedly. Remember, our definition does not say that all people will be religious, or that they will share the same object of religious value. Something may be regarded as of supreme importance to the life of one person while it is considered trivial by another.

What do you make of Barbara's assertion that she is not religious? Our definition does not say that either a person or a community has to be aware of being religious when assigning unrestricted value to something. So from our perspective it is legitimate to designate Barbara's humanistic, unrestricted value as religious, even if her own understanding of religion does not lead her to the same conclusion.

By using our functional definition of religion, and by considering the circumstances surrounding each datum, we can determine religious data and avoid two common pitfalls. First, we can avoid the situation in which data are determined by or limited to what has been studied in the past, and thus we can overcome traditionalism. It is not necessary for a belief or ritual to be associated with any of the great religions in order for us to consider it a religious datum. The weekly act of watching the Sunday afternoon football game may under certain circumstances be as much a religious ritual as the celebration of the Catholic mass.

Second, we can avoid leaving the determination of data to a instinctive or intuitional feeling that may be unconsciously biased or dogmatic. For example, a statement such as, "I feel strongly that the drug experience has nothing to do with religion and therefore will not give it any consideration in the study of religion," would prevent us from considering the relationship between drugs and religion.

In the following procedure, we do not assume a fixed number of religious data. Data may refer to individuals or a group of people; it may entail the act of voting, an extreme emotion, a star, a cross, or an idea of God. In determining the particular data—that is, what is being studied—for the field of religion, we arrive at our conclusion only as a result of our own study; we do not assume from the start that there is a fixed number of data for us to study or that anything is automatically religious in its own right.

In summary, we may say that the data—the "what" of the field of religion—can be identified only by applying our definition to an individual datum, and then investigating the particular case to determine whether the aspect of unrestricted valuation is present.

Second Order Data

When the data has been determined and study has begun, it is important to note that a second order of data becomes relevant. Second order data are those that provide critical commentary on first order data or the study of first order data. These second order data can be very significant to the student in a field of study. They relate a field to the continuum of scholarship. Let us consider two examples.

Sometimes you will find that second order data involve the work of scholars outside the field of religion. For example, if you are studying the cross as a religious symbol expressing what some people deliberately affirm as being of unrestricted value for them, and an art historian writes a book analyzing the differences between crosses bearing the crucified body of Jesus (a crucifix) and empty crosses, then this work could be of significant importance to your study. Despite the fact that the art historian may have little or no interest in the cross as a religious datum, from your perspective she or he may provide important clues for your study. The additional information this book may provide about the cross, as historical commentary or aesthetic theory, may suggest new points of view for understanding the people who created or utilized this religious artifact. We have used the example of an art historian, but second order data of importance have been produced by philosophers, anthropologists, sociologists, psychologists, literary critics, or others who are concerned to interpret the symbolic expressions and responses of the human beings. What is studied in the field of religion should include and can benefit from related areas of scholarship.

Sometimes second order data will include the comments of those within the field of religion on the efforts of their colleagues. If you are doing a study of the cross as a religious symbol, and you know that five other scholars have recently published their findings on this phenomenon, it will be most important for you to distinguish your contributions from theirs. This process develops a "critical" or "second order" tradition in a field of study. It is an ongoing phenomenon that every student in a field will want to consider. We conclude that second order data, while depending and following upon first order data, are nonetheless important in understanding what is studied in the field of religion.

Who Is Studying It?

The second question to be addressed in determining the field of religion is, "Who is studying it?" Is there any particular kind of student best qualified to participate in the study of religion? Is the student in religion required to possess some special characteristics that a student entering another academic field would not be expected to exhibit?

The invitation to study already indicated that students are both fundamental and crucial to a field of inquiry. Every field is seeking bright, energetic, interested, and committed students. A student in the field of religion does not need any special kind of insight, knowledge, attitude, or belief different from that required of students in philosophy or anthropology or any other academic discipline. A student must be willing to learn the functional definitions of a field, to develop the skills or methods for interrogating and interpreting data, and to pursue his or her work with a concern for critical understanding. While the definitions, data, and methods will differ from field to field, the responsibility of the student remains constant. The student in the field of religion shares the same responsibility as those in the natural and social sciences.

This is not to say that the academic study of religion will not expose the student to some unique challenges. For example, some students will enter the field having already made personal religious commitments. They may well be Christians, Jews, Buddhists, humanists, or something else. Others will enter with no personal disposition towards religion. Is it possible for all these individuals to engage in the academic study of religion? The answer is yes, but not without a disciplined commitment from them to treat definitions, data, and methods critically and fairly. Let us consider some examples.

If one enters the field as a member of a religious community, then she or he must recognize that the symbolic expressions of their own community are now data to be critically investigated. Such students will not only be "insiders" to a religious community, but will now be "insiders" to an academic community as well. They will be learning its language, methods of interpretation, and standards of evaluation and reporting. They will expose their own personal religious symbols and experience to discussion from a variety of perspectives such as philosophical, anthropological, sociological, and psychological approaches. As "insiders" in two communities they will be required to assess the assumptions, forms of speech, and claims to knowledge in both the religious and academic communities. This "standing on the boundary" as an insider in two overlapping communities can be an exciting opportunity and challenge. It will be effective, however, only if the student is prepared to examine critically the appropriatness of the questions asked and methods employed, demanding that all data be treated fairly and that any conclusions drawn do justice to the highest standards of academic inquiry.

For students who have rejected a previous religious commitment or have never made such a commitment, their challenge is to develop a knowledge of and appreciation for the methods and data of the study. It is important that the novel or the strange not be rejected out of hand or embraced without critical study. A student's predispositions or attitudes can affect the outcome of a study, but they need not. As one becomes an "insider" to the field of religion one accepts the responsibility for monitoring one's prejudices and reactions to assure that the data, methods, and conclusions of this field remain unbiased insofar as that is humanly possible.

The answer to the question, "Who is studying it?" is that all kinds of students pursue the study of religion. No special qualifications are required.

How Is It Being Studied?

The third basic question to be addressed in defining the field of religion is, "How is it being studied?" We want to know what method or methods we will use to study religion. By "method" we mean a systematic mode of procedure to achieve a goal or goals.*

Since the range of religious data is broad and the interests of students are various, we will use many different methods to study religion. No single method is identified with the study of religion. Several methods commonly used include the philosophical, psychological, historical, sociological, and comparative/structural approaches.

In selecting a method for study, we must take two factors into account: (1) the particular interests of the student and (2) the appropriateness of the method as a means of studying religious data.

Let us consider the first factor. If you are interested in the truth or falsity of a religious proposition, you might well select a philosophical method for studying the data. If you are interested in the documented origin or a system of belief, you may use a historical approach. If you are interested in discovering how the form of one religious community compares with that of another, you may employ a comparative/structural method. It is important to remember that the kind of question that you ask will influence your choice of method.

The second factor to consider in choosing a method—its appropriateness—is also very important. It is essential to select a procedure that suits the nature of the data under consideration. Just as we would not use a telescope to examine the structure of a cell, so we would not apply the rules of critical historical study to analyze a religious myth. Nor would we investigate the religious datum "God" using empirical categories appropriate to size, shape, and weight. Such procedures would be unsuitable because they fail to consider the sense and form in which the religious datum is considered meaningful. If religious myth does not intend to speak historically, and if the nature of God is not that of a physical object, then the methods of analysis that attempt to treat them as such are inappropriate. In selecting a method for the study of religion, we must take into account the method's capacity to respect the integrity and intention of the religious datum under consideration.

In summarizing the answer to the question, "How is it to be studied?" We must conclude that no single method is adequate for all purposes. We must select from available methods those that are appropriate to the questions being asked, to the particular interests of those engaged in the study, and to the nature of the religious data under consideration. Only then can we be sure that our method will be appropriate to the wide range of data we will consider, as well as to the wide variety of student interests.

WHY IS IT BEING STUDIED?

The fourth and final question to be addressed in determining the field of study of religion is the question, "why?"

---

*The student may find it helpful to read the chapter "Methodological Reflections" in part III in connection with the points of this section.

There are probably as many reasons for the study of religion as there are students. Some students know exactly why they wish to undertake the study, while others have no clear sense of their motivation. We will consider three important reasons why a person might study religion: emancipation from ignorance, gaining information and skill, and increasing appreciation. Let us consider each of these reasons separately.

Emancipation from Ignorance

If a liberal education in general aims at emancipating a human being from ignorance and parochial dogmatism, then a student can legitimately expect religion as a field of study also to exhibit this aim. Therefore any course in the study of religion should help the student achieve this goal by furnishing various data that express people's religious values and by providing methods for discriminating critically among them. For better or for worse, religion has powerfully affected the self-definition of people and their communities across the ages and in every recorded culture. To critically participate in the study of religion is to be introduced to the phenomenon of human self-definition in a way that adds perspective and richness to your own understanding of this quest to express what is human.

Information and Skill

A second reason for undertaking the study of religion is to gain information about the field and skill in interpreting its data. Any course in the area of religion will attempt to identify the field of study, introduce examples of religious data, and provide a method or methods for study in the field. You can expect to gain information about the field, its data, and its methods so that you can understand and then interpret them for yourself.

Increasing Appreciation

Students might study religion, third, to increase their appreciation of this form of human expression. The field of religion involves critical study of the expression of people's unrestricted valuation. A study of this field is not intended to make students religious; rather, the goal is to develop students' interpretive skills so they can discriminate the crucial elements in their own or other people's quests for ultimate value. Thus students may legitimately expect that this book will help them develop their critical skills in order to increase their appreciation and understanding of the expressions of religion.

Many fields of study will touch upon data that you, as a student in the field of religion, will identify as religious. Sociologists may study the organization of religious communities; literary critics may study the forms of expression found in sacred scriptures; a psychologist may interpret the dream state of a particular religious mystic. As a student you will treat these instances in other courses, following the questions and methods appropriate to those courses. However, in the field of religion, you will attempt to develop methods that will allow you to elicit information from religious data so that the "claims" of the data are themselves the central issue. That is to say, religious data lay claim to meaning; they symbolically express, declare or avow a judgment about the significance of human experience. It is the nature, meaning, and significance of this claim itself that the field of religion attempts to explore. As a student in this field, it is your goal to understand critically and thereby appreciate the various data of religion by sensitively and skillfully pressing the question, "What do religious data mean as they themselves claim meaning?"

THE STUDY THAT FOLLOWS

You have now been invited to participate in the study of religion, marked as it is by a specifically defined understanding of *what* is to be studied, *who* may study it, *how* it is studied, and *why* one might study it. The chapters that follow help you do this by providing one particular view of the nature of religion, with specific data and specific methods of study.

The study that follows is based on the definitions and understandings outlined above, and it discusses the nature of religion generally and generically through an understanding of major types of symbolic expressions: images of the holy, sacred story or myth, ritual, art, scripture, belief, individual and community, and morality. This list is by no means exhaustive; there are additional types of expression not mentioned here. Our attempt, however, is to identify and discuss those types that seem either most universal to religion or most important in some of the major religions. Through them, you should attain a more thorough knowledge of religion, more skill in interpreting the meaning of religion, and more appreciation for its importance in human existence.

While the various religions of humankind find important places in our chapters as examples of these expressions, we are not offering a study of particular religions. To do so would be to assume that religions define "religion" or the "what" of our study—something that has been rejected above. Of course, the religions of humanity have been the major and most obvious source of religious expressions;[3] but our definition is meant to include other cultural phenomena or data that, whether commonly called "religion" or not, give evidence of being religious.

Now, let us turn to some of the major types of the "varied symbolic expressions" that make up the primary data of our study.

NOTES

1. Karl Marx and Friedrich Engels, *On Religion* (New York: Schocken Books, 1964), p. 41.
2. This discussion of predefinitional priorities employs the categories set forth by Frederick Ferre in *A Basic Modern Philosophy of Religion* (New York: Scribners, 1967).
3. See the discussion of the nature and function of specific religious traditions in our chapter "Religions: Paths and Accents" in Part III of this book.

Part 2

VARIETIES OF RELIGIOUS EXPRESSION

CHAPTER 2

The Holy

Inescapably, human religiousness includes a "brush with mystery," a "being in touch with the holy," an "experience of sacredness." The holy is sometimes perceived as a reality beyond the self, sometimes as within the self. In either case, personal experience of the holy is qualitatively different from other experiences, and no normal language can adequately describe it. Moreover, the object of that experience so transcends the ordinary that it defies completely rational explanation.

The experience of the holy and the holy as experienced, in spite of the ambiguity of meaning, are central to all religious expressions. Most sacred stories tell of action by the gods or heroes. Belief systems are built upon concepts of a holy reality. Rituals convey a sense of the presence of the holy to the worshiping community. Moral codes are derived from and given sanction by this sacrality. Painters, poets, and musicians seek to capture the holy in their art. Behind, beyond, and within all symbolic expressions is an intimation of a "presence," a "holiness." Poet William Wordsworth captured a universal religious sentiment in the lines, "I have felt a presence which disturbs me with the joy of elevated thoughts." The philosopher Alfred North Whitehead pointed to the holy in his words: "Religion is a vision of something which stands behind, beyond, and within the passing flux of immediate things—something real, yet waiting to be realized."[1]

Expressions of the holy can be found in the cave paintings of preliterate civilizations, in the ancient religions of the Middle East, in African and Native American religions, and in the journals of individual spiritual seekers. However, expressions of the holy from within the five worldwide religions—Judaism, Christianity, Islam, Hinduism, and Buddhism—will be discussed on the following pages.

THE HOLY AS EXPERIENCED

How can we describe experiences of the holy? One answer comes from the German theologian Rudolf Otto in his book, *The Idea of the*

Holy. Otto proposes that countless people have experienced the feeling of awe, mystery, and wonder—an experience of what he calls "the numinous." Such experiences may come in crisis moments when we witness the birth of a baby, the death of a parent, an earthquake, a shockingly beautiful sunset on the ocean, or even when we feel the excitement of love. We feel in those moments what Otto calls "mysterium tremendum," an intense feeling that may gradually pass away or may continue in extended ecstasy. Although there is usually no clear intellectual conception about the nature of the holy thus felt, the person has a sense of an intensely positive experience of something sacred.[2]

The experience described by Otto appears to be common to people in the various religious traditions. In the text of the Hindu Bhagavad Gita, for example, the poetic story reports experiences of the holy. The warrior, Arjuna, after a successful battle in which Lord Krishna was his helper, exclaimed:

Ah, my God, I see all gods within your body;
Each in his degree, the multitude of creatures;
See Lord Brahma throned upon the lotus;
See all the sages, and the holy serpents.
Universal Form, I see you without limit,
Infinite of arms, eyes, mouths and bellies—
See, and find no end, midst, or beginning,

Crowned with diadems, you wield the mace and discus,
Shining in every way—the eyes shrink from your splendor
Brilliant like the sun; like fire, blazing boundless.[3]

St. John of the Cross (1542–1591), a Spanish Christian, expressed an experience of the holy and the subsequent euphoria with these lines:

I remain, lost in oblivion; My face I reclined on the beloved.
All ceased and I abandoned myself, leaving my cares forgotten among the lilies.[4]

The ancient writer of the Hebrew Bible tells his vision of God with the words recorded in Isaiah, chapter 6:

I saw the Lord sitting upon a throne, high and lifted up; and his train filled the temple. Above him stood the seraphim; each had six wings: with two he covered his face, and with two he covered his feet, and with two he flew. And one called to another and said: "Holy, holy, holy is the Lord of hosts; the whole earth is full of his glory.[5]

These few examples suggest that it is not preposterous to claim that an experience of the holy is universal. It is, of course, too much to say that all people everywhere affirm the reality of the holy in their experience, or that the experience and expression is always the same. Rather, an experience of the holy is not parochial but is present in some form in various cultures all over the world.

Within particular languages and vastly different cultures, persons report their experience of the holy. Through ritual, music, the arts, or belief systems they express their understanding of the "other" that in some manner transcends ordinary life. It is as though some people everywhere walk in a "presence" symbolically identified as ultimate reality, the eternal, the highest good, the root of all meaning, the depth dimension of existence, God, Brahman, Allah, and so forth. We can reasonably declare that a sense of the holy is affirmed in all religions in all cultures.[6]

THE HOLY EXPERIENCED IN TWO WAYS

If we were to visit religious centers throughout the world, talk with those who practice their religion, and study the sacred texts, we would find different testimonies of religious experience. Muslims, Jews, and Christians experience God as separate from the world and beyond human life. God is believed to have created the world, to influence if not control history. This God confronts persons and calls them to live morally. Yet among Buddhists and Hindus, the holy is usually experienced as internal. The yogi and the Zen monk seek to withdraw in meditation to experience that which is holy. Religious experience among Western persons seems to be on one end of a continuum with Easterners on the other. To be sure, these types are seldom purely one or the other; yet we will find it useful to consider these two types of experience of the holy: confrontation and interiority.[7]

THE GOD WHO CONFRONTS HIS PEOPLE

The Hebrew Bible begins with the sacred story of creation. "In the beginning Jahweh created the heavens and the earth." God created light, heaven, earth, all vegetation, animals, the sun, the moon, and finally human beings. Then, having put the first man and woman in a perfect garden, Jahweh placed demands on them about how they should act. When Adam and Eve disobeyed their God, they were forced to leave the garden and hence were separated from God.

The primeval stories continue with the main theme of God confronting the ancient people. Jahweh placed certain demands on Cain and Abel. The same divine One commanded Noah to build a huge boat in order to survive the coming flood. Abram (later called Abraham) was commanded to travel from his home to a new land and later was chosen to be the leader of a great nation. In additional stories, God confronts Esau, Jacob, Joseph, and many more.

The book of Exodus continues with a narrative about Moses who, having left his family in Egypt, was in the wilderness taking care of a flock of sheep. Suddenly Moses was shocked to observe a bush near him that was burning. Jahweh's voice came from the fire telling Moses, "Take off your sandals for this is holy ground." Jahweh then instructed Moses to be the leader of his people, to take them out of slavery in Egypt to their own land. When Moses asked for clarification about who was speaking, the voice of God declared: "I am who I am."[8]

Whether these stories are myth, legend, or factual history, they present experience of the holy confronting persons. Throughout the Hebrew Bible, God continues to speak, to lead, and to judge—to be external to nature and to human life. One poetic writer sums up this experience in Psalm 121:

I will lift up my eyes to the hills,
From whence does my help come?
My help comes from the Lord,
Who made heaven and earth.

During the many years of Jewish history, religious Jews have maintained their belief in the all-powerful divine being. Such a faith has continued in spite of dispersions, ghetto discriminations, and the holocaust. To this day the experience of God is recalled in every temple and synagogue when the people say the Shema: "Hear, O Israel, the Lord our God, the Lord is One."

Christianity, like the Jewish culture out of which it emerged, continued faith in the transcendent God. Christians accepted as their Bible the Jewish scriptures, along with their own New Testament. They were convinced that God was in the begining, and the same God "became flesh and dwelt among us."[9]

As Christianity spread north from Palestine toward Greece and Rome, the New Testament reports additional experiences of God. God came to the people "like a mighty wind" as reported in Acts, chapter 2. Paul, the writer of New Testament letters, was made blind and speechless by the resurrected Jesus on the road to Damascus and was converted to Christianity (Acts, chapter 9). And Christians were urged to accept the judgment and forgiveness of the God who was made known by Jesus, the Christ. No one needed to argue for the existence of God; God was experienced as creator, the one who forgives people for their rebellion, and one who is the source of peace and hope. Even in the modern world, Christians direct their prayers to God. In every kind of public worship, God is affirmed, often in the form of a creed like the following: "I believe in God the Father Almighty, maker of heaven and earth; and in Jesus Christ His only Son our Lord. . . ."[10]

Just as the scriptures of Judaism and Christianity reflect experiences of God confronting persons, so too do the sacred writings of Islam, the Qur'an. According to the sacred book, Allah created the world and all people, and this God, being kind, taught people things that were not known before.[11] God is a single being, a unified personal will who overshadows the entire universe with his power and grace.[12] John A. Hutchinson, an American philosopher of religion, writes that "any exposition of Muslim doctrine must begin—and end—with the one God, Allah, majestic, holy, transcendent, absolutely unique."[13] Faith in Allah who calls to all the faithful permeates Muslim religious life.

Affirmation of one divine being, creator and sustainer of the world and human life, who stands over against all that he has made, gives laws for the community of the faithful, and who comes to human life with grace and forgiveness, has been characteristic in the religious life of Jews, Christians, and Muslims. Thus the divine is experienced as the one who confronts the human and can be identified at one end of the continuum suggested in our typology.

PHILOSOPHIC DEFENSE OF THEISM

The experience of the holy as a transcendent and external being by Jews, Christians, and Muslims became the norm in the three religious traditions in the West. Yet a companion kind of experience developed which explained and defended this affirmation of God. The new movement was philosophy.

About the fifth century B.C.E. a group of persons in Greece became vividly aware of the processes of human reason. Beginning with Thales, Heraclitus, Pythagoras, Epicurus and coming to fruition in Plato and Aristotle, these philosophers were convinced that knowledge gained by ordinary experience needs to be refined by the processes of human reason. According to Plato, whatever is claimed to be true is mere opinion if not tested by the light of reason.[14] If the God who confronts his people truly exists, that claim can be proved by reason. Human reason, then, became part of the equipment of intellectual people in order to demonstrate that God truly exists external to subjective experience.

Throughout the literature of philosophy of religion, three major arguments for the existence of God have been emphasized. They are (1) the ontological argument, (2) the cosmological argument, and (3) the teleological argument. A brief sketch of these three arguments provides an essential part of Westerners' belief in God.

The Ontological Argument

In about the year 1078, in an abbey in Normandy, the head monk Anselm wrote a series of meditations in which he tried to provide a single basis of reasoning to support the Christian assertion of God's existence. The principle for which he was looking seemed to have appeared to him suddenly, and he wrote it in the form of a prayer. (Note that for Anselm, immediate experience and reasoning were not totally different.) Since that time his words have been known as the ontological argument and have fascinated philosophers and theologians. In brief, the statement is, "God is that than which nothing greater can be conceived." For St. Anselm, it followed that God must necessarily exist. Selections from Anselm's own words may be helpful in understanding the argument.

O Lord, you who give understanding to faith, so far as you know it to be beneficial, give me to understand that you are what we believe. We certainly believe that you are something than which nothing greater can be conceived. But is there any such nature, since "the fool has said in his heart: God is not." However, when this very same fool hears what I say, when he hears of "something than which nothing greater can be conceived," he certainly understands what he hears. What he understands stands in relation to his understanding, even if he does not understand that it exists. For it is one thing to stand in relation to our understanding; it is another thing for us to understand that it really exists. For instance, when a painter imagines what he is about to paint, he has it in relation to his understanding. However, he does not yet understand that it exists, because he had not yet made it. After he paints it, then he both has it in relation to his understanding and understands that it exists. Therefore, even the fool is convinced that "something than which nothing greater can be conceived" at least stands in relation to his understanding, because when he hears of it he understands it, and whatever he understands stands in relation to his understanding.

And certainly that than which a greater cannot be conceived cannot stand only in relation to the understanding. For if it stands at least in relation to the understanding, it can be conceived to be also in reality, and this is something greater. Therefore, if "that than which a greater cannot be conceived" only stood in relation to the understanding, then "that than which a greater cannot be conceived" would be something than which a greater can be convinced. But this is certainly impossible.

Therefore, something than which a greater cannot be conceived undoubtedly both stands in relation to the understanding and exists in reality.[15]

This argument has been the object of much controversy among philosophers and theologians up to the present time. Some critics have said that Anselm may have given an adequate definition of God but that a definition cannot prove that the object described actually exists in external reality. Philosopher Immanual Kant in the eighteenth century insisted that existence cannot be shown to be merely the result of an idea; existence can be known only from empirical data—from some kind of experience.[16]

The Cosmological Argument

Probably more persons are persuaded by the cosmological argument than by the ontological one. A contemporary man or woman might say, "Of course God exists. The world must come from somewhere; it didn't just happen without a cause." This form of the argument can be traced to Plato's dialogue, *Laws*. However, its familiar formulations are attributed to the theologian St. Thomas Aquinas who lived from 1224 to 1274 C.E.

Thomas's point of view was that the hypothesis that God exists is the only way to account for empirical data. He used five related arguments to "prove" his hypothesis. The first begins with the observation that some things about us are in motion. We can also observe that whatever is in motion is put into that state by something else that moves it. Now if everything that moves is put into motion by something else, that which did the moving would itself have been set into motion by something else. Soon we are taken back, back, and yet further back until we arrive at the conception of a first mover that was put into motion by nothing else. Such a first mover, Thomas said, is what is meant by God.

He stated his argument in another way under the title "contingency and necessity." We all observe that everything around us, even ourselves, is contingent—that is, everything we can experience depends on something else. Now if everything is contingent, nothing necessarily exists, for everything depends on something else and comes into existence and goes out of existence but is never necessary. Since this fact appears to be true, it would therefore follow in theory that at one time nothing at all existed, for nothing is necessary. But such an assertion is ridiculous, for if at one time there was nothing, then there could not be anything now. Thus we must posit a necessary being who had the power to bring about everything that is contingent.

Thomas had three other ways of stating the argument all quite similar to the two briefly sketched above. While none of the arguments are convincing to all critics, they do have positive appeal to those who believe that everything that is must have had a first cause outside or beyond that which we ordinarily know.

The Teleological Argument

The term teleological comes from the Greek words *telos,* meaning "end" or "purpose," and *logia,* which means "the science or study of." Thus *teleoligcal* refers to the study of final purpose, goal, or end. From the time Plato wrote the *Timeus* through the arguments of Thomas Aquinas about 1500 years later, arguments have been presented asserting that God must exist because the complex and intricate design in nature calls for an infinite designer. However, English philosopher William Paley (1743–1805) first presented a modern and influential teleological argument.[17]

Within his discussion, Paley used an anology that catches the essence of the argument. Anyone finding a watch lying on the ground, he said, would not be justified in explaining the watch, with all of its complex mechanisms, as just happening by chance. Rather, it is a better hypothesis to suppose that the watch implies a watchmaker—someone who designed and built it. In a similar fashion the French biologist Henri Bergson (1859–1941) in a book called *Creative Evolution,* declares that a study of evolution suggests the hypothesis of a purposive being who directed the movement from simple to more complex forms of life and is responsible even for the magnificent instincts in animals.

St. Thomas Aquinas stated the argument in a few words as follows:

We see that things which lack knowledge, such as natural bodies, act for an end, and this is evident from their acting always, or nearly always, in the same way, so as to obtain the best result. Hence it is plain that they achieve their end, not fortuitously, but designedly. Now whatever lacks knowledge cannot move towards an end, unless it be directed by some being endowed with knowledge and intelligence; as the arrow is directed by the archer. Therefore some intelligent being exists by whom all natural things are directed to their end; and this being we call God.[18]

It is worth noting again that the arguments for the existence of God all presuppose that the holy reality being defended is a God who is different from nature and human life yet encountered as person, who is the creator of everything, and who acts independently, confronting people by conscious acts of judgment, forgiveness, speech, and guidance. These arguments, then, are related to our first type of experience of the holy identified as confrontational.

THE HOLY AS WITHIN: INTERIORITY

Experiences of the holy by persons within Eastern religions—Hinduism and Buddhism and traditions growing from them—seem to a large degree to be different from Western religious visions. The holy does not confront one from the outside in much of Eastern spirituality. Rather, it is experienced when looking inward. This spirit within is experienced as the most real part of the person, as well as sacred reality itself.

Of course, some religious experiences in the West are also of this type. Mystical persons in Western religions fall quite easily into this interior type. Yet mysticism has never been the norm in Islam, Judaism, and Christianity. Moreover, expressions of God as outside the self appear also in the Hindu tradition as expressed in the Vedas, with hymns of praise offered to Savitri, Vishnu, Shiva, and Indra. Indeed, even much of popular devotional Hinduism is centered on worship of the gods. Nevertheless these two types—confrontation and interiority—are useful types for pointing out differences in the experience and expression of the holy in varied cultures. Evidences of the second type of holiness are plentiful in the Asian religions.

The story of the historic Buddha is a paradigm of the inward experience of the holy. The Buddha was a sensitive young man, rich in possessions, the proud husband of a beautiful princess, and blessed with a son. But in awareness of the miseries of sickness, old age, and the inevitableness of death, and disillusioned by the meaninglessnesss of all external possessions, he left his palace. He experimented with a life of self-denial, reflection, and conversation with well-known persons of wisdom. He found no satisfactory answers. Then while in silent meditation sitting under a tree in northern India, he became enlightened. In becoming aware of his true self, he also became aware of the truths about human life and the right paths of living.

Throughout the history of various branches of Buddhism, the image of the Buddha sitting quietly with eyes partially closed to the outside world has been the mode wherein a vision of holiness is possible. The content of that vison, however, is not of a personal God who confronts one with demands, or of one who initiates a covenant with the people. Rather the experience is an awakening of the self to one's own true nature. The experience leads to an intuitive conviction that a person can become nonattached to everything external and gain a consciousness of liberation from cravings for things. With such a new perspective, everything outside the self remains the same; yet it is different. The totality of existence is transformed by the internal vision of the self that has achieved Buddhahood.

Zen Buddhism, a sect in Japan best known by Western students, is especially characterized by inner experiences of the holy. Spiritual life in the Zen tradition is not based on belief in a God or on belief in a human soul. Moreover, Zen teachers are firmly opposed to the idea that Buddhahood is something to be searched for outside oneself. Rather, within every person there is a Buddha-nature, they believe. The technique for realization of the true self is sitting meditation, or *zazen.*

The technique of *zazen* is simple. It begins when the monk silently enters the *zendo* (meditation hall). Having removed his shoes, he bows in respect to the Zen master, bows to a statue of the Buddha, bows to others who may already be sitting, and finds a cushion on the floor or on a raised platform. The devotee seeks a comfortable upright position with legs crossed in lotus position and begins steady breathing. In a moment the master will strike two pieces of wood together indicating that the session is beginning. With eyes half-closed and focused on the floor a few feet in front, the participant, breathing slowly but deeply from the diaphragm, may count "one" upon each exhaled breath. The room is absolutely quiet; not even the sound of air entering nostrils or of saliva being swallowed is heard. For several hours the meditators sit in perfect silence. The time of sitting is then broken by the sound of a bell to indicate the termination of the period.

Why *zazen?* One ancient commentator explained that this way of meditation is a type of study of the Buddha.

To study the way of the Buddha is to study your own self. To study your own self is to forget yourself. To forget yourself is to have the objective world prevail in you. To have the objective world prevail in you is to let go of your "own" body and mind as well as the body and mind of "others." . . . The true cause of . . . enlightenment is the merit and effectiveness of sitting. Truly the merit lies in the sitting.[19]

Even a Western person who is unfamiliar with Eastern forms of spirituality can, with practice, understand at least a bit the Zen inward way of perceiving holiness. Here is a brief section from the diary of an American professor visiting Japan.

Tonight was my fifteenth zazen session with Rev. Kabori. I was finally able to forget the pain in my knees (part of the time) and even ignore the sounds outside the temple. The two hours of sitting seemed like a long time; yet I wasn't bored. It was a period which seemed empty, quiet, peaceful, and I didn't feel any sharp difference between myself and everything else in the zendo. . . . When the bell rang and I left the temple for the long walk along the familiar Kyoto streets on the still, moonlit night, I felt like I was doing walking zazen. I was vividly aware of the dim lights from tiny houses behind well-kept fences. The shadows cast from perfectly trimmed trees by the moon were striking. And the distinctly Japanese smells were more pungent than usual. I experienced something today. Is it too much to call it an experience of the holy?[20]

If the experience of the holy is an inward discovery in these forms of Buddhism, the same interiority of the holy is equally evident in Hinduism. Sociologist Peter Berger claims that "if there is a prototypical gestalt of Indian religiosity, it is surely the Yogi sitting in the lotus position —silent, withdrawn from the world, passive, turned inward in his quest of the ultimate reality within himself."[21]

Berger's sweeping statement is supported by the historian of religion Mircea Eliade, in the assertion that "no one knows of a single Indian spiritual movement that is not dependent on one of the numerous forms of yoga."[22] Each type of yogic discipline may include concentration on a single object (tip of nose, a point between the eyebrows, an external point), breathing through one nostril, mastery of body movements, or simply sitting in meditation. In spite of different techniques, the spiritual discipline of yoga has the goal of liberation from the human condition of ignorance and "to win absolute freedom, to achieve the unconditioned."[23] The widespread yogic practice, then, indicates the Hindu concern for what Eliade calls "the contents and structures of the unconsciousness."[24] Huston Smith, philosopher of religions, in a similar fashion suggests that in India the fundamental religious interest is centered on psychological problems—on the self.[25]

It should be repeated that spirituality in non-Western cultures is not totally of one type. Yet these typical expressions from the Buddhist and Hindu traditions give evidence that many experiences of the holy prevalent in the East are illustrations of the type we call "interiority."

PHILOSOPHICAL DEFENSE OF INTERIORITY

Earlier in the chapter we saw that the experience of the holy and belief in a God who confronts persons—the God of traditional Judaism, Christianity, and Islam—was supported by philosophers. Through the use of reason, the ontological, cosmological, and the teleological arguments were used by believers to substantiate their faith as well as to convince skeptics.

Buddhists and Hindus, for the most part, were less concerned with philosophic arguments to support their convictions. They were persuaded about the reality of the holy through the experience of turning inward in various kinds of yoga and meditation. Yet over the centuries many philosophic schools developed in South Asia and East Asia. These philosophers provided a thorough framework supporting the claims about the holy made by religious persons. Every college and university library contains dozens of volumes on Buddhist and Hindu philosophies. For our purposes, only two representatives will be mentioned: Acharya Sankara (pronounced "shankara"), an interpreter of Advaita Vedanta, and a modern writer, Swami Prabhavaranda.

Sankara, who lived around 800 C.E. developed a scheme of thought referred to as Vedanta, which is still dominant in India. Sankara proposed that the basic idea found in the Hindu scriptures—especially the Vedas and the Upanishads—was that all reality is one. Although the name given to this one eternal and spiritual reality is Brahman, the true self or *atman* is nothing less than the spirit of Brahman. The two are identical as expressed by the phrase, *tat tvan asi* which translated literally means "thou art that." He explained his position as follows:

The Brahman exists, eternal, pure, enlightened, free by nature, omniscient and attended by all power. . . . The Brahman's existence is well known, because it is the Self of all; everyone realizes the existence of the Self, for none says, "I am not"; if the existence of the Self is not well known, the whole world of beings would have the notion "I do not exist." And the Self is the Brahman.[26]

Although Sankara used the processes of reason to develop his system of thought, he also believed that genuine knowledge comes from the experience in which one achieves union with the holy.

It is . . . an awareness of identity with Brahman, and that as an "intuitus," a dawning of insight, our own clear-sighted realization of that which the scriptures taught. This awareness cannot be "produced." We cannot reason it out.[27]

Throughout subsequent years, Vedanta has taught that the human is essentially divine and that the only worthy goal of human life is to unfold and manifest that divinity. Swami Prabhavananda, lecturing and writing in the United States in the twentieth century, said:

According to Vedanta, there is a divine ground, Brahman, underlying the universe in name and form. It is omnipresent; therefore it exists within every creature. . . . When the mind has been purified through spiritual disciplines and is able to turn inward upon itself, man realizes that his true being is Atman-Brahman. To uncover this true being, of divinity, which lies hidden within oneself, is to become perfect.[28]

SUMMARY

Men and women in widely different cultures have experienced the holy—at least that is their claim. The names given to the holy may be Allah, Yahweh, God, or Brahman. That experience may also be called enlightenment, *satori, moksha,* or may even go unnamed. Yet each experience clearly falls somewhere on the continuum from a God who confronts one from outside the self to an inward experience by which holiness is known. While this chapter has characterized the confrontation type as Western while Eastern spirituality is one of inward awareness, observers of religion discover that both types, or combinations of the two, can be found in every tradition and culture. But whatever the type—experience of the holy as confronting the self, or the experience of the holy as within the self—such experiences are central to religion.

As students of religon we may be puzzled. Could it be that both extreme types are equally authentic and that both lead to partial insights? Could it be that the holy is both transcendent and immanent? If these two questions are answered affirmatively, then experiences of the holy characterized by confrontation and interiority may contribute to a broader vision of the holy than presented by either extreme.

NOTES

1. These two phrases are quoted in many places. The first is from William Wordsworth's poem, "Lines Composed Above Tintern Abbey." The second comes from Alfred North Whitehead's *Science in the Modern World* (New York: Macmillan, 1925), p. 192.
2. Rudolf Otto, *The Idea of the Holy* (New York: Oxford University Press, 1958), pp. 11–12.
3. *Bhagavad-Gita: The Song of God,* Mentor Edition, trans. Swami Prabhavananda and Christopher Isherwood (New York: New American Library, 1944–1951), p. 92.
4. St. John of the Cross, *Ascent of Mount Carmel,* trans. and ed. E. Allison Peers (Garden City, N.Y.: Image Books, 1958), p. 72.
5. Taken from the Revised Standard Version.
6. According to Huston Smith, each of the world's great religions has a transcendent dimension, along with personal and social characteristics. The first is the source of the other two. See "The Relevance of the Great Religions for the Modern World," in *The World Religions Speak,* ed. Finley P. Dunne (The Hague: W. Junk, 1970).
7. For a thorough discussion of this typology see Peter Berger, *The Heretical Imperative: Contemporary Possibilities of Religious Affirmation.* (Garden City, N.Y.: Doubleday, 1980), chap. 6, and Peter Berger, ed., *The Other Side of God: A Polarity in World Religions.* (Garden City, N.Y.: Doubleday, 1981).
8. It would be extremely helpful for students to read all of Genesis and the first three chapters of Exodus in the Bible.
9. John 1:14.

10. The Apostle's Creed. Tradition, not historical evidence, links this creed to the twelve apostles. However, it was used prior to the fourth century in the Christian Church.
11. Taken from the Qur'an, Surah xcvi, 1–4.
12. Huston Smith, *The Religions of Man* (New York: Harper & Row, 1965), p. 205.
13. John Hutchison, *Paths of Faith*, 2d ed. (New York: McGraw-Hill, 1975), p. 472.
14. This is the main assertion in Plato's analogy of the cave in *The Republic*.
15. Taken from John H. Hick and Arthur C. McGill, eds, *The Many-Faced Argument* (New York: Macmillan, 1967), pp. 4–6. The editors used St. Anselm, *Opera omnia*, ed. Dom F. S. Schmitt (Edinburgh: Thomas Nelson & Sons, 1946).
16. See John Hick, *Philosophy of Religion*, rev. ed. *Englewood Cliffs, N.J.: Prentice-Hall, 1968), pp. 122–34.
17. William Paley, *Natural Theology: or Evidence of the Existence and Attributes of the Deity Collected from the Appearances of Nature*, ed. Frederick Ferre (New York: Liberal Arts Library, 1962).
18. St. Thomas Aquinas, *Summa Theologica*, ed. Anton C. Pegis (New York: Random House, 1968), pt. 1, ques. 2, art. 3.
19. Quoted by William Theodore de Bary et al., eds., in *Sources of Japanese Tradition*, vol. 1 (New York: Columbia University Press, 1964), pp. 245–47.
20. From the private notes of T. William Hall, one of the authors of this book.
21. Peter Berger, *Heretical Imperative*, pp. 147–48.
22. Mircea Eliade, *Patanjali and Yoga*, trans. Charles Lam Markmann (New York: Funk & Wagnalls, 1969), p. 5.
23. Ibid., p. 115.
24. Mircea Eliade, *Yoga: Immortality and Freedom*, trans. Willard P. Trask (Princeton, N.J.: Princeton University Press, 1970), p. xvii.
25. See Huston Smith, "Accents of the World's Religions," in T. William Hall, ed., *Introduction to the Study of Religion* (New York: Harper & Row, 1978).
26. William Theodore de Bary, ed., *Sources of Indian Tradition*, vol. 1 (New York: Columbia University Press, 1958), pp. 315–16.
27. Rudolf Otto, *Mysticism East and West* (New York: Macmillan, 1960), p. 51.
28. Swami Prabhavananda, *The Sermon on the Mount According to Vedanta* (Hollywood, Calif.: Vedanta Press, 1946), p. 62.

QUESTIONS FOR STUDY AND DISCUSSION

1. This chapter proposes two types of experience of the holy: confrontation and interiority. In what ways is this a helpful typology? In what ways is it inadequate?

2. It has often been claimed that the holy in religion is a transcendent reality. Yet there are several different meanings of the word *transcendent*. In what sense, then, is the holy transcendent in your judgment?

3. Suppose you are with a group of people discussing religion and the question of belief in God comes up. Then one person says, "This is a foolish discussion. God is a private and personal belief that cannot be talked about." How would you respond to that person?

4. If you are willing, share with others in the class some personal experience that you identify as an experience of the holy.

PROJECTS

1. Find a copy of a book containing selections from the scriptures of the major religions of the world. Prepare a paper discussing selections

from each religion that illustrate both types of religious experience presented in this chapter.

2. Some Buddhist and Hindu teachers suggest that holiness can be experienced through spiritual discipline. In order to test this claim, find someone who will guide you in the discipline of prayer or mediation. After sustained experimentation, write a report on your experience.

3. Select one of the classical philosophical arguments for the existence of God in the Western tradition. Read thoroughly the argument as presented by the originator and commentators on it. Study also those who have rejected the argument. Then write an essay in which you state, in your own words, the argument for God, important refutations of the argument, and your own conclusions regarding the validity or nonvalidity of the argument.

4. Friedrich Nietzsche, the German philosopher, in an essay called "The Gay Science," has a madman declare, "Whither is God? I shall tell you. We have killed him—you and I." Write an essay in which you discuss Nietzsche's meaning. Criticize and evaluate this point of view from the perspective of a Hindu or a Buddhist.

SUGGESTED READINGS

Berger, Peter. *The Heretical Imperative: Contemporary Possibilities of Religious Affirmation*. Garden City, N.Y.: Doubleday, 1980, especially chapter 6.

Berger, Peter, ed. *The Other Side of God: A Polarity in World Religions*. Garden City, N.Y.: Doubleday, 1981.

Eliade, Mircea. *Yoga: Immortality and Freedom*. Princeton, N.J.: Princeton University Press, 1970.

Hesse, Herman. *Siddhartha*. Trans. Hilda Rosner. New York: New Directions, 1951.

Hick, John. *God Has Many Names*. London: Macmillan, 1981.

Miller, David L. *The New Polytheism: Rebirth of the Gods and Goddesses*. New York: Harper & Row, 1974.

Otto, Rudolf. *Mysticism East and West*. New York: Macmillan, 1960.

Robinson, John A. T. *Honest to God*. Philadelphia: Westminster Press, 1963.

Smith, Huston. *The Religions of Man*. New York: Harper & Row, 1965.

Watts, Alan W. *The Way of Zen*. New York: Random House, 1974.

CHAPTER 3

Sacred Stories

Long before people learned the skills of logic and the scientific method they told stories. In our time we still tell stories. The human imagination is as old as consciousness; it is as new as the most recent novel or last night's dream. Although not all stories are sacred, a story becomes sacred when its images and symbols express meaning and point to that which is affirmed as ultimate or holy. Some claim that whenever people have looked for something to base their lives on, they have chosen not the facts in which the world abounds, but the myths of an immemorial imagination.

This chapter suggests that along with scriptures, rituals, beliefs, ethical norms, and the arts, sacred stories are an important expression of religion and are interrelated with all other expressions of religious people. Stories about the gods tell of the human experience of the divine; these stories are often expressed in rituals. When explained by reason, the content of stories becomes belief. Moreover, religious painting, sculpture, and music are inspired by the images within the sacred stories. Both individuals and religious communities find sacred stories to be clues to their self-understanding. A study of religion, then, would be incomplete without an inquiry into sacred stories.

An essential source book for the serious student of sacred stories is a four-volume work by comparative mythographer Joseph Campbell called *The Masks of God.* In the volume called *Occidental Mythology* he suggests that sacred stories (he uses the term "myth") serve four religious functions. The first is that such stories elicit and support a sense of awe before the holiness of existence. They tell of the gods whose reality is wonderful, majestic, all-encompassing, and who sometimes demand human loyalty. At other times they refer to the still, small voice within consciousness. Basically these stories reflect the human experience of the holy. Second, sacred stories are cosmological, serving the human desire to know about the beginnings of the cosmos, of societies, and of human life itself. They function to provide a sense of living in an ordered cosmos rather than in a disordered chaos.

A third function of sacred stories is sociological; they tell who we are within a community and how we should behave. Finally, as a fourth function religious stories provide a way of self-understanding by helping the individual understand who he or she is; they lead individuals through crises of birth, puberty, marriage, suffering, and death; they reflect the inner life of every man and woman. A single sacred story may function in all these ways by linking, for example, mystery with cosmology, and society with the self. Many sacred stories, however, feature one or two of these functions as central themes. While every sacred story may not serve all these functions, they may nonetheless be discussed around the central themes that distinguish them. For purposes of clarity, we will link stories featuring the holy (numinological) and the cosmic order (cosmological) together. We will then examine these featuring psychological (self-understanding) and sociological (community) themes together.

SACRED STORY AND MYTH

Thus far we have avoided attention to the word "myth," not because that term is inadequate but because it is misunderstood. Most modern people, influenced by the traditions of reason and science, immediately suppose that a myth is an untrue story. News report often tell about "the myth" of something, referring to a fanciful tale that is contrary to fact. Other persons assume that a myth is an outdated story originating in some primitive, ignorant tribe.

Yet the majority of scholars in the field of religious studies mean something positive when they use the term "myth." For example, Mircea Eliade, the highly influential twentieth-century scholar, writes that "myth narrates a sacred history; it relates an event that took place in primordial time."[1] Similarly, historian of religion Charles Long, in writing about myths of creation, defines myth as "a true story—a story about reality."[2] A more complete definition providing a basis for this study comes from Alan Watts. an American interpreter of mythology and of Zen Buddhism: "Myth is to be defined as a complex of stories—some no doubt fact, and some fantasy—which, for various reasons, human beings regard as demonstrations of the inner meaning of the universe and human life."[3]

Dozens of other scholars of mythology agree that myths, ancient or modern, cannot be laughed at or pushed aside in a serious study of religion. The sacred stories, they all declare, are a profound aspect of religion, telling in a symbolic way truths about the way things really are for the people who tell them. The "reality" of myth is the reality of human experience as it probes for deeper truths and sacred realities; factual reality is not always useful in doing that. In the same way that literary fiction or poetry expresses profound truth without being fact, so also can myth reflect and invoke deep human meaning.

In recognition of the scholarly understanding of the meaning of the word myth and the importance of myth in religion, it is appropriate to use the terms "sacred story" and "myth" interchangeably. If you, the reader, tend to be intellectually uncomfortable with the concept myth and tend to give it negative meanings, then when myth is used, translate the term into sacred story. For maximum understanding, both terms will be used throughout the remainder of the chapter.

THE ORIGINS OF SACRED STORIES

Sacred stories have at least two complementary roots. The first is a general source that cannot be identified with a single person. Rather, stories have emerged as cultures have developed and as stories were orally passed down from generation to generation. The second source is the visions, hopes and dreams of individual persons—shamans or seers—whose experiences were told to the people in story form or dramatized in cultic rituals.

The first source is the society itself. People told stories just as we tell stories. The earliest of these stories were about divine beings, the processes of nature, and ancestral heroes. Stories were told of worlds being created, of birth, death, tragedy, intrigue, and love or hate among gods and humans. These myths served the purpose of providing a "sacred canopy" over individual and collective life.

Anthropological studies indicate that these ancient stories were intimately related to sacred rituals. Native Americans, for example, from as long ago as their history is known, have celebrated their stories in ceremonies around the sacred fire. Early Christians, too, performed their worship ritual every Sunday to reenact the story of their resurrected savior. Today, stories told throughout history are still found in every religious community.

The second root of myth is the inner life of highly respected religious leaders, most dramatically to be seen in the life story of holy persons in various primal cultures.[4] Accounts of these persons tell of dreams and visions that revealed the mysteries of life. John Neihardt, in his book *Black Elk Speaks*, relates the story of Black Elk, who, as a child, had a vision in which he communicated with divine powers. Following his vision, he believed it was his special calling to keep alive the vision through public rituals in order to save his Oglala Sioux nation from destruction.

The answer to the question, "What is the source of sacred stories?" is not exhausted by the simple answer that there are two roots, social and individual. Nor is each source separate from the other. The first, the stories told by people in a culture, profoundly influence the psychic life of an individual. The second, personal visions of special individuals, find their way into tribal stories and rituals. But whatever the origin of the sacred stories, they have been important religious expressions from the beginning of civilizations. Joseph Campbell emphasizes the significance of these stories in his vivid language:

Throughout the inhabited world, in all times and under every circumstance, the myths of man have flourished; and they have been the living inspiration of whatever else may have appeared out of the activities of the human body and mind. It would not be too much to say that myth is the sacred opening through which the inexhaustible energies of the cosmos pour into human cultural manifestation.[5]

ANCIENT MYTHS OF MYSTERY AND CREATION

The four functions of sacred stories have already been identified above. Each of these functions can also serve to identify four kinds of stories. The first two kinds are stories expressing convictions and featuring themes about divine mystery (numinological), and those telling about the creation of the cosmos (cosmological). Most often these two types are found together in cosmogonic or creation myths.[6] In regard to cosmogonic stories, Mircea Eliade explains that "there is no myth which is not the unveiling of mystery." Moreover, the mystery expressed is the hidden truth about the divine power acting in *in illo tempore* (at a time beyond time), and hence these stories provide a model for all eternity to those who live in time.[7]

As modern persons, we may be bothered by the assertion that sacred stories express a truth. Obviously for us, the stories are not always literally true. When we even raise the question about truth in myth we are usually thinking in a scientific way, a way not available to ancient people. For them, knowledge about how things "really are" came through their stories, and truth was an issue of *meaning* more than *facts*. We can suppose that they knew the meaning to be true because the myths provided an ordered system of meaning which corresponded with their own deepest experience.

Myths expressing the mystery of the holy and the creation of the world can be found in various cultures of the world. The stories tell of the transformation of chaos into order; out of darkness, formlessness, and void the cosmos was created. These imaginative stories may tell of the world emerging from the Great Mother or coming out of a cosmic egg. Others present the created world mysteriously arising out of nothing or being created by God or gods. But whatever the major motif may be in creation myths, they are poetic expressions about ultimate meaning, "not only of our existence, but the existence of the whole cosmos."[8]

A collection of hundreds of creation myths by Charles Long in his book *Alpha* provides an excellent introduction to sacred stories from many cultures. One such story from the Japanese tradition is given in considerable detail and can be shortened to hint at its contents.

Izanagi and Izanami, god and goddess of the heavens, stood on the floating bridge of heaven and dipped their spear into the waters below. As the spear was lifted, mud from the bottom of the sea dropped and congealed, forming a beautiful island. Wishing to live on the island thus created, and, as husband and wife, to produce other islands, they descended to the newly formed earth.[9]

Even today, at the national shrine of Ise, the sun goddess Amaterasu, an offspring of Izanagi and Izanami, is worshiped through a reenactment of parts of the ancient story. Only those insensitive to the contemporary impact of ancient myth would fail to see these dramas as a foundation of the Japanese love of their beautiful islands, the call to purification by water, and the propensity for constant personal renewal.

Similar in structure and function is the story of creation in the Jewish and Christian Bibles:

> In the beginning God created the heavens and the earth. The earth was without form and void, and darkness was upon the face of the deep; and the Spirit of God was moving over the face of the waters. And God said, "Let there be light"; and there was light. And God saw that the light was good; and God separated the light from the darkness. God called the light Day, and the darkness he called Night. And there was evening and there was morning, one day.
>
> And God said, "Let the earth bring forth living creatures according to their kinds: cattle and creeping things and beasts of the earth according to their kinds." . . . And God saw that it was good. Then God said, "Let us make man in our image, after our likeness; and let them have dominion over the fish of the sea, and over the birds of the air, and over the cattle, and over all the earth, and over every creeping thing that creeps upon the earth." So God created man in his own image, in the image of God he created him; male and female he created them.[10]

Many devout Jews and Christians who are not conscious of the mythic nature of their creation story suppose that it is a scientific description of how the world was created. Even while they argue for a literal understanding of this ancient story, however, they are profoundly influenced by the myth and maintain a sense of awe at the mysterious power of the one God who created the world out of the chaos. Whether literally understood or not, the story points to holy mystery and cosmic order.

Other Jews and Christians recognize that this story is not scientific fact, but they too affirm the profound meaning of the creation story. One of the American astronauts, upon looking down at the tiny ball of earth one Christmas Eve, took a Bible from his space possessions and read for the world to hear: "In the beginning God created the heavens and the earth." Many persons who live within the orbit of Judaism and

Christianity and are influenced by the creation story in Genesis are convinced that this universe is a cosmos, not a chaos; that all of the natural world was created good, and that humans have a responsibility to care for their sacred world. The ancient myth is still powerful, precisely in and through its poetic and storylike character.

Persons in the Hindu tradition, like those in other religions, hold sacred the storylike poems in the earliest scriptures in India, the Vedas. One myth of the beginning can be reconstructed as follows:

In the beginning there was nothing; neither being or not-being, death or immortality, night or day. There was only darkness, a void. Then whatever was—that One—was hidden by the void and came into existence by the power of heat. This One evolved, becoming desire and the first seed of mind. Bundles of seed were present, as well as powers; energy and impulse were there. Only later, by overflowing, did the gods come to be. But why and how did all this happen? Only the overseer in the highest heaven knows, or perhaps he does not know.[11]

Every reader of these sacred stories will immediately see that they have much in common. Each tells of the mystery of the divine creation. None of them is an adequate scientific account of how things began, but they were not written as science. Each, rather, seeks to communicate awe and wonder about the power or powers that turned nothing (or chaos) into something (or cosmos). Each seeks a response of devotion to the divine powers of creation. Each provides the basis for a world view holding that, at bottom, everything is spiritual, and the fundamental response of religious persons is one of respect for all that has been divinely made.

ANCIENT SOCIAL AND PERSONAL MYTHS

Ancient peoples possessed stories not only about the mystery of divine creation, but also myths about social order and personal identity. The text of the Enuma Elish, dating approximately five thousand years ago in Mesopotamia, provides a pattern for the ordering of society in accordance with the previous action of gods. Thus Mesopotamian society sought to pattern its organization after the way of the gods.[12]

Other ancient stories include moral codes to maintain social order. The Code of Hammurabi is an example originating seventeen centuries before the Common Era. It begins with an explanation that Hammurabi, appointed by the gods, was charged to bring justice to the people; therefore he provided an extensive moral code.[13] More familiar to most Westerners is the story in the second book of the Bible (Exodus), which provides a specific code for religious and moral living within society. A shortened form of that biblical story is as follows:

On the third month after the people of Israel had been led out of slavery in Egypt, they camped in the wilderness of Sinai near a great mountain. Then God spoke to Moses, and said, "If you will obey my voice and keep my covenant, you shall be my own possession." And when Moses told the people they said, "All that the Lord has spoken we will do." On the morning of the third day, as God had promised to Moses, there was thunder and lightning and a thick cloud on the mountain, and a very loud trumpet blast, so that all the people in the camp trembled. And Mount Sinai was wrapped in smoke, because the Lord descended upon it in fire. The Lord came down upon Mount Sinai and called Moses to the top of the mountain. Then God spoke all these words, saying:

I am the Lord your God. You shall have no other gods.
You shall not make for yourself a graven image.
You shall not take the name of the Lord in vain.
Remember the sabbath day to keep it holy.
Honor your father and your mother.
You shall not kill.
You shall not commit adultery.
You shall not steal.
You shall not bear false witness against your neighbor.
You shall not covet.

While the well-known story of Moses and the Ten Commandments deals with social and personal morality, another ancient Middle Eastern story, the Gilgamesh epic, concentrates on psychological identity and growth. It originated probably two thousand years before the Bible and came from the Sumerian culture in Mesopotamia. The Gilgamesh story is pieced together from many fragments rescued by archeologists and is available in a variety of translations. This epic stands as a vivid story of gods and people, struggles with life and death, the power of sex, the search for immortality, and the final decree of human duty. As you will see, the myth focuses on the god/man Gilgamesh who must have represented every person, just as Urk stood for every society. A brief version of that story follows:

There once lived a king named Gilgamesh of Urk, two-thirds god and one-third human, who as a young ruler was handsome, strong, and arrogant. Rather than live the kind of life expected of him, Gilgamesh instead spent days and nights seducing the young women and forcing their men into hard labor. Finally the people had taken their limit of abuse and requested the goddess Aruru to create a friend for Gilgamesh to occupy his time that Urk might have peace.

Granting that wish, Aruru created valiant Enkidu out of the clay of the earth. Enkidu was strong, bushy haired, and lived with animals. He was a frightening sight even to the rough hunters. Yet Enkidu was transformed into a gentle human through sexual intimacy with a temple priestess and was brought to the city in search of Gilgamesh. Of course he had to be taught to wear clothing, to eat properly, and to become civilized—all of which he was taught by the young lady. Thereupon he entered Urk: Strong, handsome, and valient, he was very much like Gilgamesh. Jointly seeking adventure, they set out together to kill the evil Huwawa who lived in the forest of the god Enlil.

With the courage of heroes, the two embarked on their journey, and quickly fulfilled their first task—killing the guardian of the forest.

Gilgamesh, resplendent in appearance, refused the seductive advances of the goddess Istar who, in her anger, sent a mighty bull of heaven to destroy Gilgamesh. The two powerful young men destroyed the bull, and Gilgamesh was hailed as hero. But in the height of his glory, Gilgamesh's friend Enkidu died at the decree of the gods. Gilgamesh was devastated in his grief over the loss of Enkidu and, in his new obsession with a fear of death, had only one burning concern—to escape the human fate of death.

In his desperation, Gilgamesh knew of one who had gained immortality and could give him that secret. This was Utnapishtim. Traveling the long and arduous journey, conquering untold dangers along the way, he relentlessly persisted until, at last, he crossed the ocean of death and reached Utnapishtim.

At first, Gilgamesh failed the test of overcoming sleep for six days and seven nights, the task given to him. Nevertheless, Utnapishtim finally told him the secret of the gods. At the bottom of the sea there is a plant which, when eaten by a person in old age, will rejuvenate life. With that news, Gilgamesh went to the bottom of the ocean, found the plant of immortality, and with great joy began his journey back to Urk. On the way, however, a great tragedy occurred. Gilgamesh, tired and hot from his travels, decided to bathe in a lake when a snake appeared, grabbed the plant, and ate it.

Gilgamesh now knew that there was no hope for him to gain immortal life. So he decided to accept the role of king which the gods had given him and return to his task of ruling his own city of Urk.

In commenting on this story, one writer, Alexander Heidel, suggests that this myth is presented to convey the bitter truth that death is inevitable for every person. Each person, then, has no choice but to do the duty assigned, leaving immortality to the gods.[14] Additional psychological dimensions are also present. The story suggests that men are often animal-like, needing the civilizing power of a women, even her sexual embrace. Men, the ancient story tells, need adventure, just as they can be enriched by friendship. And while the search for immortality is inevitable in that everyone fears death and wants to live forever, the human task is to live fully and morally in whatever role may be assigned.

MYTHIC CONSCIOUSNESS: DEAD OR ALIVE?

From the stories thus recounted, we might suppose that persons in all ancient cultures found their knowledge about the world, about society, and about themselves from their stories. If their total orientation was informed by sacred stories, we could say that they possessed a "mythic consciousness." We would conjecture, then, that the stories they were told and which they, in turn, told their children, expressed basic convictions. In short, the myths explained, for them, the way things "really are." Their worship, their world view, their place in society, their self-image all emerged from the stories preserved by the religious tradition.

We might suppose, upon first reflection, that contemporary persons no longer possess a mythic consciousness. The long period—about 2500 years—since rational modes of thought have been espoused by philosophers surely should guide us to think analytically, not mythically. Moreover, modern science has been part of Western cultures for five hundred years. Surely we want to look to empirical evidence—not to stories—for truth.

Obviously, modern people have been profoundly shaped by philosophy and the sciences. Twentieth-century technology has entered our conscious and unconscious ways of perceiving reality. Some have claimed that there is no knowledge outside of scientific knowledge, and the way to achieve all knowledge is by the scientific method. Some unreflective persons might even claim, "If you can't touch it, feel it, taste it, or program it on a computer, it doesn't exist." From this viewpoint all mythic presentations are at best naive and at worst absolute falsehoods.

Some religious persons called fundamentalists deny that their scriptures contain myth. They claim that all stories in the Bible or Qur'an or Vedas are literally true and can be proven scientifically. Still others recognize the importance of myths in ancient religions, but they insist upon the process of modernizing by demythologization. By that term they mean that modern people should seek the insights behind the myths and throw out the unscientific fantasy elements. Similarly, the twentieth-century theologian Paul Tillich suggested that myths often become broken. He meant that modern persons recognize that most myth is poetic story, not literal fact, yet it is a sacred story still possessing power in the lives of contemporary religious people.

For many people, perhaps a majority living now, the ancient stories are dead. These persons no longer feel a sense of awe and wonder when they hear creation stories. They are not inspired by stories of heroes like Moses (in the Bible), Arjuna (in the Bhagavad Gita), the Buddha, or the resurrected Christ. The term "secular" has been applied to those for whom the ancient stories and all other expressions of traditional religions are no longer meaningful.

Let us not be too quick, however, to assert that mythic consciousness is completely dead. We would find it useful, for example, to analyze current television programs, comic books, and movies to discover the stories told and believed about ourselves and our society. Professor of English and comparative mythologist Michael Sexson urges us to recognize that even modern scientists are active mythologists:

The so-called "big bang" theory of the origin of the universe, popular with most scientists today, has striking similarities to the vast number of creation stories collected by folklorists; and descriptions of such things as "quasars," "quarks," "antimatter," and "black holes" among astronomers are more curious than anything the mad mind of the mythmaker ever invented.[15]

MYTH IN CONTEMPORARY CULTURE

Contemporary mythographers, most notably those inspired by the psychologist C. G. Jung and the movement to understand mythic narrative as a means of religious knowledge, have made us aware that myth, broadly understood, remains in modern consciousness. Whether it appears in our dreams boiling up from the unconscious and uncovering mythic motifs for religious meaning, or whether it is in stories we read or tell, there still exists a mythic way of knowing—of experiencing and giving expression to the religious.

A mythic consciousness is manifested in us when we inwardly know that the real is more than what is observed with the senses or the scientific methods we use to predict and control our surroundings. The real is present in dreams as well as in waking perceptions. The real is known in the sudden creative insights we call intuition. Our knowledge of the real is expressed in images and metaphors that not only communicate but give embodiment to the real, often to the divine.

In commenting on these kinds of experiences, especially in relation to Native Americans, Jamake Highwater writes, "The individual experience of images and ideas is for almost all Indians of the Americas a communion with the 'Mighty Something' that is the abiding power of the cosmos."[16]

He then writes at length, explaining that not only Native Americans but all creative people seem to depend upon inspiration or intuition, expressed through images and dreams, for their life-supportng and life-affirming discoveries. The Native Americans especially understand their contact with the divine, the "Mighty Something," in a mythic/ritual way. And the experience of the divine is sought by every person, as Highwater here describes:

In the old days, a young person traveled to some remote area where it was known that many powers dwelled—often a mountaintop, or the shore of a remote lake, sometimes in the depths of a deep forest. There, the youth remained for several days and nights, alone and in utter silence, fasting from both food and water, humbly naked except for a loincloth since for most Indians the body is all a person owns, sometimes offering flesh from arms or legs and otherwise enduring hardships that provoked hallucination. . . .

. . . The young people in search of a vision . . . relied upon sacred songs and hardships to bring them into contact with the *orendas* [divine spirits]. If a youth was fortunate he or she would be approached by a vision that usually took the form of both visual and auditory hallucinations. An animal-power would appear and speak to the neophyte, teaching a song or revealing sacred and powerful images that he or she was instructed to paint on the body, clothing, shield, and tipi as a manifestation of personal power.

When returning to his or her people, the youth would describe the experience to close friends and relations, reconstructing it and filling in gaps, adapting it to the mythic norms of the culture.[17] The author reminds us that these experiences of dream, vision, and myth are not from an ancient culture, but of Native Americans of the nineteenth and twentieth centuries. It is a vivid presentation of how primal visionary/mythic thinking occurs.

The writing of depth psychologist C. G. Jung has provided ways of probing into our own modern, Western, mythic consciousness. Sigmund Freud opened the way for modern persons to include the dream world in the realm of the real, while Jung discovered that in dreams, these archetypal myths keep recurring and become part of what shapes our knowing, even of the divine.

In his Terry Lectures delivered at Yale University in 1937, Jung stated his conviction that human personality consists of both the conscious and the unconscious. The conscious aspect contains the observable part of the self; the unconscious is the unknown part. He continued in the following way:

My psychological experience has shown time and time again that certain contents issue from a psyche that is more complete than conciousness. They often contain a superior analysis or insight or knowledge which consciousness has not been able to produce. We have a suitable word for such occurrences—intuition. In uttering this word, most people have an agreeable feeling, as if something had been settled. But they never consider that you do not *make* an intuition. On the contrary, it always comes to you; you *have* a hunch, it has come of itself, and you only catch it if you are clever or quick enough.[18]

Moreover, in his *Essays on Analytical Psychology,* Jung made a distinction between the personal unconscious and the collective unconscious. Whereas the contents of the first come from the person's own experience, the contents of the second are common to the human race. When dreams or images arise from the personal unconscious and cause difficulty, they can be interpreted through personal associations and reflections. When, however, signals come from the collective unconscious, "They will be of the order, rather, of myth; in many cases even identical with the imagery of myths of which the visionary or dreamer will never have heard."[19]

Within the collective unconscious, then, the storehoue of archetypal myths resides, according to Jung. These archetypal myths influence the human psyche and present themselves in dreams, motivating persons toward ritualistic behavior and affirmations about the divine reality. Whether we know it or not, we think and live mythically.

Modern forms of mythic consciousness can be seen also through contemporary literature and storytelling. The spokespersons for all religions have always told stories, even as the scriptures upon which they depended were filled with stories. The humerous quip, "God created man because he loves stories," has been attributed to novelist Elie Wiesel. In commenting on that statement, historian James Wiggins points out the ambiguity of the pronoun "he" and suggests that stories may be liked by both God and man.[20]

Storytellers, whether Thomas Mann, Graham Greene, Flannery O'-Connor, Elie Wiesel, or hundreds more, have each chosen a narrative form for the expression of convictions, including convictions about something holy. Some have claimed that fiction is a more viable medium of communicating truth than any empirical account could ever be. Stories, like ancient myths, are a form of pretending, of thinking and acting "as if" something were true. In the ritualized form of myth, primal people actually put on the mask of a god and acted "as if" they were the god, thereby assuming the characteristics and power of the god. In so doing they became transformed or new creatures. The same is true in modern fiction, for we identify with the characters; becoming the other, we know what could not otherwise be known.

Fiction may well be rooted in history, and myth may refer to specific human events; in either case, however, the truth about the sacred, about the cosmos, about society and ourselves is presented now as it was for ancient people, through stories.

SUMMARY

Throughout the religious world, men and women have been informed and inspired by sacred stories. These stories tell of the wonders of the divine creation, of patterns for social order, of heroes and heroines whose struggles have been an inspiration for all who follow. Images in these stories have become symbols of faith, encouraging devotion to spiritual reality. Rituals externalize the stories, keeping them alive; scriptures preserve these sacred stories; belief systems organize the ideas into coherent creeds. Contemporary religious persons affirm ancient stories and create new ones as they express their beliefs about ultimate value.

NOTES

1. Mircea Eliade, *Myth and Reality,* trans. Willard R. Trask (New York: Harper & Row, 1963), p. 5.
2. Charles Long, *Alpha: The Myths of Creation* (New York: G. Braziller, 1963), p. 12.

3. Alan W. Watts, *Myth and Ritual in Christianity* (Boston: Beacon Press, 1968), p. 7.

4. The word "primal" rather than "primitive" is used by Jake Highwater in *The Primal Mind: Vision and Reality in Indian America* (New York: Harper & Row, 1981). His term avoids the pejorative connotation of "primitive" while suggesting that Native Americans, for example, demonstrate a basic consciousness different though not inferior to Western scientific and rational consciousness.

5. Joseph Campbell, *Hero with a Thousand Faces* (Cleveland: World Publishing, 1956), p. 3.

6. Often the terms "cosmogonic" and "cosmological" are used synonymously. In a strict sense, "cosmological" refers to theories of the universe as an ordered whole. "Cosmogony" means simply the creation of the universe. There is an obvious relationship, in that cosmogonic stories provide a sense of cosmic order. Yet for precision, the term "cosmogonic" is used here to deal with stories of creation.

7. Mircea Eliade, *Myths, Dreams, and Mysteries*, trans. Philip Mairet (New York: Harper & Row, 1960), p. 16. The same idea can be found in many works by Eliade.

8. Marie Louise von Franz, *Patterns of Creativity Mirrored in Creation Myths* (Zurich, Switzerland: Spring Publications: n.d.), p. 5.

9. See Charles Long, *Alpha*, pp. 147–49. See also for comparison William Theodore de Bary, ed., *Sources of Japanese Tradition*, vol. 1 (New York: Columbia University Press, 1964), pp. 24–29.

10. Taken from Genesis 1, Revised Standard Version of the Bible. It is worth noting that there is a second creation story, probably older, beginning chapter 2, verse 4 and continuing with the garden of Eden story.

11. The Rig Veda can be found in many translations of Hindu scriptures. A condensed version can be found in a translation by R. C. Zaehner, *Hindu Scriptures* (London: J. M. Dent and Sons, Everyman's Library, 1969), pp. 11–12.

12. See James B. Pritchard, *Ancient Near Eastern Texts* (Princeton: N.J.: Princeton University Press, 1955), pp. 37–72.

13. Ibid., pp. 164–80.

14. Alexander Heidel, *The Gilgamesh Epic and Old Testament Parallels*, 2d ed. (Chicago: University of Chicago Press, 1949), p. 11. The summary of the Gilgamesh myth presented here has been composed out of the texts in Pritchard and Heidel, along with reference to shortened versions in Gerald A. Larue, *Ancient Myth and Modern Man* (Englewood Cliffs, N.J.: Prentice-Hall, 1975), pp. 85–90 and Cornelius Loew, *Myth, Sacred History, and Philosophy: The Pre-Christian Religious Heritage of the West* (New York: Harcourt, Brace & World, 1967), *pp.* 52–59.

15. Michael Sexson, "Myth," in T. William Hall, ed., *Introduction to the Study of Religion* (New York: Harper & Row, 1978), p. 43.

16. Jamake Highwater, *Primal Mind*, p. 81.

17. Ibid., pp. 84–85.

18. C. G. Jung, *Collected Writings* (New York: Pantheon Press, 1953), 2:41.

19. Quoted in Joseph Campbell, ed., *Myths, Dreams, and Religion* (New York: E. P. Dutton, 1970), p. 170. Campbell goes on to assert that "the evidence for this in the literature of psychiatry seems to me now to be beyond question."

20. James B. Wiggins, ed., *Religion as Story* (New York: Harper & Row, 1975), p. ix.

QUESTIONS FOR STUDY AND DISCUSSION

1. Why do so many people reject the idea that their scripture and tradition contain myth? If they understood the term "myth" as presented in this chapter, would their objections be modified?

2. What does it mean to take something literally as opposed to symbolically? analogically? metaphorically?

3. What conditions must be met for fiction to be "true"?

4. Thomas Mann wrote, "In the life of the human race, myth comes at an early stage. In the life of an individual it is a late and mature one." What did he mean? Do you agree? Why or why not?

5. Why do some ancient sacred stories remain powerful for some modern people while other stories lose their meaning?

PROJECTS

1. Choose two of the books from the selected bibliography, identifying each author's definition of myth. Write a brief paper comparing and contrasting those definitions.

2. Select a sacred story from your own religious tradition and briefly tell that story. Then explain its meaning for contemporary religious people for whom it is a meaningful story.

3. Examine carefully advertisements in popular magazines. Identify images in the commercial art or language that is borrowed from ancient mythology.

4. One way to test the thesis that myth remains powerfully active in the modern world is to invent one. Compose a story that (a) accounts for the origin of the world and human beings, (b) tells of a perfect world that existed in *illo tempore,* (c) explains how, through some blunder, humanity lost this world, and (d) speaks of how, through specific rituals, this perfect world can be regained. Work out a ritual activity to dramatize the story, and select a number of other people to perform the rites.

5. Analyze a fictional film you have seen for its mythic character. How does the film, through mythic themes and images, express mystery, cosmic meaning, social reality, and/or personal identity?

SUGGESTED READINGS

Campbell, Joseph. *Myths to Live By*. New York: Viking Press, 1973.

Cassirer, Ernst. *Language and Myth*. Trans. Susanne K. Langer. New York: Dover Publications, 1946.

Coomaraswamy, Ananda and Sister Nivedita [Margaret E. Noble]. *Myths of the Hindus and Buddhists*. New York: Dover Publications, 1967.

Eliade, Mircea. *Myth and Reality*. Trans. Willard R. Trask. New York: Harper & Row, 1963.

———. *Myths, Dreams, and Mysteries*. Translated by Philip Mairet. New York: Harper & Row, 1960.

Heidel, Alexander. *The Gilgamesh Epic and Old Testament Parallels*. 2d ed. Chicago: University of Chicago Press, 1949.

Jung, C. G. *Man and His Symbols*. New York: Dell, 1964.

———. *The Portable Jung*. Ed. Joseph Campbell. New York: Viking Press, 1971.

Kirk, James A. *Stories of the Hindus: An Introduction Through Texts and Interpretation*. New York: Macmillan, 1972.

Larue, Gerald A. *Ancient Myth and Modern Man*. Englewood Cliffs, N.J.: Pren-
tice-Hall, 1975.
Loew, Cornelius. *Myths, Sacred History, and Philosophy: The Pre-Christian Religious
Heritage of the West*. New York: Harcourt, Brace & World, 1967.
Long, Charles H. *Alpha: The Myths of Creation*. New York: G. Braziller, 1963.
Murray, Henry A., ed. *Myth and Mythmaking*. Boston: Beacon Press, 1968.
Watts, Alan W. *Myth and Ritual in Christianity*. Boston: Beacon Press, 1968.

CHAPTER 4

Ritual

It has been suggested that the Western religious traditions have celebrated the *word* and the Eastern traditions the *silence*. Whatever grain of truth may exist in such an inflated generalization, however, no religious tradition is without the *act*. Indeed, it might even be argued that the ritual act is not only universal to religion, but is also the single most important characteristic of any *living* religiousness! This too may seem inflated, especially given a popular notion of ritual as "meaingless repetitive action," or a Western bias in favor of theology, doctrine, and creed. However, a look at the religion of all humankind—both historically and structurally—reveals at least the possibility, if not the truth, of the statement. Not only have all religions included ritual, but the concrete act of doing religion—especially in the heightened sense of sacredness that ritual represents—both completes and creates the very core of religion as a lived experience of what is real and sacred for someone. A ritual of marriage, for example, when religiously done, brings to experiential completion the unity of two people. In their eyes they are now "as one" and exist in a sacred wholeness with a new and renewed sense of who they are and what is real for them. In short, and as this essay will eventually show, if one looks at ritual with an empathy and sympathy for the religious meaning it may hold for its participants, one is struck by the power of ritual within any truly living religion.

This chapter reflects on a religious understanding of ritual and argues for its nature and importance as a religious expression. Of course, like any other religious expression, ritual may lose its power, degenerate into mechanical repetition, and be relatively meaningless. When this happens, however, either new and different rituals take their place, or living religiousness dies. Our own contemporary society reflects this process of religious change in which old meanings and forms die and new ones are born. While religious forms like rituals are some of the most conservative of all culture forms, they do change and, in our own culture, these changes are evident and rather rapid. Nonetheless, as will become clear by the end of this chapter, the importance and power of ritual for being human makes it difficult to envision a world without some kind of religion, and religion without some kind of ritual. In many ways, ritual represents the life of religion; it is religion lived out in concrete action.

TYPES OF RELIGIOUS RITUAL

The word *ritual* may denote a variety of things. It is therefore necessary to indicate just what kinds of expressions fall under the heading of ritual in this study. We will attempt two tasks: delimitation, or setting the boundaries of a definition, and typology, or classifying types of rituals.

The boundaries of the definition of ritual may be broad or narrow. Some people consider all ritual as religious, while others limit the definition of ritual to religious acts only. Both alternatives are possible, but both are arbitrary and unhelpful. We may define ritual as any patterned and usually repeated behavior that lies outside the daily routine; but it does not follow that all such rituals are religious. A social or cultural event such as a party or concert might, for example, be considered a ritual, but it does not necessarily hold religious meaning. Therefore, the delimiting key to a definition of ritual in this chapter will be to distinguish religious from nonreligious ritual.

For our purposes, a ritual is religious if it expresses an ultimate value, meaning, sacrality, and significance for someone—that is, if it somehow touches the foundations of what that person considers real and sacred. To quote a recent study of religious ritual: "When repetitive actions refer to essential structures of the universe, and paradigmatic modes of being, then we have genuine ritual."[1] With such an understanding, one might, for example, make sense out of the rituals of an American "civil religion" such as Memorial Day or a President's funeral. One might also find religious ritual in a college fraternity initiation or a marriage ceremony constructed completely outside any of the symbols or institutions of an established religion. Generally speaking, however, religious rituals are found within the religions of humankind—from the most "primal" and tribal cultures to the universalistic "great religions." Such rituals fall within one or more of the following types:

The first type includes rituals associated with *ecological cycles*, that is, rituals whose time, nature, and intent are closely associated with the cycles of the natural universe. For example, rituals of planting and harvesting, of hunting and animal cycles, of spring or fall, and of the movements of stars and planets fall within this type.

The second type is nonecological *liturgical calendar* rituals, that is, rituals of a given religion or culture that follow a regular cyclic pattern of repetition but are not primarily associated with the cycles of the natural universe. The Jewish and Christian year of special holy days is a good example of this, although one can find such yearly calendars in other religions too.

Third, we have rituals of the *human cycles,* that is, rituals focusing on the individual process of birth, growing up, and death. Often referred to as "rites of passage," human cycle rituals include the rituals of every culture associated with birth, naming, initiation, marriage, and death.

Noncyclic *crisis rituals* make up the fourth type. These are rituals that, while often repeated, do not necessarily follow any regular cycle of repetition but are done "on demand" whenever necessary. Good examples of such rituals would be divination techniques, curative rituals, and certain kinds of fertility rituals.

This typology is not exhaustive, and some rituals may fall into two or more of these categories at the same time. However, it is important to describe the phenomena we include under the expression ritual. In summary, religious rituals usually belong to one or more of these types: ecological cycle rituals, liturgical calendar rituals, human cycle rituals, and crisis rituals.

UNDERSTANDING RITUAL

In spite of the universality and importance of ritual within the religions of humankind, the study of ritual is only now coming into its own in the general study of religion. While the reasons for this are varied, an important one is that the immediacy of the living act (verbal or nonverbal) is more difficult to study than the words, symbols, and institutions that make up religion. Until recently, at least within the academic field of religion, the study of ritual had been sporadic at best. Now, however, increasingly sophisticated work has begun to open a deeper understanding of the importance, nature, and function of religious ritual. Let us look briefly at some of these views or interpretations of ritual.

RITUAL IN HISTORY

One view of ritual focuses on the relationship of ritual and history. This historical interest proceeds in several ways. One approach examines the function ritual plays in the transmission of cultural and religious symbols, values, and self-understandings—or the transmission of a culture's history and tradition. Another examines the historical relation between myth and ritual, that is, the question whether ritual precedes or comes out of myth. While such historical questions are now a dead issue—the answer is more "both/and" than "either/or"—they have enlivened religious studies for some time.[2] A third historical concern has been the relation between ritual and the arts. Many scholars have pointed to the close affinity between ritual and drama, for example, while others have focused on literature. In any case, these concerns indicate the importance of ritual as a point of origin for many of the arts.

RITUAL AS PLAY/PERFORMANCE

Another view of ritual relates it closely to either play or performance. Analyzing the play element of culture, the cultural philosopher Johan Huizinga[3] includes ritual as one primary type of play. He understands genuine play as finally serious in that it both reflects and helps order a culture's world: using such interpretive categories as make-believe, ordered activity, and play space as sacred space, he draws parallels between play and ritual that are both interesting and suggestive. A related kind of view draws parallels between drama, performance, and ritual.[4]

RITUAL AS RELIGIOUS POWER

Still other views have arisen from phenomenological studies of religion focusing on the religious power of ritual, as well as its important relationship to myth.[5] (This view is expanded below.)

RITUAL AS SOCIAL/PSYCHOLOGICAL FUNCTION

Finally, social scientific views, especially from anthropology, have been very important. These views stress the sociological-cultural functions of ritual. The exemplary models of this approach are Clifford Geertz and Victor Turner, so we now look briefly at their interpretations.

Geertz's view is best summarized by his own statement: "The anthropological study of religion is therefore a two-staged operation: first, an analysis of the system of meanings embodied in the symbols which make up the religion (or ritual) proper, and second, the relating of these systems to social-structural and psychological processes."[6] For Geertz, religion is a complex symbol system reflecting, creating, and integrating a culture's sense of reality, meaning, values, and social ordering. It is a powerful mediating and ordering force bridging the gap between the ethos of a culture (the actual state of affairs) and its mythos (or its ideals and "imagined world"). Within this system, ritual is crucial to the fusing of these worlds and to the establishing of religious conviction. He says of ritual, for example:

In a ritual, the world as lived and the world as imagined, fused under the agency of a single set of symbolic forms, turn out to be the same world, producing thus that idiosyncratic transformation in one's sense of reality.... It is, primarily at least, out of the context of concrete acts of religious observance that religious conviction emerges on the human plane.[7]

Victor Turner, who has perhaps contributed more to ritual studies within anthropology than any other single person, shares some of the general approach of Geertz, but he has focused much more on the nature of ritual specifically. Building his generalizations about ritual from very specific studies of particular rituals (in this case the Ndembu tribe in Africa), Turner offers insightful interpretations of the nature and value of ritual for human culture and society. Central to this interpretation is the notion of ritual as a dramatic process whereby normal social structure is transcended and a temporary unity is attained beyond all usual social distinctions. In addition, the central values and structures of society are reinforced and/or charged with creative power. More specifically, he uses the central categories of "liminality" (living on the threshold) and "communitas" (sense of communal oneness) to speak of the power of ritual:

Communitas breaks in through the interstices of structure, in liminality; at the edges of structure, in marginality; and from beneath structure, in inferiority. It is almost everywhere held to be sacred or "holy," possibly because it transgresses or dissolves the norms that govern structured and institutionalized relationships and is accompanied by experience of unprecedented potency.... There is a dialectic here, for the immediacy of communitas gives way to the mediacy of structure ... [for] men are released from structure into communitas only to return to structure revitalized by this experience of communitas.[8]

While Turner's understanding of communitas and liminality will be explained further below, it is important to realize here the power that he suggests ritual has for both breaking out of the normal and for creatively revitalizing the normal. Like Geertz, then, Turner believes that ritual does not simply reflect social ordering but is a powerful tool for both reflecting and creating the deepest cultural values and for revitalizing and even changing social structure itself.

We have spent some time with the anthropological view because it has been such an important source of contemporary ritual studies. While it is impossible to discuss or even mention here all the people and theories connected with this viewpoint, we have suggested key models that seem to represent these views.

LOOKING AHEAD: THIS CHAPTER'S VIEW

The view of ritual discussed below is one that owes much to the anthropological and phenomenological views briefly characterized above, and to the definitions of religion offered by this book. We understand ritual to be an important and distinctive symbolic expression within the religious life, one that both expresses people's deepest values or faith and functions to move them toward their religious goals or ideals. In fact, together with myth or sacred story (with which ritual is often associated in the actual religious lives of people), ritual is perhaps the most important and most universal of the religious expressions. Within the context of the religious life, or for people who experience religion as a living reality, ritual might be thought of as *a specific and usually repeated complex "language" of paradigmatic word and gesture.* Such a way of describing or defining ritual points to the fact that it is generally highly specified and often repeated action, is constituted by more than just bodily actions (namely words, art, and so forth), forms a complex "language" full of meaning for people, and is religiously powerful or paradigmatic.

Before expanding this understanding of ritual in greater detail, an explanation of the word "paradigmatic" may be helpful. "Paradigm" refers to a concept or action that serves as pattern or model for all that is related to it. Thus a religious paradigm will provide a pattern for understanding religion as well as for living religiously. More specifically, a religious paradigm will point to whatever is sacred, that which has power and which is of unconditioned value. It will also clarify what is understood as true, meaningful, and real. While all religious expressions are paradigmatic in some sense, ritual—as lived religion—is perhaps the best example. Ritual embodies or enacts the sacred or ultimate in an immediate way and thereby has immediate power to both express the holy and transform people.

AN INTERPRETATION OF RITUAL

Ritual becomes religious or paradigmatic when three elements are present: (1) the sacred context within which it normally takes place; (2) the transcendent power that marks the core of its meaning; and (3) the transformative power that makes it effective. These elements also show how complex ritual can be as well as why it is a repeated act.

RITUAL IN SACRED CONTEXT

The first element present in a religious ritual is its sacred context. Within a sacred context, the central words of the Latin Mass, *"hoc est corpus meum"* ("this is my body"), are filled with power and meaning for believing Catholics. Outside of that context, those same words become mere hocus-pocus. While this rather dramatic example may overstate the case, it succinctly points to the importance of a sacred context for contributing to the religious meaning and power of ritual. This sacred context includes sacred times, sacred places, a sacred tradition, and sacred participants. In short, ritual does not usually take place in a vacuum but in particular places at particular times, within particular traditions, and involving certain kinds of participants.

Sacred Time

Time is not experienced by religious traditions or people as homogeneous or the same throughout; certain times are more auspicious and sacred than others—more correct and right for rituals to take place. Perhaps the clearest example is the idea of sabbath in the Jewish and

Christian traditions. Such times are sacred not only by traditional usage, but because God, or the gods, has established it so. Also, certain times are sacred and proper for ritual because whatever is considered holy and/or divine has made its presence known then. Thus holy days in any religious tradition, or even particular times of any given day (for example, sunrise or sunset), are sacred times because the holy ordained it as such, or the sacred presence is felt then. In other cases, such as the birth and maturation of a human being, certain times are considered sacred since they mark important turning points in that life.

In these ways, the time of a ritual may add to its power, meaning, and sacrality, and thus to its paradigmatic character. An Easter sunrise service, for example, is perhaps more powerful and meaningful because of its performance at dawn, for not only is Easter the time of Christ's resurrection, but dawn is the time of the resurrection of light and life. The time of ritual—as a sacred time—contributes to the sacred context of a religious ritual and therefore to its religious power.

Sacred Place

Similarly, certain places carry sacred value and significance. For example, in noting the parallels between play and ritual one author says:

We found that one of the most important characteristics of play was its spatial separation from ordinary life. A closed space is marked out for it, either materially or ideally, hedged off from everyday surroundings. Inside this space the play proceeds, inside it the rules obtain. Now, the marking out of some sacred spot is also the primary characteristic of every sacred act. Whenever it is a question of taking a vow or being received into an Order or confraternity, or of oaths and secret societies, in one way or another there is always such a delimitation of room for play. The magician, the augur, the sacrificer begins his work of circumscribing his sacred spot. Sacrament and mystery presuppose a hallowed spot.[9]

Ritual space thus implies a break in normal space, just as ritual time implies a break in normal time. Whether designated as such by the gods or recognized as a place where sacrality is felt, ritual space is a sacred space for a ritual. This space, whether a church, a mountain top, a grove in the jungle, a city, or even a home, then becomes a significant part of the general sacred context.

Sacred Tradition

The particular symbols, actions, or words of a ritual are usually taken from a particular religious heritage or tradition (for example, Judaism or Islam). By their very presence in the ritual, they make the whole tradition a part of the context. *"Hoc est corpus meum"* in the Latin Mass, for example, points not only to some particular ritual words of long-standing importance within Roman Catholicism, but to the Latin language itself as a part of that sacred tradition. These words, when spoken, imply the whole sacred tradition of Roman Catholicism back through a sacred history. Sacred tradition thus points to any part of, or the whole of, that which has gone before but still plays a part in the ritual. By tradition, therefore, we mean the mythology, history, particular symbols, practices, persons, gestures, community, and set of institutions of a specific religion, especially as represented in a ritual. The sacrality of the tradition, then, lends to the sacrality, meaning, and power of the ritual.

Sacred Participants

Sacred participants are the "specialists in the sacred," such as priests or shamans, rabbis or ministers, diviners or sorcerers. These people become a part of the sacred context by virtue of their special sacred power and authority. Whatever the nature of such power within any given religion, or however it has been attained, these human participants—as themselves symbolic expressions—are not only important to the sacred context, but are in some instances absolutely critical to the effectiveness of the ritual itself. The exemplary model of a sacred participant in almost every culture is the priest, or his or her equivalent. The priest is the one who, almost by definition, "handles the sacred" or is the "ritual doer." This does not mean all rituals must have priests, or even that all rituals must have some religious authority in charge, but it does suggest how important is the role these figures play in the sacred ritual.

Sacred participants might also refer to especially sacred implements or objects without which a ritual lacks power. Within many Native American religious rituals, for example, the sacred pipe is such a participant.

Together, the four elements or aspects of the sacred context described briefly above—time, space, tradition, participants—contribute to the general sacrality, meaning, power, and paradigmatic character of the ritual.

TRANSCENDENT POWER

In addition to a sacred context, a religious ritual involves transcendent power. The power of a religious ritual takes two forms: (1) an ability to bring into presence that which is considered holy or ultimately real, and (2) an ability to suspend and go beyond the normal mundane world of time and space, and to create a world that is whole, true, ordered, sanctified, and celebrated. Together, these factors make up the "transcendent power" of ritual, for, though they are distinct, both elements localize true power in transcendence—either the presence of transcendent reality or an experience of transcending time and ordinary life.

Both aspects of the transcendent power of ritual are perhaps best expressed by the historian of religions, Mircea Eliade. Eliade emphasizes ritual as a reversal of time in which the primordial, creative acts of the gods—told in myth—are reenacted and brought into the present. In this view, myth (that is, the acts of the gods) represents a divine and paradigmatic model for ritual, and it is by repeating such models that the sacred (that is, the gods or whatever is considered transcendent) is made present, giving the ritual its power. Eliade says, for example, that "every ritual has a divine model, an archetype." Then, quoting Hindu scripture, he says:

"We must do what the gods did in the beginning." "Thus the gods did, thus men do." This Indian adage summarizes all the theory underlying rituals in all countries. We find the theory among so-called primitive people no less that we do in developed countries.[10]

For Eliade, myth reveals the primary locus of ritual power, for it is in the creative acts of the gods—particularly "in the beginning," or in the primordial time—that true power, reality, being, and creativity lie. To show this, Eliade focuses on the tendency to repeat the cosmogonic myth, or the myth of the creation of the world. The creation of the world was the creative act *par excellence,* and ritual, by entering into that primordial time *(illo tempore)* and by repeating or reenacting the myth, participates in the power of the original acts of creation. As Eliade says:

Thus the cosmogonic myth serves . . . as the archetypal model for all creations, on whatever plane—biological, psychological, spiritual. But since ritual recitation of the cosmogonic myth implies reactualization of that primordial event, it follows that he for whom it is recited is magically projected *in illo tempore,* into the "beginning of the World"; he becomes contemporary with the cosmogony. What is involved is, in short, a return to the original time, the therapeutic purpose of which is to begin life once again, a symbolic rebirth.[11]

The reenactment of myth indicates how ritual can symbolically make present the sacred as well as draw the human out of ordinary time and life into a time beyond time via a breakthrough experience.

The presence of the holy in ritual does not just depend on mythic reenactment, however. Rituals invoke the presence of sacred reality in other ways too—by sacred words and gestures, or by symbols that point to and invoke the presence of the transcendent, sacred, and powerful. In Tibetan Buddhist rituals, for example, the various enlightened beings called bodhisattvas, are symbols or aspects of buddhahood itself. Invoking the presence of the bodhisattvas thus brings the divine Buddha itself into presence. Here, myths or "acts of the gods" are not as important as the transcendent power of a particular mode of being called enlightenment, symbolized by buddhas and bodhisattvas. However conceived, the "presence" of the sacred remains a significant part of the transcendent power of ritual. The historian of religions Evan Zuesse puts it this way:

Ritual obtains its special effect through its adherence to models. What is repeated in ritual is the creative constitution of the real ... [With] a sacred antiquity and a primordial quality.... To do the rite again is to join with the ancestors and regenerate the ideality of their lives.... The particular is made paradigmatic, and the archetypal is made concrete and bodily present. Time is broken through.[12]

While Zuesse's language sounds like Eliade, he avoids limiting these models to myth and the "acts of the gods." His view of the sacred presence might include such transcendent ideals as love or buddhahood as well as myths made present in the ritual.

Zuesse also points to the power of ritual to draw people beyond ordinary time. Like Eliade he speaks of breaking out of ordinary time into another kind of time, or another kind of life and situation. He refers to a particular quality of religious experience in the ritual, a breakthrough experience of transcending the normal and mundane character of time, space, and social order that makes all things new and whole. This shift in focus allows us to understand better the experiential and existential character of ritual, and the contribution of that character to the meaning and power of ritual as religious and paradigmatic. Speaking for this point in terms of African ritual, the historian of religions Benjamin Ray says:

The ritual sphere is the sphere *par excellence* where the world as lived and the world as imaged become fused together, transformed into one reality. Through ritual man transcends himself and communicates directly with the divine. the coming of divinities to man and of man to divinity happens repeatedly with equal validity on almost every ritual occasion. The experience of salvation is thus a present reality, not a future event. In short, almost every African ritual is a salvation event in which human experience is recreated and renewed in the all important ritual Present.[13]

This comment on African ritual describes precisely our point about the transcendent power of ritual, in both elements of bringing transcendence into presence, and of breaking through ordinary life. On the one hand, the holy becomes present—divinity comes to humanity and humanity to divinity. On the other hand, ritual brings about the breakthrough experience of a moment in and out of time, a "salvation experience" of transcending self and world and of realizing the unity of all worlds, both actual and ideal.

More specifically, however, the transcending of normal time and space refers to what Turner calls liminality or being "on the threshold." To be liminal is to have broken out of normal social order and hierarchy, normal individual identity, and normal temporality. To be liminal in ritual, at least for Turner, is thus to have transcended both time and the normal social order. The peyote pilgrimage of the Huichol Indians of Mexico is a good example of liminality. In the ritual, not only is normal time and space transcended as the people walk in the time and place of the gods *(Wirikuta)*, but social roles are reversed and, for example, the old man is called "the baby."

Closely related to this breakthrough experience is the experience of unity and wholeness, or the "fusion of the worlds" as expressed by Ray above. The experience of transcending is not merely a going beyond, but also a coming to something—in this case an experience of wholeness, unity, order, sanctity, and celebration. On this point, Zuesse emphasizes that ritual is concrete, bodily, and experientially immediate, and that it brings togther the prereflective world of sensation and feeling with the reflective world of self- and cultural-consciousness. Zuesse suggests, for example: "Since ritual is a paradigmatic way of the body knowing itself to be in the world, ritual acts have a crucial importance for consciousness and existence, binding together things and awareness into a unity."[14] A ritual may bring together not only the worlds of feeling and reflection, but also the microcosmic world of our immediate experience and the macrocosmic world of universe or cosmos, and the worlds of self and others. Ritual helps us to "locate" ourselves in the world; in ritual the inner self meets the external world.

In this sense, Zuesse echoes Turner's understanding of communitas, or the sense of communal oneness. In Turner's view, the transcendence of time and social order in liminality leads, through ritual, to the sense of true community, shared world, and shared equality. Turner suggests this state of true community might best be described through Buber's understanding of I-Thou relationships. The Huichol pilgrimage again provides a good example. During the time of the pilgrimage, a special group unity is attained; it is literally done and undone before and after the pilgrimage by a ceremonial binding and unbinding. More generally, such notions as the Christian "communion of the saints," or the Jewish sense of "peoplehood" and family, are experienced in Christian and Jewish rituals and expressed there.

The experience of communitas and a new unity or wholeness is a powerful result of the breakthrough experience of ritual. It helps people "locate" themselves in a meaningful world.

Ritual gestures forth the world as meaningful and ordered. It establishes a deep primary order which precedes the world that can be spoken, and out of which the word proceeds, to which it returns. . . . Every gesture . . . is a revelation of a way of being located in the universe; each gesture points out a universe too, and makes spaces in it for human life.[15]

Finally, the transcendent power of ritual, as both the presence of the holy and the breakthrough experience, sanctifies and celebrates the world that it creates. In ritual, the world is not only whole, but it is holy, sacred, and good. The festive character of many rituals points especially to this sanctification and celebration.

The transcendent power of ritual, therefore, marks the core of its religious meaning and power. Without this transcendent power, ritual would indeed be "merely ritual"—that is, empty gesture and relatively meaningless form. With it, however, the holy, transcendent reality becomes present, and ordinary time, life and social/psychological existence is broken through and transcended. Together, these two types of transcendence create the transcendent power.

TRANSFORMATIVE POWER

A distinct form of ritual power, yet one closely related to the transcendent power discussed above, is its power to change, transform, and affect people and their world. Turner speaks of this transforming power in social and cultural forms, while Eliade calls it the potential for recreating worlds. Either way, ritual is understood as having the power to change, especially if seen from the point of view of the participants. The transformations that ritual brings about can be discussed in four distinct ways: (1) the personal or individual; (2) the collective or group; (3) the natural ecosystem; and (4) the cosmic totality. As with the types of rituals mentioned above, these categories are neither exhaustive nor mutually exclusive. Any single ritual may involve all of them, while other rituals may involve effects that don't exactly fit any of them. Nonetheless, the transformative power of ritual may be understood in these four ways.

The Individual

In our modern and individualistic society, we may naturally begin by considering the effects of ritual on the individual—effects going all the way from "I feel better" to "I'm born again!" The kind of individual effects we point to here, however, refer less to emotions and feelings than to deep transformations in identity and social or religious role. These effects are often expressed in terms of rebirth, renewal, healing, or wholeness.

Perhaps the clearest examples of these rituals are the rites of passage, or "rituals of the human cycle." Rituals of birth, naming, initiation, marriage, and death—to mention only the most obvious—are processes by which the individual passes through life in a series of transformations; indeed, they help establish a spiritual path through life. In many cultures, these rituals not only signal the process of growing up but of moving "upward" toward a more spiritually fulfilling existence. Singling out the symbols of death and rebirth in such rituals, Eliade discusses initiation as a process of death and rebirth whereby the child dies to an old mode of being and is reborn to a new and more sacred one, adulthood. He says, for example: "Initiatory death provides the clean slate on which will be written the successive revelations whose end is the formation of a new man. . . . This new life is conceived as the true human existence, for it is open to the values of spirit.[16]

In a less dramatic yet nonetheless important understanding of this characteristic of the effect of ritual, Zuesse focuses on self-definition as one of the primary intentions of rituals. He suggests on the one hand the importance of connections, relationships, and links with others in the process of self-definition. On the other hand he points to the significant understanding of ritual as a primary place where these links happen. Zuesse concludes that "ritual is therefore part of an elemental process of self-definition and self-maintenance."[17] In short, we come to know deeply who we are in relation to others, and ritual is a crucial place for establishing true relationship and true selfhood.

Other important expressions of transformative power reside in images of healing and wholeness. This can be seen, for example, in the words of the Catholic Mass: "Lord, I am not worthy to receive you, but only say the word and I shall be healed." Taking their cue from the unity and wholeness represented in the transcendent power, these images suggest the power of ritual to heal at various levels: physically, psychologically, or spiritually.

The Group

Taking a cue from the unity and wholeness discussed under transcendent power above, and from Turner's view of communitas in ritual, we may conclude that ritual creates a sense of true and shared community among its participants, and perhaps between them and others as well, both living and dead. Whether in the form of a marriage covenant between two people, a tribal ritual in a group, or a larger notion such as the "communion of the saints" in Christianity, ritual helps restore and create a sense of sacred community.

Both Turner and Zuesse describe the particular character of individual relationships within ritual as I-Thou, that is, as a relationship of shared, mutual humanity and integrated relatedness. This factor was discussed under the sense of unity in the transcendent power, but it is relevant here too insofar as it continues after the ritual and affects the whole sense of community and social cohesiveness.

Zuesse points out that this sense of community may also result in ethical beliefs and actions. To take a Christian example, if ritual helps establish not only the sense of the communion of saints but also a more general sense of our total common humanity bound ideally in love, then one effect of the ritual might well be whatever good works issue from it for the good of all. Words near the end of the Mass thus say, "We have heard God's Word and eaten the body of Christ. Now it is time for us to leave, to do good works, to praise and bless the Lord in our daily lives." Similarly, Confucian ritual points toward an ethical stance of filial piety, and a Buddhist ritual ideally results in compassion for all beings. In short, whether the particularistic ethic of a given tribe or culture, or a more universal ethic such as found in the world religions, ritual affects the group by inspiring ethical sensibilities and patterns of behavior.

The Ecosystem

In the eyes of many religious people, ritual can affect the nonhuman order too, for example, the fertility and growth of plants and animals, and the workings of sun, moon, and stars. In fertility rituals (including human fertility), the power of ritual is understood to restore and/or recreate the growth and flow of all natural life. The rain and sun dances of Native Americans, the rice-transplanting rituals of Japan, the hunting rituals of tribal Africa, and the spring rituals of many cultures suggest the pervasive character of this interest in ritual's transformative power. In speaking for the Dogon tribe of Africa, for example, the historian of religions Benjamin Ray shows the importance of the creation mythology and the creator god Amma for all aspects of Dogon life, and especially for the major rituals that reflect or repeat these creative acts. In one particular example, the ritual that re-presents Amma's "signs" (that is, important gifts of Amma at the time of creation) brings plenitude and order to the whole world. Ray summarizes thus:

The placement of these Signs on sacred objects is an efficacious act that "produces" the things to which the Signs refer. . . . The painting of these signs upon the altar helps to maintain the world of existence. . . . Signs are also painted upon the major totemic sanctuaries in order to perpetuate the totemic animals and natural species associated with them. . . . During the spring agricultural rites, the head of the family inscribes at the center of his fields a pattern representing the 266 Signs and cosmic Seeds. This, together with Amma's blessing, will fructify the newly sown fields. In this way, Signs revealed in the myth function as the archetypal forms enabling the Dogon to both comprehend and control this universe.[18]

Just if and how ritual might literally function to create things (like rain, or children, or good harvests) is not at all clear to the modern mind. In many cultures and religions, however, rituals are understood to do just that.

Cosmic Totality

Many rituals express an intent to renew, change, or transform the cosmos in general. This intent perhaps includes all the others described above, but goes beyond them in trying to get at the very core of time and life itself. Eliade focuses on the New Year's ritual, for here the sense of time itself winding down and being recreated is most present. In this view, "the New Year is a reactualization of the cosmogony, it implies starting time over again at its beginning, that is, restoration of the primordial time, the "pure" time, that existed at the moment of Creation. . . . It is also a matter of abolishing the past year and past time."[19] In short, New Year's time is the ritual time *par excellence* when a new creation follows on the degeneration and demise of the year and of time itself, and the totality of existence is made new, whole, fresh, and sacred again.

A functional equivalent for the New Year ritual is the fire altar sacrifice of ancient Hinduism. Here the cosmos itself, represented by the god Prajapati, is rebuilt and renewed annually in the building of the fire altar and the creative sacrifice of Prajapati. These and similar rituals have been especially important among primal and traditional cultures. Often in these major rituals the cosmogonic myth is repeated, for the very character of life and time is at stake. Our own greatly weakened version appears in our New Year celebrations, with the chaos of a New Year's Eve party (symbolizing the demise of time and year), and the New Year's Day resolutions (symbolizing renewal and order). More appropriately, however, our equivalent rituals probably reside in our dominant religious traditions, exemplified in Easter and Rosh Hashanah.

In whatever form they appear, these rituals become models of transformative power; for the participants life and time itself are restored and renewed.

CONCLUDING REMARKS

We have discussed three elements of religious ritual: its sacred context, its ability to make transcendence present, and its power to transform life. Because it is so complex, and because it undergirds the rest of the religious life, ritual itself may be understood as paradigmatic. It reflects and builds powerful paradigms of experience, belief, and behavior; it touches the truly real and meaningful; and it creates and renews life. It lies at the heart of religious life, and it is therefore appropriate, even necessary, to repeat. As Zuesse says:

Repetitive actions are the clearest expression of the will to be and to be human. The random behavior of the general organism is adjusted and articulated in a specific, emphatic fashion. It is because this fashion is *true*, and *necessary*, that it must be repeated.[20]

Ritual thus reveals not only a "thirst for (pure) being" or a "need to plunge periodically into this sacred and indestructible time" as Eliade emphasizes, but also a means by which humanity controls or creates a way to be fully human; indeed, humanity fashions a meaningful world having sacrality and power. Perhaps every genuine religious ritual is a "salvation event" as suggested by Ray for African ritual, for ritual renews and makes things right; it saves, heals, and makes whole again.

NOTES

1. Evan Zuesse, "Meditation on Ritual," *Journal of the American Academy of Religion,* 43 (September 1975): 529.
2. See a rehearsal of this discussion by Clyde Kluckholm, "Myths and Rituals: A General Theory," in William Lessa and Evon Vogt, ed., *Reader in Comparative Religion,* 2d ed. (New York: Harper & Row, 1965), pp. 144–58.
3. See Johan Huizinga, *Homo Ludens: A Study of the Play-Element in Culture* (Boston: Beacon Press, 1956).
4. Richard Scheckner, *Essays on Performance Theory (1970–1976)* (New York: Drama Books, 1977). Cf. works by Grimes listed in suggested readings below.
5. See the suggested readings for references to Brenneman, Eliade, and Zuesse.
6. Clifford Geertz, "Religion as a Cultural System," in *Anthropological Approaches to the Study of Religion,* ed. Michael Banton (London: Tavistock, 1966) p. 42. Parenthetical phrase added.
7. Geertz, p. 28.
8. Victor Turner, *The Ritual Process: Structure and Anti-Structure* (Chicago: Aldine Publishing, 1969), pp. 128ff.
9. Huizinga, pp. 19f.
10. Mircea Eliade, *Cosmos and History: The Myth of the Eternal Return,* trans. Willard R. Trask (New York: Harper & Row, 1959), p. 21.
11. Mircea Eliade, *The Sacred and the Profane: The Nature of Religion,* trans. Willard R. Trask (New York: Harper & Row, 1961), p. 82
12. Zuesse, p. 529.
13. Benjamin Ray, *African Religions: Symbol. Ritual and Community* (Englewood Cliffs, N.J.: Prentice-Hall, 1976), p. 17.
14. Zuesse, p. 519.
15. Zuesse, pp. 518f.
16. Mircea Eliade, *Rites and Symbols of Initiation: The Mysteries of Birth and Rebirth,* trans. Willard R. Trask (New York: Harper & Row, 1968), p. xiv.
17. Zuesse, pp. 524ff.
18. Ray, pp. 31f.
19. Eliade, *Sacred and Profane,* p. 78.
20. Zuesse, p. 528.

QUESTIONS FOR STUDY AND DISCUSSION

1. Central to the theory of ritual offered in this chapter is the notion of transcendent power. Discuss the two types of transcendence referred to here, as well as just how (and for whom) such power is working.

2. Important in this chapter is the notion of embodied action as crucial to the religious life. What does it mean to talk about "embodied action," and why do you suppose it is so central to religion?

3. What does this chapter mean by transformative power? How, do you suppose, is it both related to and distinct from transcendent power?

4. The most difficult element to understand in this chapter's analysis of sacred context is sacred tradition or heritage. Discuss what this idea means, and how it becomes a part of the sacred context of a ritual.

PROJECTS

1. This chapter tries to provide a theory or model for understanding the nature of ritual both generally and in any specific case. While a

general understanding might be interesting or useful, it is in applying such models or typologies that the theory becomes truly useful. Projects, therefore, should center around the application of this theory to specific cases of ritual.

Therefore, read a description of ritual, see a film where a ritual is present, or observe a ritual firsthand. In each case write a report in which you do one or more of the following:

a. Categorize this ritual in terms of the four types of ritual offered at the beginning of the chapter.
b. Describe the various kinds of symbolic expression present in the ritual.
c. Discuss the ritual in terms of one or more elements of sacred context found there.
d. Describe what kind of transformative power is intended by this ritual.

2. Consider the definition of religion offered in this book, as well as the definition of ritual, and write a self-assessment journal in which you try to identify the religious and paradigmatic "gestures" in your own life.

SUGGESTED READINGS

Brenneman, Walter. *Spirals: A Study in Symbol, Myth, and Ritual.* Washington, D.C.: University Press of America, 1978.
Eliade, Mircea. *Cosmos and History: The Myth of the Eternal Return.* Trans. Willard R. Trask. New York: Harper & Row, 1959.
_____. *Rites and Symbols of Initiation: The Mysteries of Birth and Rebirth.* Trans. Willard R. Trask. New York: Harper & Row, 1958.
_____. *The Sacred and the Profane: The Nature of Religion.* Trans. Willard R. Trask. New York: Harper & Row, 1961.
Gaster, Theodor. *Thespis: Ritual, Myth, and Drama in the Ancient Near East.* Rev. ed. New York: Harper & Row, 1961.
Grimes, Ronald. *Beginnings in Ritual Studies.* Washington, D.C.: University Press of America, 1982.
_____. "Sources for the Study of Ritual." *Religious Studies Review* (April 1984): 134–45.
Huizinga, Johan. *Homo Ludens: A Study of the Play-Element in Culture.* Boston: Beacon Press, 1950.
Leeuw, Gerardus van der. *Sacred and Profane Beauty: The Holy in Art.* Trans. David E. Green. New York: Holt, Rinehart and Winston, 1963.
Stall, Frits. "The Meaninglessness of Ritual," *Numen* 26, no. 1 (1979): 2–22.
Turner, Victor. *Dramas, Fields, and Metaphors: Symbolic Action in Human Society.* Ithaca, N.Y.: Cornell University Press, 1974.
_____. *The Forest of Symbols: Aspects of Ndembu Ritual.* Ithaca, N.Y.: Cornell University Press, 1967.

————. *The Ritual Process: Structure and Anti-Structure*. Chicago: Aldine Publishing, 1969.

Watts, Alan W. *Myth and Ritual in Christianity*. Boston: Beacon Press, 1968.

Zuesse, Evan. "The Absurdity of Ritual." *Psychiatry* 46 (February 1983): 40–50.

————. "Meditation on Ritual." *Journal of the American Academy of Religion* 43 (September 1975): 517–30.

————. *Ritual Cosmos: The Sanctification of Life in African Religions*. Athens, Ohio: Ohio University Press, 1979.

CHAPTER 5

The Arts

For purposes of this chapter, we will use the word *art* to refer to all forms of what have generally been called the arts: the visual arts, the performing arts, and the literary arts. All of these forms of artistic expression, each in its own distinctive way and each in an appropriate context, can be understood as religious expressions. In fact, religion and art can be said to be intimately connected, even inseparable, on at least two grounds. On the one hand, art is historically grounded in religion and has played an important role within the history and practice of all the religions of humankind. On the other hand, much of art—whether or not it is connected to some particular religion—can be said to be religious by virtue of the definition offered in chapter 1. These two ways of speaking about the arts as religious govern the structure of our discussion in this chapter; one way is pursued in the first general section ("Art within the Religions"), and the other in the second section ("Art as Religious").

ART WITHIN THE RELIGIONS

When thinking of the arts in religion, there is no more obvious place to look than within the various religions of the world. Art is a universal religious expression that, in one form or another, has played an important role in all religions. Often, of course, these arts have not been distinguished from religion and called "art" in our contemporary Western sense of the term but have simply been one more form of either a culture's religion or its play. Only as cultures and human history developed did there come to be something distinct called "art."[1]

We need not define art, however, in order to discuss it as a religious expression; it is sufficient to describe, as we have above, the kinds of human expressions we mean by "the arts" and then look at them in terms of religion. In doing so we find that the arts, within the religions, are no mere museum pieces or forms of idle entertainment; they serve important symbolic and transformative functions just as do sacred stories, rituals, and all religious expressions. Like all religious expressions, they perform important religious functions and operate centrally in the service of religions.

THE SHAMAN AS ARTIST

We begin with the shaman for two reasons. Shamanism represents both one of the earliest forms of religion, and a type of religion within which the arts were (and are) central. In fact, many people would argue that the arts have their origins in shamanism. The shaman (male or female) is, after all, the paradigmatic religious visionary and practitioner of primal cultures; the one who, as the nineteenth-century Native American shaman, Black Elk, says, "sees in a sacred manner the shapes of all things in the spirit."[2] In turn, it is the shaman who invokes and/or expresses this seeing in story, poetry, song, instrumental music, drama, mask, painting, sculpture, costume, and body decoration.[3]

Some of the earliest records of human artistic efforts—for example, the paleolithic cave paintings of Europe and elsewhere—clearly reflect shamanic or visionary experience and practice. The most ancient levels of Asian culture reflect the same thing. The mythology of ancient Shinto, in fact, places shamanic possession and dance at the center of one of its most important stories: The female shamanic goddess Uzume becomes possessed, utters sacred words, and does an erotic dance on an overturned wooden tub in a successful attempt to entice the sun goddess Amaterasu out of a cave she has retreated into. This mythic event has become the paradigmatic model for much of Shinto ritual, and even today one finds Shinto music and dance (kagura) as central to Shinto practice. These rituals are done, moreover, by historical descendants of ancient female shamen called miko, young women especially trained and assigned to Shinto shrines.

These brief examples only begin to uncover the rich and ancient relationship of the arts to religion and to shamanism. This relationship has continued throughout human history, especially wherever shamanism has continued to thrive. Even today, for example, Eskimo art carries on this tradition. The shaman is the one who has a unique relationship to the spirit world, including the animal world, and is able to represent those "hidden" worlds to the people by way of carving, painting, or storytelling.

The Oglala Sioux shaman Black Elk, already mentioned above, is an excellent example of a more contemporary manifestation of this relationship of the shaman to the arts. By his own account Black Elk had numerous shamanic visions by which he was taken into the spirit world, shown both past, present, and future, and called to help his people renew their life as a sacred nation. These visions, when expressed for his people to see and participate in, took a variety of artistic forms: ritual dramas, sacred songs, tepee paintings, and stories.

Shamanism is, of course, a very diverse and widespread phenomenon in the history of religions. The generalizations above are not meant to oversimplify a complex matter but only to suggest a type of culture and religious form in which the arts were indistinguishable from religion and played a central role in it. The shaman is both a paradigmatic example of this relationship and a historical example of the beginnings of art in religion.

ART AS RELIGIOUS SYMBOL

Beyond the issue of the shaman, however, we find a more familiar situation in which identifiable artistic forms (music, literature, painting, and so forth) not only function as art but serve within religion as well. From the architecture of Islam to the music of Bach, from the literature of Judaism to the iconography of Hinduism, and from the poetry of Zen Buddhism to the medieval morality plays of Christianity, the arts have functioned and flourished in the religions in two distinct though interrelated ways. On the one hand, the arts have symbolically pointed to and expressed that which is sacred, unrestricted, or holy in a people's experience. On the other hand, they have functioned transformatively in helping people move toward religious goals. In both cases the arts have been inseparable from the actual practice of the religious life.

The symbolic function of the arts within the religions is the same as that of any religious expression. As we learned in chapter 1, all religious expressions are symbolic in that they point beyond themselves to some particular meaning and/or reality related to a people's faith or religious experience. They are understood as expressions of and responses to what individuals and communities have experienced as ultimate, sacred, or holy.

Symbolic expressions function differently, of course, according to their particular context. In general, symbols range from *representational* to *presentational* in terms of the degree to which they "carry" sacrality or holiness with them. Representational symbols tend to "represent" rather than "present" the holy itself; they tend to represent and transmit the various elements of a religious tradition as its history, its theology, its mythology, its whole symbol system. As such, representational symbols could be said to perform a more didactic or teaching function as the tradition or religion is passed on down through history.

Presentational symbols, on the other hand, tend to "present," invoke, or more directly and immediately embody sacred reality. To use an obvious Christian example, we have a presentational symbol when the wine and bread of the eucharist are thought of as the blood and body of Christ; we have a representational symbol when they are thought of as the last supper of Christ. To use an artistic example, we could say that the icons of the Eastern Orthodox Church are presentational in that they are thought to embody the living presence of the figures they represent; the paintings of Michelangelo on the roof of the Sistine Chapel, on the other hand, are more representational of a traditional view about the nature of God.

Such a distinction is, of course, not always easy to make or to hold. What may be presentational in one context may well be representational in another. In general, a good test of the applicability of the distinction can be found in relating any given artistic symbol to ritual. Since ritual in general is more presentational, the artistic forms that play a central role in ritual are more presentational in function.

Examples of the arts functioning symbolically in the religions are, of course, easy to find. We have already mentioned one excellent example above, and that is the Shinto music and dance *(kagura)* which, by being central to Shinto ritual, is a performing art functioning as a presentational symbol. Shinto *kagura* is designed both to call the Shinto gods *(kami)* into presence and to entertain them so that peace and prosperity might reign. *Kagura* performances point beyond themselves to the nature and power of the *kami* while, at the same time, they symbolically bring that power/reality into presence.

Another religious tradition within which the arts have played a significant role is Hinduism. Beginning with the cosmic, divine dancer (Shiva as Nataraj or "king of the dance"), moving through the great Hindu literature and coming to the complex iconography, one finds all the arts well represented there. Hindu literature, for example, is rich in amount and variety.[4] No doubt there are many reasons for this, but certainly two of them are the Indian fascination with language, story, and mythology on the one hand, and with a kind of sensual devotion to the gods on the other. These and other factors converge to produce the great hymns and poetry found in the earliest scriptures, especially the Rig Veda. The following excerpts from an extended hymn to the god Indra are but one example.

Let me proclaim the valient deeds of Indra;
    the first he did, the wielder of the thunder,
when he slew the dragon and let loose the waters,
    and pierced the bellies of the mountains. . . .
When, Indra, you slew the firstborn of dragons,
    and frustrated the arts of the sorcerers,
creating sun and heaven and dawn,
    you found no enemy to withstand you. . . .
Indra is the king of all that moves or rests,
    of tame and fierce, the wielder of thunder.
He is the king of mortals, when he rules,
    encircling them as a wheel's rim the spokes.[5]

Another genre of Hindu literature consists of the great epics, the Mahabharata and the Ramayana. While there are certainly secular or nonreligious themes and events narrated in these epics, religious themes and influences are abundantly present. Perhaps it is enough to say that the famous Bhagavad Gita of Hindu scripture is simply one extended episode within the Mahabharata, and that the central hero of the Ramayana, Rama, is an incarnation of the great god Vishnu. In any event, these epics can minimally be understood as representational, literary symbols; they contain cultural and religious themes and ideals that have been passsed on to countless hearers and readers, and they have inspired, in turn, countless other artistic expressions in drama, painting, or dance.

As literary symbols these Hindu epics perform similar functions to the Christian Bible—here understood as literature. From the narrative power of the Genesis stories to the ecstatic visions of the book of Revelation, and from the poetry of Psalms to the parables of Jesus, the literary and religious power of the Bible is manifest. As God's word, especially in a ritual context, it is a presentational symbol bringing the holy to the faithful. In other contexts, for example a Sunday School, it performs the teaching and transmitting functions of a representational symbol as it passes on the ideals, stories, models, and visions that make up the foundations of Christianity.

It is questionable whether such written works would have the sacred power they do without their literary form. Literature, by its very nature, has the power to draw people beyond the mundane, ordinary, descriptive world. It has unique symbolic power to point beyond itself to the realms of the spirit, the imagination, the transcendent. Like any good art, literature "speaks" out of the depths and heights of human experience—experience which can, in many cases, be understood as religious. By the power of metaphoric language literature can "see" and express in ways not available to other written forms. The psalms in the Bible are an obvious example. Psalm 121 says:

I lift up my eyes to the hills.
From whence does my help come?
My help comes from the Lord,
   who made heaven and earth.
He will not let your foot be moved,
   he who keeps you will not slumber. . . .
The Lord is your keeper;
   the Lord is your shade on your right hand. . . .
The Lord will keep you from all evil;
   he will keep your life.

Shifting our attention back to Hinduism, however, we can look at another major religious art form called "iconography." Generally speaking, iconography refers to those visual arts (sculpture, painting) in a religion that depict the gods, spirits, or other special beings in some particular shape and manner. The iconography of Hinduism is particularly rich and significant in the practice of Hinduism, and particularly pervasive throughout the religion.[6] Like any iconography understood as religious symbol, it points beyond itself by the power of its significant form to a sacred reality, yet it expresses or gives shape to such reality and thus brings it into visual presence. Especially in popular Hinduism, the Hinduism of the masses of Indian peoples, it becomes a visual theology that replaces written, verbal expressions of the faith. It is a holy "text" to be "read" by seeing and participating in the power it expresses. In a ritual context, iconography becomes a presentational symbol as an immediate epiphany (appearance, manifestation) of the holy. Appearing in children's books and comics, and purchased in a magazine shop of contemporary Bombay, for example, it becomes a representational symbol helping to keep alive and pass down through history the beliefs, ideals, and shapes of the gods and heroes of Hinduism.

Some people might think that the iconography of a religion, especially a religion not their own, represents an idolatry or worship of idols. Idolatry, however, can exist in *any* religion, since it is the idea that the form itself is the sacred and no longer functions as a symbol pointing beyond itself. Idolatry is a greater temptation, however, in religions rich with iconography, but where these artistic forms genuinely function symbolically, they are not themselves the object of worship.

That the image or icon is not itself the object of worship in Hinduism can readily be seen in how such images are treated. Temporary images made for annual festivals, for example, are unceremoniously thrown out when the festival is over and the indwelling spirit of the image has been ritually removed. Without that indwelling spirit or god-power, the image is just so many sticks and stones.

A less obvious artistic form found as religious symbol is the traditional Japanese garden. The gardens of Japan have been and remain an important art form, yet they have served very conscious religious purposes as well, especially in their connection to Buddhism. In the latter context, gardens have symbolized everything from the paradise of the cosmic Buddha Amida to the nothingness *(mu)* or emptiness *(ku)* of Zen.[7] An appreciative walk through such gardens, or the quiet contemplation of them, invokes a kind of geography of the spirit and opens one to the sacred realms the gardens represent.

Perhaps unique among the arts as religious symbol—particularly as presentational symbol—is the music of religion, including both vocal and instrumental music. Music has a unique experiential and participatory immediacy that lends itself to lifting people out of the mundane world and expressing to them the sacred realities. Perhaps unlike the visual, literary, and performing arts, music does not seem to demand or suggest some meaning; it more easily sweeps people into an experience of *ekstasis* (standing outside)—a religious, experiential ecstasy. From the religious drumming of tribal Africa to the profound grandeur of a

Bach chorale, from the solemn rhythms of Buddhist chant to the rich melody of Jewish song, music may be uniquely able to "see" and express things "in the spirit."

Within music, vocal music (from groan to chant, and song to yell) may have a special power to give "voice" to humanity's deepest soul and highest visions. When words or other expressions fail, the human voice remains the most natural "instrument" available for significant symbolic expression. Being very close to us, it becomes a natural vehicle for putting us in touch with the holy.

In short, through artistic forms, the religions have possessed a host of important expressions serving symbolically to represent and present the holy. The arts have served well within the religions.

ART AS RELIGIOUS PRACTICE

To speak of art as religious symbol, as we have above, is only one side of the coin in art's service to the religions. Though very closely related to its function as religious symbol, it is important to consider art's practical function in religions, that is, its transformative function as a part of religious practice. Whether from the point of view of the artist who creates such art, or of the person who participates in or religiously uses such art, the transformative function is critical for understanding art's relationship to religion.

One obvious beginning point is to look at the relationship of the arts to ritual. As this book's chapter on ritual tries to make clear, the actual practice of religion often centers on ritual. Other religious expressions are brought into play there, and the arts are no exception. Ritual both uses the arts centrally and nurtures them; it is the primary religious context within which the arts function religiously—whether symbolically or transformatively. To this extent, all religious art is first and foremost ritual art, and therefore its primary religious function is transformation and renewal.

In a simple but beautiful documentary film called *Pilgrimage to a Hindu Temple,* scholar/director H. Daniel Smith shows us how Hindu iconography plays a central ritual function.[8] A lone devotee travels to a particularly sacred temple on a special festival day. After certain preparatory rituals of purification, he moves on into the temple itself. This journey is a journey of the spirit as he gets closer and closer to the central holy spot of the temple. As he moves through the dark passageways, carvings on the walls remind him of central beliefs and sacred stories. At the very center of the temple, deep within the sacred spaces and hidden even from the camera's eye, the devotee comes face to face with the god Vishnu in iconographic image. Here the central transformative experience takes place, and the devotee feels renewed and spiritually reborn by the encounter. Art has clearly served its transformative function in this case.

The rich and complex ritual and meditation practice of Vajrayana (sometimes referred to as Tibetan) Buddhism is importantly centered on the arts. Through sacred chant *(mantra)* and sacred pictures *(mandala)* important meditative practices take place. The arts, in this tradition, become vehicles *(yana)* and disciplines *(yoga)* for entering into spiritual realms, and for realizing or awakening to buddha-reality.

The place of the icon in the Eastern Orthodox Church is yet another obvious example. Where the icon is, there is the presence of God (in one form or another) working in transformative ways to renew life and the spirit. To kiss the icon is not an act of idolatry but a ritual and religious act of coming close to God and feeling the divine presence.

Again, no one who has participated in or appreciatively heard the music of the Black Church in American can miss the ritual and transformative power of music. The "amazing grace" that one of the great gospel hymns sings about is brought into play partly by the very singing and hearing of the song! Ritual art, like this hymn, is designed to move us somehow; to change, open, shift, alter, or otherwise transform our lives that we might be better "in tune" with the holy. Such ritual art is a part of the power of salvation, even for "a wretch like me."

ART AS RELIGIOUS

Up to this point we have primarily been interested in the more obvious sense in which the arts have been religious expressions, that is, the role the arts have played in the religions of humankind. The opening section of this chapter, however, suggested that there might be another way to view the arts as religious, and that is to see the arts themselves— outside of any connection to some religion—as religious. Certainly our definition of religion in chapter 1 allows us to contemplate this point of view since religion is not defined merely in terms of particular religious traditions; *any* phenomenon may be potentially religious if it expresses someone's unrestricted value or faith! We take the latter point seriously as we turn our attention away from the religions within which art has served and toward the arts themselves as potentially religious in their own right.

THE ARTIST AS SHAMAN

When, in the previous sections of this chapter, we focused on the arts within religion, it was useful to discuss the shaman as an artist and as a paradigmatic example of that relationship. Here, to indicate the shift in our attention to the arts themselves, it is useful to discuss the artist as shaman. To do so is to claim something quite special, religiously, for the artist—deeply and ideally understood. It is to claim that the true artist serves a religious purpose by "seeing" deeply into the spirit of things and by expressing that seeing in significant ways. It is also to claim that the expressions thus presented have transformative power for those who truly "enter" them. On these very points the cultural analyst Theodore Roszak says:

> The essence of good magic—magic as it is practised by the shaman and the artist—is that it seeks always to make available to all the full power of the magician's experience. While the shaman may be one especially elected and empowered, his role is to introduce his people to the sacramental presences that have found him out and transformed him into their agent. His particular gift confers responsibility, not privilege. Similarly, the artist lays his work before the community in the hope that through it, as through a window, the reality he has fathomed will be witnessed by all who give attention. For the shaman, ritual performs the same function. By participating in the ritual, the community comes to know what the shaman has discovered. Ritual is the shaman's way of broadcasting his vision; it is his instructive offering. If the artist's work is successful, if the shaman's ritual is effective, the community's sense of reality will become expansive; something of the dark powers will penetrate its experience.[9]

Several points are raised in these comments that directly relate here. One, of course, is to see the artist as a kind of shaman, that is, someone with special experiences, a deeper vision, or "a magician's experience"; one who has come face to face with "sacramental presences" and has been made their agent. Like the shaman, as Black Elk told us, the artist is one who "sees in a sacred manner the shapes of all things in the spirit."

This deeper seeing, however, is taken before the community in works of art rather than in works of ritual; nonetheless they express to the community the artist's vision, faith, unrestricted valuing, or religious experience. The work of art is the artist's "instructive offering" to the community, whether understood as representational and presentational symbol, or as transformative power for others. The artist's responsibility (not privilege) is thus to bring this deeper seeing forth for all to see and be transformed thereby.

Of the many excellent examples, one of the best is the twentieth-century European painter Pablo Picasso. In our understanding, Picasso —an avowed atheist—was a religious painter and shamanic artist. His works reveal his deeper vision into the spirit of things, especially the human spirit. Picasso "saw" beyond the surfaces and into the depths of human reality and expressed a prophetic/shamanic vision in his art for the community to see and be transformed. The holy or sacred he saw and expressed may not always be "good" or "beautiful," but such terms are only relative and may not necessarily indicate the religious in any case.

The artist's vision is thus translated into works of art for all to see. They become, for the sensitive viewer who "enters'" them, a "window" not only into Picasso's genius but into his particular depth-experience of the human spirit. Thereby, as Roszak says, the community comes to know what the artist has seen, and its own sense of reality is transformed and expanded.

Similarly, the philosopher of art T. R. Martland suggests that religion is art and art is religion when a certain "jarring" takes place.

Transformation, or that jarring kind of sense which does away with old structures and understandings, has always been the latch on the door to religion. . . . Religion and art are activities that open their followers out from an inherited way of seeing things, from an inherited structure of reality, and "get" them into a new way of seeing things, into a new world. They upset. They jar. They impose. They reconstruct the world with new fundamentals. When the transformation is complete, those who have gone along will change their view of the field, of its methods and goals.[10]

One can find literary shamans everywhere, especially in the contemporary world. From Carlos Castaneda to Wallace Stevens, from Yukio Mishima to Annie Dillard, and from Elie Wiesel to Margaret Atwood, poets and novelists take us into deepr worlds and thereby "jar" and change our world as well.

Other great artists do the same. From Igor Stravinsky to Isadora Duncan, and from Strindberg to T. S. Eliot, music, drama, and dance expand horizons and move people to deeper levels of awareness. The power of great art, like the power of aesthetic experience, is a religious power; in these similar powers the arts become intrinsically religious.

To this point, however, we have focused on the unique insights and abilities of individual artists. There is another way, though less dramatic and obvious, to see the artist as shaman—or at least as a religious functionary—and that is to look at the artistic vocation and discipline as a religious vocation and discipline.

The model for this view of the artistic vocation is found in the Far East, particularly in Japan. There, many of the arts—though influenced by the religions—are understood as religious disciplines and processes in and of themselves. This is expressed by attaching the term "way" (Chinese *tao;* Japanese *do*) to many Japanese words for the arts, all the way from the martial arts (for example, *judo, aikido, karatedo),* to the fine arts (for example, *kado* or poetry, and *gado* or painting), and even to other arts usually not recognized as such (for example *chado* or tea ceremony). The word *way* in traditional China and Japan has often indicated a spiritual or religious way, path, or journey. In fact, the word is used to indicate the religions themselves, as in *butsudo* or "Buddhism." Connected to the arts, however, the word indicates that artistic discipline and creativity carry religious meaning and power. Art is never a mere copying of nature but an attempt to plumb the depths of spirit and reality that undergird this life. Artistic pursuit is a meditative discipline by means of the techniques and forms of the art. It seeks to see and awaken to the deeper or larger realities of life.

It is out of such training and ideals that, for example, the great seventeenth-century haiku poet Matsuo Basho wrote his "religious" verses that almost never mention any obviously religious themes. His most famous poem has only to do with old ponds and jumping frogs!

Old pond!
Frog jumps in.
Water sound.

Basho has, here, become absolutely one with this instant of time, and this instant of time, if we listen carefully, is a splash heard in eternity. The poem is a religious expression of spiritual insight and meditative experience, and it is left to us by Basho that our world might be changed thereby.

ART AS CULTURAL PARADIGM AND STYLE

Yet another way of understanding art as intrinsically religious is to see it as expressing or revealing a whole culture's "way of seeing," or paradigm—a whole culture's conscious or unconscious sense of reality, world view, deep valuing, or faith. The arts of a culture (a society or people) can be seen as a window into that culture's deepest experience of itself and the world. The art historian William Fleming has said, "If one desires to understand the spirit and inner life of a people, one must look at its art, literature, philosophy, dances, and music, where the spirit of the whole people is reflected."[11]

This spirit and inner life of a culture can be seen as a people's religious and spiritual foundations, their faith and basis for a meaningful world. It is not the individual's vision so much as a collective, communal, cultural vision that is expressed, and art—as a paradigm—reveals it.

The idea of cultural paradigm is important to twentieth-century theologian Paul Tillich. He writes,

Every style (or paradigm) points to a self-interpretation of man, thus answering the question of the ultimate meaning of life. Whatever the subject matter which an artist chooses, however strong or weak his artistic form, he cannot help but betray by his style his own ultimate concern, as well as that of his group, and his period. He cannot escape religion even if he rejects religion, for religion is the state of being ultimately concerned. And in every style the ultimate concern of a human group or period is manifest.[12]

A small but graphic example of art as paradigm and style, and thereby as a window into a culture's personality or religious attitude, can be found in a comparison of flower arranging in Japan and America. The typical American floral arrangement, for example at a wedding or funeral, is a rather large display filled to overflowing with a variety of flowers and greenery; it is symmetrical in shape, and it exudes abundance, color, variety, and a grand beauty. The individual differences

that might occur from one type to another, from one person to another, from one geogrpahic region of America to another, and from
one historical period to another, all reflect differences in style. That
there is an underlying similar (though general) pattern in all, however,
indicates a paradigm.

A typical Japanese arrangement, on the other hand, is very different.
It consists of merely two or three rather bare branches, with few flowers
and little greenery, placed in an asymmetrical pattern. The variety of
types of flowers and colors is minimal, and the general impression is a
sparse economy that highlights the few items in the arrangement. Less
seems better, and the arrangement—like its artistic cousin the traditional landscape painting—has rather extensive open spaces. Again, there
are, of course, stylistic differences within this general pattern, and, in
Japan, this has much to do with the various schools of flower arranging.
Nonetheless, the general pattern is maintained and could be said to
represent a paradigm.

But what do these two different paradigms reveal about these two
cultures? On the one hand, the American (or Western) paradigm shows
a deep valuing of being and of things. The paradigm says that the
created world is filled with the glory and abundance of life in all its
plenitude and variety. Moreover, being or life has a rational, descriptive
order as seen in the symmetry of the bouquet. On the other hand, the
Japanese (Eastern) view affirms both the created forms (flowers,
branches beauty) and the emptiness between those forms. The open
spaces in the arrangement and in the landscape painting allow the hidden spirit to breath through. As the Taoist scripture called the Tao Te
Ching says, expressing the thought of the Far East in general, it is only
by virtue of a spiritual nothing (no-thing) that we have the authentic
function of use of something.[13] The asymmetry of the arrangement
indicates the primacy of an intuitional, aesthetic, subjective appropria-
tion of reality.

Still another example of art as paradigm, as a window into a culture's
spirit and inner life, can be found in literature, and again a comparison
between West and East helps to make the point more clearly.

It could be argued that the dominant form of Westsern (European
and American) literature has been the narrative story, of both fiction
and nonfiction. By contrast, the dominant literary form in at least traditional China and Japan has been a particular style of poetry, generally
nonnarrative, nonepic, and very brief (as, for example, the haiku given
above). Insofar as these broad generalizations are true, these two very
different literary forms may reveal two diverse paradigms. On the one
hand, there is an orientation in the West to a temporal, "objective,"
descriptive, "narrative" reality; to events and people sequenced through
time (whether historical time or sacred, mythic, fictive time). On the
other hand, the Far East reflects an orientation to a more "subjective,"

immediately experienced poetic reality in which time stands still, as it were, or is transcended in the eternity of the moment.

To say this does not mean, of course, that one cannot find the narrative story in the Far East or nonnarrative poetry in the West. It does mean, however, that two very different paradigms exist, each tending to dominate in its own cultural context. If one looked further into these paradigms, as well as into other arts similarly understood, one would be looking into fundamental orientations to reality, conscious or unconscious world views, deep cultural values, and ways of seeing by which the world is known and made meaningful. While these paradigms might change and shift as time, history, and cultures develop, nonetheless they remain important forms of religious expression as defined in this book.

SUMMARY

Among the variety of religious expressions are the arts—painting, sculpture, architecture, iconogrpahy, music, the novel, poetry, flower arrangement, music, drama, and all the other arts. These arts have, on the one hand, been an integral part of the religions; they have been symbolic expressions of that which is sacred, holy, or unrestricted in value. On the other hand, the arts themselves are religious as they see deeply into the spirit of things, provide a window for all to grasp a depth dimension of the human spirit, or even as they "jar" one into some transforming experience. As a paradigm, the arts express a culture's world view, its values, and its faith. As Paul Tillich said, the ultimate concerns of a culture are often expressed in the arts.

NOTES

1. See Gerardus van der Leeuw, *Sacred and Profane Beauty: The Holy in Art* (New York: Holt, Rinehart and Winston, 1963). His major thesis is that all the arts were at one time inseparable from religion. Only as cultures and societies became more complex and less theocentric did a distinctive, nonreligious artistic form develop.
2. John Neihardt, *Black Elk Speaks: Being the Life Story of a Holy Man of the Oglala Sioux* (New York: Pocket Books, 1959), p. 30.
3. For a survey of the shaman as artist see Andreas Lommel, *The World of the Early Hunters* (London: Evelyn, Adams & Mackay, 1967), pp. 105–49.
4. See the convenient survey of Hindu literature in A. L. Basham, *The Wonder That Was India: A Survey of the Culture of the Indian Sub-Continent Before the Coming of the Muslims* (New York: Grove Press, 1959), chapter 9.
5. Ibid., pp. 400f.
6. For a look at Hinduism in terms of iconography, see Diana Eck, *Darsan: Seeing the Divine Image in India* (Chambersburg, Pa.: Anima Books, 1981).
7. For a survey of the Japanese garden as religious symbol see Mark Holborn, *The Ocean in the Sand: Japan, from Landscape to Garden* (Boulder, Colo.: Shambhala Publications, 1978).
8. For more information on this film see Robert A. McDermott, et al., *Focus on Hinduism:*

Audio-Visual Resources for Teaching Religion, 2d edition (Chambersburg, Pa.: Anima Books, 1981), p. 46.

9. Theodore Roszak, *The Making of Counter Culture: Reflections on the Technocratic Society and Its Youthful Opposition* (Garden City, N.Y.: Doubleday, 1969), p. 260.

10. T. R. Martland, "When Is Religion Art? When It Is a Jar," in Diane Apostolos-Cappadona, ed., *Art, Creativity, and the Sacred: An Anthology in Religion and Art* (New York: Crossroad, 1984), p. 259.

11. As quoted in James Karman, "Art," in T. W. Hall, ed., *Introduction to the Study of Religion* (New York: Harper & Row, 1978), p. 110.

12. Paul Tillich, *Theology of Culture,* ed. Robert C. Kimball (London and New York: Oxford University Press, 1959), p. 70.

13. D. C. Lau, trans., *Lao Tzu: Tao Te Ching* (Baltimore, Md.: Penguin Books, 1963), p. 67.

QUESTIONS FOR STUDY AND DISCUSSION

1. In order to clarify the major distinctions in this chapter, review and discuss as well as compare and contrast the following pairs:

a. The nature and function of the arts within the religions as distinct from the arts as religious.

b. Similarly, the shaman as artist as distinct from the artist as shaman.

c. Art as religious symbol as distinct from art as transformative.

d. Representational as distinct from presentational symbols.

e. Art as cultural paradigm as distinct from art as cultural style.

f. Art as iconographical symbol as distinct from art as idolatry.

2. Taking any one of the central categories of the chapters listed above (in question 1), discuss if and how it might be applied to some art forms with which you are familiar.

PROJECTS

1. Take a real or imaginary trip to some religious institution at the time of an important ritual. As a participant/observer, note for later discussion the variety and function the arts play in this context. If there is opportunity, interview some of the participants in the ritual to find out how these arts worked religiously for them.

2. Go to a museum, theater, concert hall, or other place where visual and performing arts take place (including fine films). Watch and/or listen for the symbolic power of these works. Can you "enter" them? Do they expand your world? Can you see any paradigms operating?

3. Read some so-called secular (but fine) literature. Does it create a new world? Does it draw you out of yourself? Does it point beyond itself to a deeper experience of things? Does it "jar"you?

SUGGESTED READINGS

Apostolos-Cappadona, Diane, ed. *Art, Creativity, and the Sacred: An Anthology in Religion and Art.* New York: Crossroad, 1984.

Armstrong, Robert P. *The Powers of Presence: Consciousness, Myth, and Affecting Presence.* Philadelphia: University of Pennsylvania Press, 1981.

Burkhardt, Titus. *Sacred Art in East and West.* London: Perennial Publications, 1967.

Halifax, Joan. *Shaman: The Wounded Healer.* New York: Crossroad, 1982.

Leeuw van der, Gerardus. *Sacred and Profane Beauty: The Holy in Art.* New York: Holt, Rinehart and Winston, 1953.

Martland, Thomas. *Religion As Art: An Interpretation.* Albany, N.Y.: State University of New York Press, 1981.

Moore, Albert. *Iconography of Religions: An Introduction.* Philadelphia: Fortress Press, 1977.

Pilgrim, Richard. *Buddhism and the Arts of Japan.* Chambersburg, Pa.: Anima Books, 1981.

CHAPTER 6

Belief

Wherever religion is found, it is expressed in one form by beliefs about God or the gods, human beings, the nature of the cosmos, and the purpose of life. An inquiry into religious belief, then, is surely an important aspect of the study of religion. However, this inquiry is no easy task, since religion is a complex field that includes very different sorts of data, issues, and methods. For instance, there is probably no living religious tradition that does not involve some set of myths, rituals, doctrines, ethical teachings, and writings that record and interpret the history of the tradition's social and cultural interaction. Within the context of these religious expressions we will try to establish the meaning of religious belief, focusing on the basic beliefs of some of the major religions of humanity. These beliefs, objectified in the myths and rituals of the various traditions, give expression to the distinctive "visions of life" or religious interpretations.

The ambiguous term *belief* must first be carefully defined. Many definitions are possible, since definitions are simply rules of usage. For our purposes, a definition should not only clarify and stabilize the meaning of the term belief but also prove to be a useful tool in an attempt to identify basic beliefs in the world's religions.

An analysis of religious beliefs constituting different "visions of life" also requires a definition of the rather vague phrase "vision of life." To understand the term "vision of life" we will propose a "conceptual model," that is, a model made of concepts or thought rather than clay or plastic. This model will function like a "recipe" to indicate exactly what elements go into making a "vision of life." The religious expression of all traditions appears in some way to represent the style or pattern of interpretation indicated by our model. Thus when the expressions of a particular tradition illustrate the elements identifed by our model, we will cite these expressions as evidence of one tradition's "vision of life." We do not claim that this model is the only one that might function in this way. We do claim, however, that it does not abuse, distort, misrepresent, or prejudice the analysis of any of the beliefs to be considered.

Two things must be kept in mind throughout this inquiry into religious belief. First, the task of defining belief in general is distinct from the task of analyzing specific religious beliefs. A definition of belief gives us a formal or abstract understanding of the term; it does not examine the content of particular religious beliefs. For example, an examination of the Muslim belief in Allah the Creator lies outside the task of defining religious belief in general. To analyze particular beliefs we must move beyond the realm of definition to a critical investigation of the religious traditions themselves.

Second, the phenomenon of religious belief may itself be approached from a number of different perspectives. For example, a philosopher of religion may ask about a certain belief, "Is religious belief X true?" While this is certainly an important question, it is not the major question of this chapter. We are not concerned with demonstrating the truth or falsity of specific religious beliefs, or with evaluating arguments that one religious vision is superior to another. The sole purpose of comparing and contrasting religious beliefs is to appreciate the relative similarities and differences among various religious visions. We will not recommend, judge, or defend any particular set of religious beliefs.

Similarly, the historian may ask the important question, "What is the origin and particular historical development of religious belief X?" This is not a central question here. Rather, we will ask what difference religious belief makes in the life of the believer. How does a vision of life lead people to understand the obstacles to complete and satisfying living? How does this vision determine their goals? How and under what conditions can people achieve the desired ends contained in their vision?

Since people hold many different beliefs and visions, we must be selective. Beliefs discussed later in the chapter have been chosen because they are relevant to the modern experience and because they are expressed universally rather than in localized settings only.

THE TERM *BELIEF*

THE AMBIGUITY OF THE TERM

The term *belief* is ambiguous, and its usage differs in various contexts. Consider some of the diferent emphases found in a few familiar usages: "I believe so; I don't know for sure ..." (suggesting that belief is a tentative attitude or opinion to be contrasted with certain knowledge); "You had better believe it; it's as plain as the nose on your face" (suggesting that belief entails a perception or a recognition that something is the case); "I believe in you, Mark, and therefore I am giving you responsibility for . . ." (suggesting that belief is a personal disposition to trust or have confidence in); "You are making a believer out of me, Jane" (suggesting that belief is characteristic of a person who has been persuaded or led to a conviction); "The Nicene Creed expresses the Christian belief" (suggesting that belief is a credal or doctrinal statement).

These examples are not intended to be exhaustive. I believe (the latter word implying probability rather than certainty) that you could add to them if you were asked. They demonstrate enough diversity of usage, however, to establish the need for a functional definition.

The first step in defining belief is to clarify our purpose in studying the phenomenon of religious belief. In this way we can construct some criteria or standards for evaluating definitions.

CRITERIA

We want to study religious belief in a way that aids in identifying, comparing, and contrasting the beliefs that comprise the respective visions of life of some of the world's religions. Our main concern is the significant effect that an individual's belief has on his or her understanding of the human condition, on his or her ideal goals within this condition, and on the means of realizing those goals within this condition.

In light of chapter 1, a definition of religious belief must show it to be one aspect of a religious person's "deliberate affirmation" of the unrestricted value. Religious belief can thus be characterized as the assertion of an alleged fact of such unrestricted importance that the believer orients his or her whole life around it. For example, the assertion of the "fact" that God acted in the Exodus to free a people from a specific mission may be considered—if one makes it the focus of one's personal life—an expression of religious belief. Further clarification of the notions of assertion, belief, and fact will help illumine their significance in a religious context. First, let us distinguish between belief and faith.

BELIEF AND FAITH

Belief and faith, as understood here, are not identical. By faith we mean the experience of the holy, while belief refers to a symbolic expression or external representation of that faith. Belief is thus one step removed from the experience of faith. The terms *belief* and *faith* are often used interchangeably, but this practice is inadequate for several reasons. First, it does not allow us to distinguish between religious beliefs, which are related to the experience of faith, and beliefs in general, which are not. Second, while religious beliefs presuppose the experience of faith, that experience is not exhausted in the expression of religious belief. Third, the experience of faith yields a degree of certainty inappropriate to religious or secular belief. Let us consider each of these points.

First, not all beliefs are religious. Not all beliefs attempt to communicate something of unrestricted value. Religious beliefs, as contrasted with secular beliefs, do attempt to express the experience of an unrestricted value.

Second, the experience of faith, understood as the self's experience of the holy, the sacred, or the unconditional value, is the source of the various expressions of religious belief. Religious beliefs are symbolic objectifications or externalizations of the experience of faith; they are not themselves what is valued unrestrictedly. Rather, the religious belief is a representation, an interpretive and conditioned artifact, that attempts to express within the limits of language the unconditional value.

Third, while certainty may arise from the subjective experience of faith, it is not appropriate for the interpretation of that experience given in a particular belief. The truth of any proposition may be doubted. Religious belief is born in the self-evident and self-authenticating experience of faith, but once it is given expression in a particular interpretation or belief it is subject to doubt. Belief may be mistaken.

Distinguishing religious belief from belief in general helps to clarify the significance of religious belief.

BELIEF IN GENERAL

All belief, whether religious or nonreligious, holds certain factors in common. These include (1) assertion, (2) symbolic expression of the assertion, (3) a relationship between the subject and object of the assertion, (4) the possibility of being mistaken, and (5) the need to be distinguished from knowledge.

Assertion

An assertion is a symbolic expression that declares, avows, or claims that something is in fact the case. Assertion may be defined as "a symbolic expression of alleged fact."

In this definition the term *fact* denotes an accurate statement (that is, one that is true, needs no correction, and has avoided error) signifying a real, objective state of affairs. A fact signifies conditions that are not exclusively private or simply a matter of subjective expression.

An *alleged fact* may be contrasted with a *demonstrated fact*. An alleged fact is a statement that claims to be an accurate or true representation of an objective state of affairs but has not yet had its claim demonstrated or proved. This is not to say that its claim is false, only that its truth or falsity has not yet been demonstrated by an appropriate method. A demonstrated fact is a statement whose claim to represent accurately an objective state of affairs has been proved or sufficiently established by appropriate procedure. What these methods might be, who decides when a demonstration is sufficient, or what is to be done when different methods appear to produce different demonstrations, are questions that will not be discussed in this chapter. We are not concerned here with the question of demonstrating the truth of specific beliefs.

A fact (alleged or demonstrated) may or may not be regarded by someone as personally important. Thus the demonstrated fact that "Jim has a wart on his nose" expresses what is actually the case, regardless of what Mary wants or likes. A factual statement claims that some experience has public consequence. It is effective beyond the idiosyncratic experience of one subject. A demonstrated fact reveals such a state of affairs to anyone who adequately uses an appropriate method of demonstration.

Symbolic Expression

Every act of assertion implies the explicit or implicit use of human language in the interpretation of a situation. Humans use symbol systems—here language—to give order, theme, or meaning to the contents of their experience. At this point we are concerned only with explicit, written symbolic expression as opposed to behavior resulting from the spoken word. The latter, however, is a legitimate expression of belief. For example, if a highway patrol officer asks me, "Do you have a license?" I may either orally assert, "Yes, I do," or, without benefit of the spoken word, simply take out my license and display it. In the latter case I am making an assertion without speaking. Nevertheless, my specific action implies that I have understood the question and am making an intentional response to it. If we were to study religious belief by observing religious rituals, we would make use of this distinction.

In review, all belief involves assertion, and an assertion is a symbolic expression of an alleged or demonstrated fact.

The Belief Relationship

By saying that belief always involves assertion, we are also saying that belief is always a relationship consisting of at least two poles. The first pole represents the subject for whom the relation is internal; the subject holds and affirms the relationship. The subject has a positive attitude toward the object, holding enough confidence and trust to make an assertion. The subject of the relationship is the believer or one who does the believing. The second pole represents the object of belief, what is believed, or the assertion of an alleged fact. In the belief relationship the subject perceives, understands, or "sees" the object to be an accurate expression of an objective state of affairs.

Let us consider an example of the belief relationship: "Siddhartha Gautama the Buddha believed that all life is suffering." In this example Siddhartha is the historical subject or believer because he was confident enough in his perception of experience to affirm the assertion "all life is suffering" as true. The belief relationship involves a confident subject who deliberately affirms the truth of a symbolic assertion.

Belief May Be Mistaken

Another important element of all belief, however, is that it may be mistaken. Consider the following example: "John believed that Mary loved him." Is this in fact the case? John has alleged that it is. Has he demonstrated this fact? As far as our example goes he has not brought forth such a demonstration. Does this mean that John should not have said that he "believed" that Mary loved him? No, because belief may be mistaken and still be belief.

As long as the subject (John) is in a positive psychological state with regard to its object (Mary loves John), he may legitimately say that he believes the assertion to be true. The condition of intentionality or awareness is the essential characteristic of belief. The issue is not whether the assertion has been or could be demonstrated. Even if John has deluded himself about Mary, or Mary has deceived John, it is still true that John believes Mary loves him. In sum, belief may be mistaken. Belief that involves error is nonetheless belief.

Belief and Knowledge

Any definiton of belief must clearly distinguish between belief and knowledge. The primary difference between belief and knowledge is that while belief may be mistaken, knowledge may not be mistaken. Knowledge includes what we have already described as belief. Knowing is belief plus an additional factor, the ability to demonstrate the truth of an alleged fact. For example, NASA once *believed* that it was possible to place people on the moon. We now *know* that it was correct.

RELIGIOUS BELIEF

According to our definiton of religion in chapter 1, an assertion expresses a subject's religious belief only if the subject regards it as expressing something of unrestricted personal value. The feature that distinguishes religious belief from other belief is that the subject of religious belief "perceives" the object of belief as being of unrestricted importance for his or her life. "Perceiving" here does not mean that the eyes of the religious believer see some state of affairs that the eyes of a nonreligious believer do not see. Both the religious and nonreligious believer may agree on the expression of an alleged fact. Rather, perceiving refers to the discovery of a pattern of pivotal importance within an experience. For example, on looking at many colored tiles on a wall I suddenly realize that it is a mosaic showing the pattern of a man's face that conveys a central insight into a human condition.

The perception of religious belief requires that a person discover a meaningful pattern in his or her experience of life that becomes all-important. Such a perception organizes the person's attitude, his or her understanding of life, and the pattern of behavior within his or her life. Thus Gautama the Buddha, upon empirically observing the sights of an old man, a sick man, a corpse, and a monk, "perceived" (that is, had the insight of interpretation) that ultimately all life is suffering and that the essential meaning of life is found in the liberation from this suffering. Similarly, the prophets of Israel looked upon the economic and civil corruption of their community and "perceived"in this the inevitability of judgment by a righteous God who demanded that human life reflect justice in all its aspects. Through the "perception" of an order or pattern of meaning in the facts of life, the religious believer understands and evaluates life differently from those who are not religious believers.

The object of belief has an intense and comprehensive effect on its subject. For example, Gautama the prince must give up his kingdom and devote himself completely in body and mind to the quest for nirvana, that is, the state of complete release from suffering. Similarly, the prophets must endure painful rejection by their community without the possibility of compromise in word or deed. The subject of religious belief positively affirms this object in the quest to realize a full, meaningful life.

A Functional Definition of Religious Belief

We will now define religious belief as "the varied symbolic assertion of alleged fact, the unrestricted value of which is so perceived and positively affirmed as to shape the attitude, understanding, and intentional behavior of a subject's life."

Understood against the background of the discussion above, this definition is specific, inclusive, and without narrowness, compartmentalization, or prejudice. However, this definition represents an ideal standard for religious belief. We may find no people whose beliefs constantly and completely direct their whole disposition, understanding, and activities. Yet if people hold beliefs that they think should be functioning in this way, then we are dealing with religious belief. The religious life often includes the tension between ideal expression and actual realization. In this chapter we will concentrate upon the ideal conceptual expression of belief and not on the effectiveness of the application of such belief.

This definition also stresses the notion of "fact regarded as being of unrestricted importance," because it seeks to avoid interpreting religious belief as merely emotional language, or as simply language expressing a policy of behavior or a commitment to a way of life. Important as emotion and volition are in religious belief, they do not exclude the intellectual element. When a person decides that the world is the result of an intentional act of creation, or that the world is an illusion, it becomes important whether or not the world is actually a creation or an illusion. If one believes that the world is in fact an illusion, it makes no sense to orient one's whole life toward a proper relationship to its creator (since the world is not a creation). Rather, it would make sense to seek to liberate oneself from the ignorance of this world by turning inward to the depths of one's own being, a view that becomes genuinely important to the believer.

However, religious belief is open to a wide variety of interpretations of these facts. While fact is genuinely important to religious belief, specific interpretations of facts often show a range of differences; the same "fact" may be understood very differently by different people. What does not vary is the believer's perception of the unrestricted value of his or her belief.

Classification of Religious Beliefs

Our functional definition of religious belief indicates precisely what we mean by *religious belief*. No definition, however, reveals what particular believers in the past or present have believed or do believe. In order to obtain this information it is necessary to conduct a careful study of the religious expressions of particular religions. It is often helpful in initial investigations to attempt to locate and describe the beliefs that come under the following common but important classifications:

Anthropological beliefs. Beliefs that belong in this category include assertions about the nature of humanity. For example, is the human being the body, soul, spirit, or some combined relationship of them? What is the origin and nature of the body? Is humanity a product of evolution? Is the human being mortal, immortal, or both in different respects? Does a person normally experience more than one life on earth, in heaven or hell?

Cosmological beliefs. Beliefs that belong in this category indicate the nature, order, or patterns of significance constituting the world or worlds known to humanity. Was the world intentionally created or an accident? Is it real or illusory? Is it temporal or eternal? Is there more than one level or dimension to the world? Is there an underworld, hell, heaven, or paradise? Is the world regarded as good, bad, ambiguous, or some combination?

Numinological beliefs. Beliefs that belong in this category indicate the specific nature of the sacred, the holy, or the divine. For example, is the divine asserted to be personal or impersonal, one or many, eternal or temporal, loving or indifferent? Is the divine understood to be an aspect of or separate from nature, individuals, groups, history, or some combination of these?

Soteriological beliefs. Beliefs that belong to this category indicate the means by which salvation, liberation, or final human fulfillment is achieved. For example, is salvation an act of divine grace, or is it secured by the efforts of human beings, or both? Does final human fulfillment take place outside history or within history? Is liberation a phenomenon of the individual, or are communities the focus? Does judgment, reward, and punishment play a role in understanding salvation?

Sociological beliefs. Beliefs that belong in this category indicate how the individual is or should be related to various human groupings and the roles that are expected of him or her therein. For example, how is the individual related to the family? Is there a caste system and what are its responsibilities? What is the relationship of the priest, shaman, prophet, or guru to his or her community? How is a person identified for one of these religious "offices"? What role does a community's rituals, liturgy, preaching, and teaching play in the formation and nurture of human beings? Is the community the locus of salvation?

VISION OF LIFE

Having considered the nature of religious belief, we are now ready to turn to the question of how religious belief becomes a vision of life for the believer. While some studies are concerned with the truth or historical development of belief, we are concerned here with the difference various beliefs make for the life of the believer. We ask what difference it makes for the life of a subject whether he or she believes that an object is true and of unrestricted importance.

This concern is reflected in such questions as the following: How does a set of religious beliefs inform a person's understanding of the world and his or her own possibilities within it? What aspirations, ideals, or goals is a person admonished to realize if she or he affirms a set of religious beliefs? How does a set of religious beliefs suggest that a person might realize his or her ideal?

Our definition of religious belief stipulates that belief will shape the thinking and intentional response of the believer to the situations that make up his or her life. It provides the subject with an overall orientation to life, an interpretation of "what it's all about." For this reason we will call the general category of religious belief a "vision of life." This designation indicates that religious belief functions to give the believer a wholistic interpretation of the meaning of life itself.

THE TRANSFORMATIONAL MODEL

This model is called "transformational" because it indicates that a person moves from an understanding of the essential problem confronting life toward an ideal "goal" by means of some mode of activity. In this sense the essential problem of life is changed, resolved, overcome (that is, "transformed") for persons who move toward their ideal in the process.

The three essential elements comprising this transformational model are as follows: (1) the essential problems confronting people's lives, (2) the essential ideal to which people feel they ought to aspire in life, and (3) the essential mode or means for the realization of those ideals in people's lives.

The term *essential* indicates that which is most basic or fundamental. An essesntial aspect of life is one that is so pervasive that it touches every part of life. No situation of life is free from its presence, involvement, or effect. Essential elements in life relate to unrestricted values.

Essential Problems

Many religious beliefs indicate that human beings find life to be different from what it ideally ought to be. Humankind is confronted with such an "essential problem" that the ideal it aspires to is in some way blocked. Life is in some way fundamentally and essentially "wrongheaded."

Finding the "essential problem" in any particular religious vision involves asking such questions as: What is the basic road-block to life's genuine satisfactions? What obstacle prevents a person from achieving his or her highest aspirations? What principle defect must be removed before life can realize its essential goal? Let us consider, now, some of the diverse answers to these questions from the various religions. However different the answers, all are reflecting an understanding of "essential problems."

In the religions of India generally, the essential problem of life revolves around the experience of suffering. Indian religions examine the particular and finite nature of an individual's existence that makes him or her vulnerable to suffering. The Hindu traditions assert that so long as a person remains ultimately concerned with or attached to the desires of the finite self, either as an individual seeking personal pleasure and worldly success or as a public servant seeking through a sense of duty to rid the world of pain and evil, this person will remain bound to the wheel of suffering and rebirth *(samsara)*. From this perspective, the essential problem is a fundamental ignorance of the self, powerfully perpetuated by the surface delights of distractions of worldly "illusions" *(maya)* experienced through the individual body, personality, memory, and so forth.

Similarly, the Buddhist tradition is informed by the insights of Siddhartha Gautama the Buddha ("awakened one") whose first truth asserts that life is suffering *(dukkha)*. From the trauma of birth to the experience of sickness, decrepitude and death, our body, senses, ideas, feeling, and consciousness teach us that life is estranged and real happiness is precluded. His second truth identifies self-desire and mental attachments *(tanha)* as the cause of life's suffering and estrangement. Thus the essential problem is that this distorted, misplaced attachment fuels the fires of inappropriate passion for the world and the self.

In Judaism, Christianity, and Islam the essential problem is not the individuality of the self in the finite world, but the injustice and the insensitivity in relationships between the self and the "other," whether God, nature, society, or individual persons. While there are significant differences between and among these religious traditions, they share a common belief structure emphasizing both a monotheistic God who is creator and primary historical agent, and a human being who, though in covenant with God, is a covenant breaker or a "fallen" creature. In these traditions neither creaturehood, nature, nor history is understood as *maya* (illusory); they are not the essential problems to be overcome. Rather, the human as specific creature, individually and socially, in action and intention, misses the mark, breaks the covenant, or "sins" within God's creation. This inappropriate intention and behavior violates the relations of mutuality, justice, and love most appropriate to the divine creation. It thereby produces a fundamental estrangement between humankind and God. This estrangement is understood as the essential problem that blocks the deepest hopes and expectations of humanity.

Essential Ideals

Our model indicates, as its second element, that a vision of life contains an interpretation of the "ideal" that huanity ought to seek in order to overcome its essential problem and realize its hope for almost meaningful and valuable life. The single term *ideal* has three very important emphases. First, the expression of the ideal indicates the believer's understanding that there is in fact a genuine possibility open for his or her life; the subject can experience a new and ideal life. Second, the ideal within a "vision of life" is experienced as a "normative" (ideal standard) possibility directing or leading one's life. The believer experiences the idea as something she or he is obligated to realize. Thus the ideal represents both a possibility for personal life and what ought to be realized as the highest goal of life. Third, to live contrary to this ideal is to be an inauthentic, incomplete person. One would be missing the mark and failing to experience the highest value open to one.

To locate this element in the religious beliefs of a particular religious vision one might ask such questions as: What would result if the chief obstacle to the fullest personal realization were removed, bringing about the highest personal satisfaction? What would the most valuable experience open to humanity consist of? Toward what end should a person aspire if he or she would find the most fruitful culmination of personal or communal life?

Hinduism and Buddhism answer these questions in terms of the individual's search for a true self, or a state of no-self, where the individual self has disengaged itself from all that makes it vulnerable to suffering and is therefore free from pain, death, and the frustrations of the world. In the Hindu traditions the soul (*jiva*) of the individual can escape transmigration and reincarnation in this less-than-ultimate world of *maya* and *samsara* by attaining *moksha* or "release." This is often expressed as an experience of union that collapses all individuality into Brahman, the cosmic "soul." The possibility and superiority of this release represents the overcoming of the essential problem confronting the human, and is the central ideal of the Hindu tradition.

Similarly in Buddhism, as the Buddha's third and fourth truths make clear, the extinction of the fires of selfish desire in the experience of nirvana—the emptying of the self—is both possible through religious practice and normative as an ideal standard for Buddhists. Mahayana Buddhism expresses its religious belief in the essential ideal through symbols of communion, emphasizing love and relationship, while Theravada Buddhism expresses its belief through the symbol of no-self. In either form it is clear that the experience of the ideal is possible and represents the unrestricted value for the believer.

Judaism, Christianity, and Islam respond to questions about the essential ideal with religious beliefs about judgment, punishment, grace, forgiveness, salvation, resurrection, and so forth. Such beliefs indicate a transformation within and/or beyond history, from the conditions of estrangement to an ideal experience of communion or mystical union, a fulfillment or peace that passes all understanding. In each of the traditions, religious beliefs express the clear expectation that humankind's essential problems can and will be overcome in real and essential fulfillment.

Essential Modes of Realizations

The third element of our model indicates that religious beliefs claim there are effective means by which persons may be transformed from the essential problem of life toward the essential ideal. The means to accomplish this transformation may be understood as the "vehicle," "procedure," or "mode of realization" involved in the fulfillment of the ideal.

In order to locate this element in the religious beliefs of a particular religious vision, one might ask such questions as: What is the nature and location of the resources necessary to realize the ideal solution of a person's essential problem? Do people possess such power within themselves, or must it come from beyond them? What are the chances of the ideal solution being realized by an individual or a community in the world or beyond it? Is such a realization inevitable, not likely, or singly dependent on what humanity itself does or does not do?

Specific religious traditions themselves often provide a variety of responses to the question of the vehicle, procedure, or mode for essential realization. The Hindu tradition recognizes the vast differences among people and thus acknowledges that there are many methods (yogas) to

overcome false attachment and experience liberation as union or communion with Brahman. Therefore, whether you are primarily reflective, active, emotional, or experimental in disposition, you would follow
the practice of *jana yoga, karma yoga, bhakti yoga,* or *raja yoga* respectively.
Any combination of these or other yogas is also possible. A person must
identify, practice, and develop an effective discipline (a training or
yoga) that allows and provides for the essential realization of liberation.

Buddhism also emphasizes yoga, although it focuses on the yogas of
meditation rather than devotion. Morality and right views are also a
part of what Buddhism calls the eightfold path or threefold training.
Theravada Buddhism emphasizes individual attainment, whereas
Mahayana emphasizes helping others attain the ideal through compassion and wisdom. The vehicles or procedures may be different, but the
goal made possible through them is the achievement of an essential
realization.

Judaism, Christianity, and Islam also display diverse responses to the
question of means or vehicle. In these three traditiions, essential realization is always associated with the formula of divine initiation and human response. Whether called Jahweh, God, or Allah, the Western
deity initiates realization out of grace by creating and urging a new
self-understanding, a new manner of being and acting, a new life. Sub-
communities within each of these traditions emphasize God's grace over
human works, while others reverse the emphasis; some emphasize the
meditative, while others stress social action; some emphasize the community and the necessity to participate in its rituals and sacraments,
while others stress the individual. The central idea in this diversity of
expression and emphasis, however, is that the vehicles are believed to
be effective channels of power that bring about the essential ideal for
humankind.

In summary, the transformational model is a way of understanding
how religious beliefs may work in people's religious life, and how beliefs
reflect essential problems, essential ideals, and essential modes of realization; it does not tell you what specific content is to be given to these
categories by Hinduism, Buddhism, or other religions. Specific reading
and study of these religions will provide the data on which one must
exercise judgment. The model is intended as an aid; only the student
can perform the study. Similarly, while our model provides a basis for
comparison, only one's study and judgment can lead to an appreciation
of the similarities and differences that appear among the religious beliefs of humanity.

SUMMARY

Religious belief may be defined as "the varied symbolic assertion of
alleged fact, the unrestricted value of which is so perceived and posi-

tively affirmed as to shape the attitude, understanding, and intentional behavior of a subject's life." Because a religious belief functions to provide an all-encompassing interpretation of life, it has been called a vision of life. A model, called the transformational model, then described the specific aspects of a vision of life. These aspects included (1) the essential problem confronting the life of a person or group, (2) the essential ideal to which a person or group ought to aspire in life, (3) the essential mode for the realization of this ideal in one's personal life. Sample questions indicated how to locate each of these elements within a particular religious vision. Examples from the religious traditions of Hinduism, Buddhism, Judaism, Christianity, and Islam illustrated how the model might apply in specific instances.

Ignorance is never a virtue, and students in the field of the study of religion must attempt to break down the barriers of parochial prejudice. Toward this end we have developed means for identifying and focusing discussion on religious belief, a phenomenon that has played and continues to play a crucial role in the evolution of human experience. Through this discussion we encounter the assertions of human hope and expectation that affirm the nature of life's meaning amidst its many challenges and threats. While this study does not intend to produce religious believers, the understanding that can result provides insights into human tears and laughter, fears and confident action.

QUESTIONS FOR STUDY AND DISCUSSION

The answers to the following questions will depend, in part, on a close reading of this chapter and, in part, on readings you may find outside this book that relate to the world's great religions.

HINDUISM

1. What does humanity desire, according to Hinduism? How is your answer revealed in the anthropological beliefs of Hinduism? in its cosmological beliefs? How is desire linked with the essential problem of *maya* and the wheel of suffering and rebirth *(samsara)*?

2. What should be aspired to in Hinduism as the essential ideal of a person's life? How is your answer revealed in the numinological beliefs of Hinduism? in its soteriological beliefs?

3. What is the role of the individual in the essential mode of realization for Hinduism? Where is the "power" of transformation located? What is the role of the community in Hinduism? How does Hinduism's sociological beliefs effect its understanding of the essential mode of realization?

BUDDHISM

1. How do the anthropological and cosmological beliefs of Buddhism express Siddhartha Gautama's first and second truths? What is meant by the terms *dukkha, tanha, anatta,* and *skandas?* What is the essential problem that confronts the person according to Buddhism?
2. What are the numinological beliefs of Buddhism and how do they affect the understanding of an authentic self?
3. What are the major differences between Mahayana Buddhism and Theravada Buddhism in understanding the essential mode of realization? How do these differences affect the expression of anthropological beliefs? soteriological beliefs? sociological beliefs?

ISLAM

1. How do the anthropological and cosmological beliefs of Islam compare and contrast with those of Hinduism? Do these differences affect the way these religious traditions understand the essential problem confronting a person's life?
2. Compare and contrast the numinological beliefs of Islam and Buddhism. How do the differences and simularities you find here affect the understanding of the essential ideal to be aspired to?
3. In what ways are Judaism, Christianity, and Islam similar in their expression of the essential mode of realization? In what ways are they different? How do the sociological and soteriological beliefs of Islam differ from those of Christianity? or Judaism?

JUDAISM

1. How do the anthropological and sociological beliefs of Judaism reflect the importance of history? Compare and contrast those beliefs with those of Buddhism. How do these differences affect the understanding of the essential problem confronting a person's life?
2. Contrast the numinological beliefs of Judaism with those of Hinduism. How do these differences inform a different understanding of the essential ideal to be aspired to in a person's life?
3. How are the soteriological beliefs of Judaism and Christianity different? similar? Are the sociological beliefs of Judaism important to understanding the essential made of realization?

CHRISTIANITY

1. How do the anthropological and cosmological beliefs of Christianity affect its understanding of the essential problem confronting a person's life? Contrast these religious beliefs with those of Buddhism.

2. What are the numinological beliefs of Christianity? How are they similar to and different from those of Judaism and Islam? How do these beliefs affect Christianity's understanding of the essential ideal to be realized in a person's life?

3. What is the role of the sociological beliefs of Christianity in its understanding of the essential mode of realization? Do these beliefs differ significantly from Buddhism? If so, in what ways? Are they similar in any respects?

PROJECTS

1. Read the first chapter of Huston Smith's *The Religions of Man* and make notes on Hindu beliefs in regard to

a. the essential problem in human existence.
b. the goal, or what the Hindus really want.
c. the various means or modes they have for achieving their aspirations.

After you have done this you should have an outline of the basic beliefs in Hinduism.

2. Read carefully all of the chapters in *The Religions of Man*. As you read, make notes on

a. the problem in the human condition confronting all people.
b. the essential ideal to which a peson ought to aspire in life.
c. the essential mode or way for the realization of the ideal.

3. After you have completed your study of *The Religions of Man* and outlined the key beliefs in each major religion, select another text, such as *Man's Religions* by John Noss. Add to your list of major beliefs of the world's religions in each of the three areas. Then make a list of all major assertions that are not included in the three categories of problem, goal, and mode of achieving the goal.

4. Select a novel or play that reflects the belief system of one of the major religions of the world. The book might be Chaim Potok's *The Promise* (Jewish); T. S. Eliot's *The Cocktail Party* (Christian); Tanizaki Junichiro's *The Makioka Sisters* (Japanese Buddhist-Shinto); or *Nectar in a Sieve*, by Kamala Markandaya (Hindu). After reading the book, write an interpretive essay demonstrating how it expresses

a. the problem.
b. the ideal.
c. the mode of achieving the ideal.

SUGGESTED READINGS

Comstock, W. Richard, ed. *Religion and Man: An Introduction.* New York: Harper & Row, 1971.

Dye, James W., and William H. Forthman, comps. *Religions of the World: Selected Readings.* New York: Appleton Century Crofts, 1967.

Frost, S. E., Jr., ed. *The Sacred Writings of the World's Great Religions.* New York: McGraw-Hill, 1972.

Hutchison, John A. *Paths of Faith.* New York: McGraw-Hill, 1975.

Noss, John B. *Man's Religions.* New York: Macmillan, 1974.

Smart, Ninian. *The Religious Experience of Mankind.* 2d ed. New York: Scribners, *1976.*

Smith, Huston. *The Religions of Man.* New York: Harper & Row, 1965.

Spiegelberg, Frederic. *Living Religions of the World.* Englewood Cliffs, N.J.: Prentice-Hall, 1956.

Streng, Frederick J., Charles L. Lloyd, and Jay T. Allen, eds. *Ways of Being Religious: Readings for a New Approach to Religion.* Englewood Cliffs, N.J.: Prentice-Hall, 1973.

CHAPTER 7

Scripture

Scripture is the sacred literature of a religious community, an authoritative basis for belief and practice, and a major resource for creative symbolic expression. It is sacred for the religious community in that it is believed to have been revealed in some special way. The claim may be that the words were given to some leader by God or that the writer was religiously inspired. Moreover, scripture is sacred in that it is thought to reveal to the faithful what is holy and what is true about the cosmos and human existence. Thus scripture is that body of literature considered to be different from all other writings. It is different because it is sacred and at the same time reveals what is sacred.

Many of us who live in a secular society find it difficult to understand fully how some literature can be considered sacred while other important writings are not. Two illustrations may, by analogy, be helpful. There is an old saying that "one's home is one's castle." This means that home is a special place where people feel comfortable and secure. Being at home is qualitatively different from being anywhere else. One feels as if there were a presence of some protecting spirit guarding the domestic tranquility—a presence that is transcendent.

There is also sacred space in a church, temple, or synagogue. When one enters such a building, a sense of quietness pervades. As movement continues toward the high altar or most holy spot, that special mood intensifies; a quality of sacredness prevails, in contrast to the ordinary or mundane space outside. In fact, for many people sacred space is the only truly real space, giving meaning to profane space.[1]

Just as our experience shows us that there is a special meaning in certain spaces which is extraordinary, so too certain literature seems to contain an unusual kind of writing and becomes a manifestation of the sacred—a hierophany. As people naturally treat with respect a sacred space, to too do they show respect to sacred texts. Scripture is respectfully read at religious services or in private spiritual devotions. In both cases readers expect that insights or truths will be presented. Surely a sensitive person in the religious community would not stand on a sacred text or use pages of scripture for ordinary purposes such as a substitute for facial tissue or as fuel for lighting a barbecue fire!

Scripture is authoritative in matters of belief and practice. We would be incorrect in asserting that religious belief and practice originated in scripture. Historical investigations show that the religious communities existed prior to the writing of their scripture; belief and practice preceded sacred texts. Although religions produced scripture and scripture did not produce religion, these sacred writings quickly became extremely important. At first, the writings legitimated beliefs and practices that were already present. In years that followed, scripture communicated to later generations the traditions and beliefs that had been significant for the people. The scripture, then, is not only a sacred document, but it continues to be a manual of inspiration and instruction for the people—an essential body of writings for the continuing tradition. Sometimes it provides specific rituals for the community and warns against impure ceremonies that would be spiritually offensive and ineffective. Other parts tell stories of heroes and heroines who were venerated in their own time and who remain models for people to follow. Scripture is prized by the people as the authoritative document of belief and practice.

Scripture is also a major source of new imaginative and symbolic expression. Not only are sacred writings filled with images and symbols from early religious expressions, but, through the years, scriptures have "fired the imagination, and inspired the poetry, and formulated the inhibitions, and guided the ecstasies, and teased the intellects, and nurtured the piety, of hundreds of millions of people in widely diverse climes over a series of radically divergent centuries."[2]

Western people know that much of the literature and the arts have been inspired by biblical images and themes. The writings of Dante, Chaucer, Shakespeare, Faulkner, Updike, and many others have been influenced by the scriptures of Judaism and Christianity. Painting, at least until the modern era, was saturated with biblical persons and symbols. The arts in Asia also reflect the sacred writings. Bronze statues of Hindu gods, statutes and etchings of the Buddha, the quiet spirit of Japanese *noh* darama, and popular art and film of India are all shaped by sacred texts. Scriptures are therefore not merely ancient relics. They remain alive in every tradition, inspiring new forms of imaginative expression.

The definition of scripture, then, can be stated again: *Scripture is the sacred literature of a religious community, an authoritative basis for belief and practice, and a major resource for creative symbolic expression.*

IDENTIFICATION OF SCRIPTURES

A vast body of sacred literature is connected with all of the great religions. This fact alone makes the study of scripture difficult. In addition, each text was originally written in the language of the people for whom it was intended (Arabic, Hebrew, Chinese, Pali, Japanese, Greek, Egyptian, and so forth). In some cases we have only fragments of early texts, increasing the difficulty of transcribing and translating the documents. Moreover, the transition from oral tradition to written texts often continued over centuries. Much of this material has survived, but some written documents have been lost or destroyed, and bits and pieces of such writings are still being discovered by archaeologists. The gathering of data from these writings promises to continue during the foreseeable future.

The study of scripture is also difficult in that not all scholars agree on which writings have the status as scripture. Even the people of a given religion have not always agreed. We may therefore ask, "Who decides when a body of literature becomes scripture?" Two related answers help clarify the problem.

First, literature becomes sacred when prized by the people of a particular community as treasured texts revealing hidden mysteries about the cosmos, the holy, society, and themselves. When the message, its origin clouded in the vagueness of history, seems to transcend ordinary human understanding, it is judged to be "above" all other literature—to be sacred. In short, literature is sacred when so judged by the people in a specific culture.

Second, texts are sacred when they are accepted by the religious leaders. Leaders are influenced by popular religion, and the popular faith is, at the same time, shaped by leaders. Therefore the second basis for constituting a text as "scripture" is related to the first. On several occasions religious leaders have decided that a canon (a "closed" body of scripture) be created. For example, a group of rabbis, meeting in council in 90 C.E., agreed that only twenty-four books make up the official Hebrew scripture. Similarly, the official list of books to be in the Christian Bible was disputed by various early Christian leaders. Finally by about 400 C.E. they agreed on twenty-seven books as the canon. Certain apocryphal books are now considered scripture by the Roman Catholic and Greek churches, whereas Protestant denominations eliminate those books in their official Bible.

Even if problems of diverse languages, original manuscripts, and official canons could be resolved, the vast array of texts remains an obstacle for a thorough study of scriptures. We might limit our study to the scripture of one tradition alone, yet most experts spend a lifetime investigating the scriptures of a single religious community. Since that is not possible for most of us, we must depend on those scholars for our generalizations about scripture.

We will therefore develop this discussion about scripture in full realization of the dangers of generalizations. In this study we will keep in mind and draw illustrations from the most well-known texts. From Islam, Judaism, and Christianity we will draw upon the Qur'an, the Hebrew Bible, and the Christian Bible. From Hinduism we will draw upon the Vedas, the Upanishads, and the Bhagavad Gita. And from Buddhism we will consider selected sutras (scripture) from the Pali Canon of Theravada (or earliest) Buddhism relating to the teachings of the Buddha. A reference will also be made to the Analects of Confucius and the Tao Te Ching, both from China. Selections from Asian scriptures have been chosen because of their availability to students and their familiarity to many Western people.

THE FUNCTION OF SCRIPTURE

The introductory paragraphs of this chapter sought to answer the question, "What is scripture?" The second part identified selected scriptures of major religions for reference. An additional step may now be taken by answering the question, "What does scripture do for people?" We can answer by asserting that scripture functions to:

1. give evidence of and inspire experience of the holy.
2. preserve the great myths, legends, and rituals of a religious tradition.
3. define moral behavior.
4. prescribe right attitudes and beliefs. In so doing scripture answers such questions as,
   a. what is real?
   b. what is the self?
   c. what is human destiny?

TOWARD EXPERIENCE OF THE HOLY

Throughout human history, people have had experiences which they interpreted as experiences of a holy reality. Those experiences have transformed people and served as a motivation for religious life. For example, when Moses heard the voice of God in the burning bush (Exod. 3) he changed from a desert shepherd to the leader of his people, guiding them out of Egypt into the wilderness and into a new covenant with God. When the descendants of those ancient Hebrews read the account many years later, they are inspired by the same God and seek to listen to the divine voice.

A similar transforming experience is recorded in the story of the transfiguration in the Christian scripture in the Gospel of Luke, chapter 9. In the narrative, Jesus is praying with several of his disciples. During the prayer,

the appearance of his countenance was altered, and his raiment became dazzling white. And behold, two men talked with him, Moses and Elijah. . . . and Peter said to Jesus, "Master, it is well that we are here; let us make three booths, one for you and one for Moses and one for Elijah"—not knowing what he said. As he said this, a cloud came and overshadowed them; and they were afraid as they entered the cloud. And a voice came out of the cloud, saying, "This is my Son, my chosen; listen to him."

Whatever the actual event was, it is presented in Luke as a hierophany—a manifestation of the holy with Jesus. The Christian reader, inspired by this account of the transfigured Jesus, is encouraged to accept the holiness of Jesus.

The Bhagavad Gita, popular Hindu story and scripture, has as its major theme the relationship of the hero, Arjuna, with the divine being, Krishna. Arjuna and his Lord Krishna assist each other in battle until they are successful. Arjuna praises his Lord Saying:

Ah, my god, I see all gods within your body;

. . . .

Universal Form, I see you without limit,
Infinite of arms, eyes, mouths and bellies—
See, and find no end, midst or beginning.

. . . .

By your grace, O Lord, my delusions have been dispelled.
My mind stands firm. Its doubts are ended. I will do your bidding.[3]

The universal love for the Gita in India suggests that Arjuna's experience of identification with Lord Krishna is a continuous inspiration to persons who seek guidance and strength in the midst of difficulty. Additional examples from every scripture could demonstrate that sacred scripture both reveals experiences of the holy and provides inspiration to the people for similar experiences.

PRESERVATION OF SACRED STORIES AND RITUALS

We have already seen in the chapter on sacred stories (chapter 3) the importance of myth for religious communities. Those stories express for the people the meaning of life and how things "really are." Stories would eventually be forgotten, however, unless preserved in some written form, so the scriptures include many of the stories. Myths of creation, of human failures, of great catastrophies, of courage, death, and rebirth, along with a larger plan for liberation, are preserved and remain alive for the people.

Sacred stories, in addition to their power to inform, inspire, and transform human life, often become the foundation for ritual action. Two of the most familiar rituals—one in Judaism and another in Christianity—illustrate the connection of biblical stories with ceremonies and rituals.

The Passover story, told in the twelfth chapter of Exodus, is no doubt a mixture of historical fact and the human imagination. It tells of Israel's final days in Egypt and God's judgment upon the firstborn of the

Egyptians. In the story, each household was instructed to kill a lamb and put blood on the doorposts. The people were to eat the flesh that night, along with unleavened bread and bitter herbs. Jahweh (God) then passed over every household of the Hebrews, while the firstborn of every Egyptian died. The next day Moses and Aaron led the people in their escape from slavery.

This great story of liberation continues to inspire people who struggle against limitations of body and spirit. Yet it is more than a story. It is dramatized once each year in the ritual of the Passover seder according to the specific instructions given in the Bible:

This day shall be for you a memorial day, and you shall keep it as a feast to the Lord; throughout your generations you shall observe it as an ordinance forever.... You shall observe the feast of unleavened bread, for on this very day I brought your hosts out of the land of Egypt.[4]

On Passover, Jewish families throughout the world join together around the candlelit table, reciting the sacred story from the Bible, eating the prescribed lamb, bitter herbs, and unleavened bread, and celebrating freedom.

The Christian community, with equal seriousness, finds that the central New Testament story of the Last Supper gives them identification with Jesus. The story is found in each of the first three gospels (Matthew, Mark, and Luke), and is referred to in John as well. According to the story, Jesus and his disciples were celebrating the Passover meal as prescribed in Exodus. During the meal Jesus took the loaf of bread, broke it, and gave pieces to each disciple saying, "This is my body." Then he took the cup of wine, blessed it and gave it to each to drink, saying, "This is my blood of the covenant which is poured out for many for the forgiveness of sins."[5] People in all branches of Christendom have been inspired by this biblical story, and each tradition—Orthodox, Catholic, or Protestant—celebrates the Eucharist in the ritual of Mass or through Holy Communion. Whenever Christians in worship devoutly accept the bread (Protestants also receive the wine), they remember and act out the story of Jesus and the Last Supper from their scripture.

PROCLAMATION OR RIGHT MORAL BEHAVIOR

Even a limited study of religion uncovers a moral component. The moral dimension is as important as the experience of the holy, rituals, or belief systems. Scripture serves to communicate these moral commands for all to follow.

The human family does not live in perfect harmony with one another. People often conduct themselves in such a way that other people's property and even their psychic and physical selves are violated. Moral codes in scripture provide norms of right behavior and right attitude by which people can live together harmoniously. If life is moral, not only will divine laws be followed, but justice may be achieved in the community.

We would need to be historians and sociologists to make an adequate study of the way moral codes developed in early societies. We would probably conclude such a social scientific study, however, with data showing that gradually every group of people developed codes or acceptable standards of behavior among themselves. Insofar as those codes were followed, there would be a tolerable absence of violence and presence of reasonable decency so that the society could exist in relative stability. As religious literature gradually came forth, and as those texts dealt with moral problems, they legitimated the highest ethical ideals by giving them sacred status. Thus the scriptures helped preserve the highest codes of moral action already in existence.

In addition, most if not all scriptures include a prophetic element. Either inspired by some divine source, or coming from the pen of sensitive moral persons, moral behavior is either commanded or ideals are proposed as guides for human interaction.

In the Jewish and Christian traditions this moral dimension is found in the Ten Commandments; in the teachings of the prophets such as Amos, Micah, and Hosea; and in the moral guidelines of Jesus. Equally apparent is the moral dimension in the scriptures of Buddhism with the Buddha's notion of the eightfold path. The Qur'an is filled with specific moral teachings, not only for individuals but for the officials of the state as well. In Chinese scripture, no element is more prominent in the writings of Confucius than the moral teachings. We can safely conclude, then, that scripture functions to proclaim right conduct for the people for whom its writings are sacred.

RESOURCE FOR RIGHT BELIEFS

Scripture also functions to answer fundamental human questions related to belief. At least three such questions appear to be universal: (a) What shall I believe about reality? (b) What shall I believe about myself? and (c) What is my ultimate destiny? Seldom do individuals have to be prodded to ask these questions. They are the perennial religious questions and seem to be built into our human consciousness.

In early monolithic cultures where pluralistic truth claims were unknown (for example the tribal cultures of Africa) these questions were answered before they became conscious. Views of reality and human existence were inculcated as part of the socialization process. Answers were self-evident through sacred stories, traditional ceremonies, and community-regulated attitudes.

When the beliefs of a community came in contact or conflict with other belief systems, however, questions quickly emerged. Biblical scholar James Williams, writing about the problems of scriptural origins, states, "The process of scripture formation is rooted in the interplay between crises of history and the answers of the tradition."[6] He suggests that whenever the answers to human questions given by a religious tradition were no longer adequate, dialogue developed giving rise to fresh answers for perennial questions. These answers then became part of scripture. The scripture, as preserved for later generations, therefore gave answers to these three constant questions: What is real? Who am I? and What is my destiny?

What Is Ultimately Real?

Wherever and whenever that question is asked in a religious context, the answer is most often the same: At bottom, reality is not matter but spirit. Of course, some philosophers have denied the spiritual reality of all things. These materialists have declared that ultimate reality is matter, motion, and the laws that govern them. Ancient Zoroastrian texts support a dualism, often interpreted as a view that reality is spirit and matter. Many Buddhist scriptures avoid all discussion of metaphysical issues but nonetheless posit the basis of reality in a spiritual state of mind.

But the answer proclaimed by the majority of sacred writings is that the world and everything in it is essentially spirit because it is rooted in a spiritual creator. "In the beginning God" are the first four words of the Bible. The Gospel of John in the New Testament begins with the phrase, "In the beginning was the word *(logos)* and the word was God." The Qur'an also affirms that reality is spiritual because Allah is the creator of all.

He . . . created the heavens and earth.
He . . . made the earth a fixed place.
He . . . guides you in the shadows of the land and sea.
God is He that created you. . . .
He is the All Knowing, the All Powerful.
God holds the heavens and the earth.[7]

Within the Hindu scriptures—the Vedas, the Brahmanas, and the Upanishads—religious knoweldge or insight is considered to be of extreme importance. As later philosophers interpreted those texts, the philosophic writings became authoritative as well. Writings of the Hindu philosopher Sankara (about 800 C.E.), then, are a kind of scripture, and his interpretation of reality is clear: There is only one reality, and that is spirit. He claims that the scriptures teach a radical nondualism. Everything is Brahman—spirit.

Down through the years religious thinkers in every culture have struggled intellectually with the question about reality. Many philosophers have referred to the physical world, human bodies, and all material things as part of the phenomenal world; yet they affirm a reality deeper than that which appears in material things. When the question is precise: "What is the ultimate nature of reality?" the scriptures and most commentators on them answer, "Reality is spirit."

What Is the Self?

The major scriptures respond similarly to the question, "Who am I?" The answers, however, are in three parts: (1) the self is essentially spirit; (2) every human being is caught in the predicament of suffering, ignorance, or rebellion, and hence has lost his or her original nature; and (3) human transformation is possible through spiritual discipline.

The Self Is Essentially Spirit. The essential nature of every person is spirit, most scriptures teach, because human life is created by the divine eternal spirit. While persons have a body, they are not merely a body; they are also spirit. Muslim, Jewish, and Christian scriptures are clear in this matter: "Mankind, fear your Lord, who created you of a single soul" are words in the Qur'an. The Bible preserves the ancient answer: "God created man in His own image, in the image of God He created him; male and female He created them." Since the Bible declares that God is spirit and that all creation is originally good, it follows that persons are spirit and in their original nature are good.

The answer is less clear in the Hindu scriptures. The Rig Veda, in its songs of praises to the god Visvakarman, the All-Maker, gives thanks to the One who created life. In the Atharva Veda, in the section on primal humanity, dozens of questions are asked: "Who fashioned feet, ankles, body, arms, neck, head, brain, etc." The answer given is that the supreme One, Brahman, did. There is evidence, then, that in the ancient Hindu scripture human life is believed to be—like all nature—spirit.[8] This interpretation is most clear in the Vedantic philosophers who insisted that the true self is the *atman* or spiritual self, and the *atman* is in essence one with Brahman, although, in ignorance, humans may not be aware of it.

In Buddhist scriptures an even more radical statement is made: There is no self *(an-atman)*, spiritual or otherwise. The self is "dissolved" in meditative awareness; it is "emptied" of any status in reality.

The human predicament. The second answer to the question, "Who am I?" is given in the sacred writings of all great religions. Although not identical, they all indicate that human beings are caught in limitations. Suffering, attachment to material things, craving, ignorance, arrogance, and disobedience are seen as fundamental aspects of the human condition. The self is mired in a predicament that hinders full personhood.

No statement is more clear than that of the Buddha. In fact, his four noble truths are the foundation of Buddhist thought and practice. The first truth is that "all life is suffering." The second truth gives the cause of the first: "Suffering is caused by craving"—sometimes called desire or attachment. For the Buddha, the fate of every person is to be caught within this web of pain and imperfection that the self brings on itself by craving and subject/object attachments.

In Hindu scriptures, following the thought of the Upanishads, people are considered limited by *samsara*, the wheel of birth, death, and reincarnation. Moreover, persons are limited by anxieties for gain and safety, as well as by pride. Equally serious is the human problem of ignorance, that is, of supposing that the material world is ultimately real when matter is only *maya* or illusion. Even the supposition that the human body is ontologically real is part of human ignorance. It is the *atman*—the soul—which is real. So the task of humankind is to overcome *samsara*, anxiety, pride and ignorance.[9]

The Bible is equally clear about the human condition. In the garden of Eden story in the book of Genesis, the first man and woman lived in happy innocence within a perfect environmnet. In their arrogance and self-sufficiency, however, they disobeyed God. They were then punished by being forced to live outside paradise. The man was forever condemned to hard work while the woman must expect pain in giving birth to children. Interpreters of this story insist that it is telling us more about the human condition generally than about any historic event. The condition includes the pride of thinking that to be human is to be like the gods, and the result is disobedience and separation from the divine spirit. Humans must forever seek for salvation from this primordial sin and separation.

The Qur'an says there are three states in the human condition. The first and primary one is the uncontrollable drive that leads one to evil. Because of it, people tend to harm others and to be hindered from attaining high moral goals. While this is a physical state only, it is a severe human limitation.[10]

Scriptures, then, give this second answer to the question, "Who am I?" I am caught in a web of limitations; liberation or extrication is thereby a primary goal of the religious life.

Transformation is possible. The third part of the answer about the self from varied sacred texts is clear: human transformation is possible. People can overcome or at least "answer" their condition, either in this life or in some eternal realm. Since religion claims to be a means of ultimate transformation, this view of the self is central.

Many Christians see in their scripture one continuous story of salvation. It begins with creation, quickly presents the fall in the story of Adam and Eve, continues with God's activity in history through the people of Israel, and reaches a high point in Jesus, the Christ. Jesus, who is presented as the incarnation of God, dies on the cross. This act of selfless suffering is seen as a redemptive act "saving" people from their sin. Through Christ's death and resurrection, Christians believe they are forgiven, transformed, and "reborn" so that they will live with Christ forever.

Other Christians understand the teachings of Jesus as a way of life which, if followed, will lead to a kingdom of God on earth—a world where justice and peace will prevail. Whatever the interpretation of the Bible, Christian scripture is held to provide an answer to the question, "Who am I?" Though sinfull because of the fall, human life can be transformed and returned to its true nature through identification with Christ.

Jews also understand the Bible (what Christians call the Old Testament) as providing a plan of salvation. Jewish history begins with Abraham's covenant with God and God's promise to make Abraham the father of a great nation. But the people were enslaved in Egypt, just as Jews have been persecuted throughout history. God, through Moses, led the people out of Egypt and established a covenant with God. God promised to be their protector if the people would keep his laws, the commandments given on Mount Sinai. Thus the way of continous transformation from slavery to freedom is loyalty of God through worship of the one true God and moral action.

The Qur'an of Islam similarly answers that people can be saved from the condition of animal-like, barbaric existence. The stages of this transformation move from the first step of learning simple rules of morality through higher stages of moral action, until one gives complete devotion to Allah. The person is transformed when submission to the will and service of God leads to forgetfulness of the self.

Verily he is saved who sacrifices his life for the sake of God and submits himself to His will; who does not rest satisfied with mere lip-sincerity, but proves it by righteous conduct. Such a one will surely have his reward with his Lord. and there shall come no fear upon him, nor shall he be grieved.[11]

Within Asian scriptures, the variety of answers all affirm that transformation from suffering, ignorance, *samsara,* or evil is possible through disciplined life. Buddhist texts in general lay stress on the personal, spiritual discipline of meditation. They discuss the goal variously as absence of the ego, liberation, correct attitudes, purity, wisdom, and emptiness. These are all ways of describing nirvana or enlightenment *(bodhi).* But a constant theme is the discipline of meditation. While it is an oversimplification to say that Buddhism is a religion of the practice of meditation, that claim has symbolic merit. The Buddha reached enlightenment while in meditation under a tree. Statues all over the Buddhist world depict the Buddha in a contemplative posture. Zen Buddhism, a late sect in Buddhist history, places *zazen*—seated meditation—at the center of spiritual practice.

The scriptures in the Hindu tradition no less vividly declare that overcoming *samsara* and ignorance in *moksha* or liberation comes through the yogas. There are, of course, various kinds of yoga.[12] Whether directed toward knowledge, work, physical postures, or devotion, each yogic discipline is a way by which one can overcome the limitations inherent in being human. The traditional sitting posture, characteristic of one form of yoga, is specified in the Svetasvatara Upanishad as follows:

Holding his body steady with the three upper parts erect, And causing the sense with the mind to enter into the heart, A wise man with the Brahma-boat should cross over all the fear-bearing streams. Having repressed his breathings here in the body, and having his movements checked, One should breathe through his nostrils with diminished breath.[13]

It is no wonder that the image of a yogin, sittin in lotus position, is a paradigmatic figure in Indian spirituality.

In China the problem of the self is located in human relations. People in that crowded society were perpetually faced with the tensions involved in human interaction. It is no wonder that the Analects of Confucius prescribe in detail correct behavior. Such behavior, essential in the Chinese way, includes exact details for every realtionship and every occasion. Through such behavior life can be fulfilled and lived in harmony both socially and in relation to the underlying will or law of the cosmos called heaven *(Tien)*.

The Tao Te Ching, a basic scripture of Chinese Taoism, finds human limitation in the contending will or ego-self, and suggests a spiritual way to achieve human fullness. These ideals include harmony with nature, clamness, living simply, having no desires, and being spontaneous. The result of living in harmony with *Tao* (way) is a virtue or power called *te*.

In summary, when people ask the question, "What can I believe about the self?" scriptures give three answers: (1) The self is spirit; (2) the self is limited by sin, ignorance, suffering, or some other hindrance; and (3) limitations can be overcome by spiritual and moral discipline.

What Is Our Human Destiny?

Scripture functions also in answering the third basic question: "What is human destiny? For what may we hope?" The scriptures of the world are a repository of teachings that speak to this haunting question. Although life is caught in the web of limitations, and some transformation or liberation is possible, what is the ultimate goal? What is the final end or destiny? The answer is multiple: It is nirvana, *moksha,* heaven, the messianic age, the kingdom of God, ultimate peace, even oneness with the holy. The book of Revelation in the Bible provides the vision of a new heaven and a new earth. Isaiah offers a similar vision of human destiny in chapter 2, verse 20.

Your sun shall no more go down,
nor your moon withdraw itself;
for the Lord will be your everlasting light,
and your days of mourning shall be ended.

The *sutras* or scriptures of the Pure Land sect of Mahayana Buddhism tell of a perfect paradise as beautiful as one can dream about, a place where all wishes will be fulfilled. In other Buddhist texts, nirvana is described like cool water that removes all fever of passions and quenches all thirsts.[14] The Qur'an describes paradise as the garden of delight where there is only peace. And scriptures in varied traditions, in vivid symbolic imagery, describe the end of those whose disciplined life has conquered all limitations. It is as though human destiny is like the beginning, pure spirit—thought of either as a fulfillment within this earthly life or as a culmination beyond this life and time itself.

SUMMARY

This chapter began with a definition of scripture as the sacred literature of a religious community, authoritative in matters of belief and practice, and a major resource for symbolic expression. Second, we explained that written texts are accepted as scripture when people recognize them as revealing the sacred and inspiring religious experience. Third, a selected number of texts were identified as most commonly referred to in the study of religion, and accessible for our consideration.

The question was then proposed: "How does scripture function in human life?" Four answers were given. Scripture functions (1) to give evidence of and inspire experiences of the holy, (2) to preserve great myths and rituals, (3) to define moral behavior, and (4) to answer fundamental questions of belief about reality, the self, and human destiny. One final topic will conclude this chapter.

METHODS FOR THE STUDY OF SCRIPTURE

The scholarly study of scripture demands a mastery of the original language used to write these texts, as well as thorough knowledge of the historical contexts within which they arose. No less important are the sophisticated tools of hermeneutics (theories and practices of interpretation) needed to discover meaning. While that task may be exciting for a few people and essential for the advancement of knowledge about scripture, it is not possible for most of us. How, then, can we who are less specialized and who have limited time study scripture? Consider the following steps:

1. First, select one small part of scripture, probably a book from a familiar text. For example, choose Genesis in the Bible or the Gospel of Matthew in the New Testament as a place to start. Read the section over and over until you are thoroughly familiar with the entire text you have selected.

2. Now that you are familiar with a section of scripture, imagine that

you are on the inside of the religious community at the time the scripture was written. Ask yourself the question: "What did it probably mean to the people for whom it was first sacred?" More specifically try to answer: (1) What does it affirm about the Holy? (2) What stories are included and what do they mean? (3) Does it give ethical norms? If so what are they? (4) How does it answer the three basic questions about reality, the self, and human destiny?

3. Since scripture is a special kind of literature, make a preliminary analysis by identifying different literary forms such as myth, historical narrative, poetry, parable, and so forth. In this literary analysis remember that religious language is most often filled with images, similes, and metaphors. Therefore identify images (water, breath, dove, rainbow), similes (for example, "it is like the chaff which the wind blows away," or "like a rock"), and metaphors (for example, "God is light," or "the Lord is my shepherd"). With those images, similes, and metaphors in mind, identify which have become important symbolic expressions for the religious community to which they belong.

4. If you have not already done so, and wish to know what scholars have said, consult a biblical commentary having the reputation of excellence, such as *The Interpreter's Bible* or *The Jerome Biblical Commentary*.

5. If you wish to go deeper into your study, find a book on the history of the scripture you are studying. Try to discover key historical information such as when it was written, who was the author, where was it set, and what was its intended purpose.

6. In each of the steps above, you have already started the process called exegesis and hermeneutics. Exegesis is the process of explaining in detail what the text is saying. Hermeneutics is the art of interpreting what is meant.

A strange and unexpected thing may happen to you in this study of scripture. You may become involved in it, for scriptures have lived because of their power. You may also become increasingly open to the claim that scripture is sacred literature.

NOTES

1. This analysis depends upon Mircea Eliade's writings, especially *The Sacred and the Profane: The Nature of Religion*, trans. Willard R. Trask (New York: Harper & Row, 1961).
2. This statement by Wilfred Cantwell Smith was written in consideration of the Qur'an, the sacred text of Islam. The comment is also appropriate for all scriptures. See W. C. Smith, *Religious Diversity: Essays* (New York: Harper & Row, 1976), p. 46.
3. *The Bhagavad Gita*, trans. Swami Prabhavananda and Christopher Isherwood (New York: New American Library, 1963), pp. 92, 130.
4. The Bible, Exodus, Chap. 12. All quotations from the Bible are taken from the Revised Standard Version.
5. Compare the story of the Last Supper in each of the synoptic gospels: Matthew 26, Mark 14, and Luke 22.

6. See James G. Williams, "Scripture," in T. William Hall, ed., *Introduction to the Study of Religion* (New York: Harper & Row, 1978), p. 86.
7. Quoted from the Qur'an, trans. A. J. Arberry in Mircea Eliade, *From Primitives to Zen: A Thematic Sourcebook of the History of Religions* (New York: Harper & Row, 1967), pp. 75–77.
8. See the Rig-Veda and Atharva-Veda in *The Hindu Scriptures*, trans. R. C. Zaehner (New York: Dutton, 1966), pp. 5, 17.
9. An examination of the Bhagavad Gita will provide ample evidence supporting these statements.
10. This view of the human condition is discussed by the Indian Muslim philosopher, Mirza Ghulam Ahmad (1835–1908) and printed in *The Philosophy of the Teachings of Islam* (Washington: The American Fazl Mosque, 1953), pp. 14–32, reprinted in James W. Dye and William H. Forthman, comps., *Religions of the World: Selected Readings* (New York: Appleton Century Crofts, 1967), pp. 578–88.
11. The Qur'an, Al-Bagara Surah, verse 113, trans. by Mirza Ghulam Ahmad, quoted in Dye and Forthman, p. 585.
12. For a brief but clear explanation of the four major yogas, see Huston Smith, *Religions of Man* (New York: Harper & Row, 1965), chap. 2.
13. See the Svetasvatra Upanishad quoted by Ninian Smart and Richard D. Hecht, eds., *Sacred Texts of the World: A Universal Anthology* (New York: Crossroad, 1982), p. 195.
14. Ibid. See the anthology of texts including those of Buddhism, pp. 231–75.

QUESTIONS FOR STUDY AND DISCUSSION

1. People who misunderstand a scholarly definition of myth often resent having that term applied to stories in their scripture. How would you explain to them the meaning of myth and the importance of myth in their scripture?

2. A point of view presented in this chapter is that the scriptures of various religions give similar answers to fundamental questions. If you agree, how do you account for the similarity? for differences?

3. What literature do you consider sacred outside the official scriptures of your own tradition? Why do you consider them sacred?

4. Under what conditions is it appropriate and inappropriate to use the title, "The Old Testament"? How crucial is this issue?

5. Review the outline of the chapter given below and discuss each section with other students.

A. What is scripture?
   1. Sacred literature
   2. Authoritative
   3. Source of creative expression
B. Identification of Scripture
   (Idenfity key texts in at least five traditions.)
C. The function of scripture
   1. To inform and inspire about the holy
   2. To preserve sacred stories
   3. To define moral behavior

4. To answer questions of belief
   a. What is real?
   b. What is the self?
      (1) Spirit
      (2) Under condition of limitation
      (3) Possibility of transformation
   c. What is human destiny?

PROJECTS

1. Make a survey among five or more friends by asking the following questions: (a) What is your definition of scripture? (b) Identify scriptures of at least three of the world's great religions. (c) Identify famous works of art that include images from some scripture.

2. Write a paper on one of the following sacred texts: Genesis, Micah, the Gospel of Mark, the Bhagavad Gita, the Lotus Sutra, or the Tao Te Ching. Use at least the first three steps proposed in the section, "Methods for the Study of Scripture."

3. Controversy rages in the United States between those who believe the Bible should be taken literally and those who believe it must be interpreted. Organize a simulation game in your class in which a group of teachers are planning a high school class to be entitled "The Bible as Literature." Divide into two groups: (1) One group wants the class to be built on the assumption that each word is literally true and needs no interpretation. (2) The other group believes that students should be helped to interpret the Bible. Permit the discussion to continue until the problem has been resolved or until a stalemate is reached.

4. Problem for a paper: The scriptures of each religion are considered authoritative for people in that religion, yet not all scriptures present the same convictions. Does this mean that some sacred texts are true and others are false? If some are true and others false, what are criteria for decision? Can they all be authoritative and true? In your paper, use illustrations from various scriptures.

SUGGESTED READINGS

Conze, Edward, ed. *Buddhist Scriptures.* Baltimore, Md.: Penguin Books, 1973.

Dye, James W., and William H. Frothman, comps. *Religions of the World: Selected Readings.* New York: Appleton Century Crofts, 1967.

Eliade, Mircea. *From Primitives to Zen: A Thematic Sourcebook of the History of Religions.* New York: Harper & Row, 1967.

Frost, S. E., Jr., ed. *The Sacred Writings of the World's Great Religions.* New York: McGraw-Hill, 1972.

Frye, Northrop, *The Great Code: The Bible and Literature.* New York: Harcourt Brace Jovanovich, 1982.

Nasr, Seyyed H. *Ideals and Realities of Islam*. Boston: Beacon Press, 1972.

Neusner, Jacob. *The Way of Torah: An Introduction to Judaism*. Belmont, Calif.: Dickenson, 1970.

Smart, Ninian, and Richard D. Hecht. *Sacred Texts of the World: A Universal Anthology*. New York: Crossroad, 1982.

Smith, Wilfred Cantwell. *Religious Diversity: Essays*. New York: Harper & Row, 1976.

Thompson, Leonard L. *Introducing Biblical Literature: A More Fantastic Country*. Englewood Cliffs, N.J.: Prentice-Hall, 1978.

Zaehner, R. C., trans. *The Hindu Scriptures*. New York: Dutton, 1966.

CHAPTER 8

Morality and Ethics

Religion is expressed in a variety of ways—in sacred stories, in scripture, in ritual action, in art and literature. Virtuous living or morality is also a mark of religion. Wherever religion is found, in individuals or groups, one component will be moral codes providing norms for right attitudes and actions. These principles are the "oughts" for sentiments and behaviors. Morality can thus be defined as the aspect of the religious life that prescribes how people ought to feel, think, and behave. To live morally is to obey these principles.

Ethics, as distinct from but related to morality, is the systematic and self-conscious process of understanding, evaluating, and interpreting morality. While morality is a style of living based on principles believed to be right, ethics is a theoretical way of explaining and defending (sometimes criticizing) moral action. The relationship between morality and ethics is similar to that between belief and theology. Religious belief is the affirmation that something is true, such as the belief that reincarnation and karma express a fact about life. Theology is the explanation, interpretation, and often the defense of that belief. Morality, then, is what we will call later in the chapter a "first order" enterprise while ethics is "second order" in nature. Morality is living according to standards of conduct; ethics is the evaluation and interpretation of morality, often aiding in the establishment or revision of moral codes.

The fact that there are "oughts" at all in human life indicates that human beings (and religion) recognize a gap between how life is often lived and how it ideally should or might be lived. All religions recognize that human existence is not necessarily all that it might be, and expressions of this can be found in notions of evil, suffering, immorality, sin, or other "failures" within the human condition. Religions recognize an "essential problem" that seems to continually keep humanity from realizing its potential ideals, and this problem is often understood as the opposite of morality, the opposite of living as one ought to live. Humanity does not live, as the Genesis story tells us, in the garden of Eden. Disobedience and selfishness permeate the foundations of human life, and it is over against these that religion offers a vision of healing, hope, and an authentic, moral life. This chapter discusses some of those moral ideals while recognizing—as religion does—that human beings often fall short of them. As the Native American shaman, Black Elk, has said, "But if the vision was true and mighty, as I know, it is true and mighty yet; for such things are of the spirit, and it is in the darkness of their eyes that men get lost."[1]

Morality and ethics as defined above are not necessarily or automatically religious. They only become religious when they are understood as expressions of or responses to that which is experienced or perceived as ultimate or transcendent. (See the definition of religion in chapter 1.)

Morality, like religion generally, is both personal and social, relating both to individual experience and behavior as well as to the individual as part of a larger group. In ethics this twofold aspect has led to the distinction between personal and social ethics. More generally, however, this polar character of morality implies that morality (and religion) operates at the intersection of the person and the world (human and nonhuman), and within a mutually dependent and mutually influencing matrix.

Ironically, to think of morality in an academic context is to attempt to be "value-free," unbiased or nonjudgmental, allowing any particular claim to be true as long as it is true for someone. This approach seems contrary to religious moralities which are "value-full" and often make absolute and exclusive claims about what is true and good. We can overcome this apparent contradiction by asserting that an academic analysis carries its own morality which, on occasion, may be at odds with religious morality. The "ought" of academic morality is the demand to know and understand in such a way that one's own biases are bracketed out insofar as that is possible.

THE MORAL IMPERATIVE

By "moral imperative" in religion we mean the basis upon which a moral demand arises and upon which particular oughts or actions are grounded. To find the moral imperative in any religion would be to answer the following questions: What motivates the moral religious life? By what religious authority are any particular actions understood to be right, good, or true actions? By what command, demand, obligation, or "imperative" does the religious life have a moral dimension and a prescription for moral action?

As religions themselves have suggested, this grounding, authority, or imperative can be located at any number of places along a continuum extending from "internal" human experience to "external" religious expressions. An example or two of this distinction may help clarify just what is at stake.

In the biblical book of Job, which in many ways deals precisely with the question of what constitutes moral action and the moral imperative, a distinction (and even tension) is set up between the Jewish tradition (and its expressions) on the one hand and direct experience of God on the other, an experience unmediated by expressions. Three of Job's friends represent the "wisdom of the fathers" and hence the tradition's already-formulated expressions or responses to what Job is going through (that is, his inexplicable suffering). Job himself, however, soon discovers that this wisdom is not true wisdom; true wisdom, as the book says, begins in the "fear" or awe before God, and in the indwelling spirit of God.

In short, for Job's friends the imperative or ground of authority in deciding upon the morality or immorality of Job's life lies in the expressions (beliefs, wisdom, stories) of the tradition. For Job, on the other hand, the ultimate ground for such decisions (and for the religious life itself) lies in direct, unmediated religious experience of God.

Jesus makes a similar distinction in Mark 7:6–8:

> Well did Isaiah prophesy of you
> hypocrites, as it is written,
> "This people honors me with their lips,
> but their heart is far from me;
> in vain do they worship me,
> teaching as doctrines the precepts of men."
> You leave the commandment of God, and
> hold fast to the tradition of men.

Here, we must realize that the "commandment of God" is a command to love God, and that the authority or ground for moral (here, non-hypocritical) action is "in the heart" or in the loving and not in the precepts, rules, or "tradition of men." Again, as in Job, a distinction is being set up between an internalized basis and an externalized one. Let us look more closely at these two tendencies or "poles," realizing as we do so that most moral imperatives fall somewhere between the two extremes.

THE EXTERNAL POLE

The fact that the basis or imperative for moral action can be understood to reside in traditional religious expressions themselves can be seen in the Latin etymology for the word *morality*. The word *mores* or *moralis* indicates, among other things, "custom." For our purposes, therefore, customs, traditions, or expressions passed down from people to people can be one basis of morality.

An excellent example of this first pole on our continuum can be found in Hinduism. Much of Hindu life, including what we might call moral action, is grounded in what has been called the *varna* (caste) as-

rama (life stage) *dharma* (duty) system. In this system, tradition dictates one's duty (moral action) in light of the context of one's caste and one's stage in life. In the Hindu scripture Bhagavad Gita, for example, the legendary warrior Arjuna faces a difficult moral decision: Shall he fight the enemy when it so happens that the enemy is led by his own brother? The answer the story gives is yes since, as a member of the warrior caste, it is his righteous duty to fight and kill. Here, it is clear that traditional expressions of *dharma* as duty are being passed down and offered as a basis upon which moral decisions are made.

Another example can be found in Confucianism. Insofar as Confucianism is based in traditional prescriptions of appropriate behavior or "decorum" *(li)* and insofar as this decorum has been expressed in carefully prescribed rules of social intercourse and social order (for example, filial piety), Confuciainism represents a moral imperative found in the tradition of expressions. The status of the Confucian classics as a scriptural basis for moral action in traditional China certainly emphasizes this point. The training of the educated "gentleman" began and ended in these classics and, for many, these classics were the authoritative basis for all moral action.

Yet another example, from a very different kind of religious world, can be seen in traditional black African religions. In his novel on Ibo culture in the late nineteenth century, called *Things Fall Apart,* the contemporary African writer Chinua Achebe describes a situation in which "things are falling apart" precisely because the authority of traditional expressions as the basis for all actions is being challenged from several sides. It is being challenged from within by the main character who, due to his own personal obsessions, commits crimes (immoral action), and it is challenged from without by European Christianity which calls for a whole new understanding of morality.[2]

Some of the most obvious instances where the externalized religious expressions become the basis or imperative for moral action are found in religious traditions having scriptures as foundations for religious authority. Nowhere is this more true than in the Western religions (Judaism, Christianity, and Islam), which all affirm scriptural authority as one basis for the religious life. For both Jews and Christians, for example, the Ten Commandments (Exodus 20:1–17) have functioned prominently as a norm, basis, or imperative by which moral action can be determined. In general, moral action in all the Western religions could be said to be based in God's commandments—commandments one can find expressed in many different ways in the Jewish Bible (Torah), the Christian Bible (Old and New Testament), and the Islamic *Qur'an.* These various religious expressions can thus be called a moral imperative.

In fact, we might claim that *all* religions include this tendency to find the authoritative base for moral action in the expressions that make up a religious tradition—scriptural expressions or not. By one form or another—by myth or oral tradition, by stories or epics, by priests or practitioners, by ritual or beliefs—religions establish norms, principles, and authoritative bases for knowing what one ought to do. Among the Ibo mentioned above, for example, not written scripture but stories in an oral tradition transmit the duties, obligations, or norms for leading the correct life. Women's stories are told to young girls so those girls know how they are to act; men's stories are told to young boys for similar reasons.

Additional examples are readily available, but the principle remains the same: religious expressions found within and passed on through a religious tradition establish for people the authoritative basis upon which moral action is distinguished from immoral action, and the oughts of one's life are established.

THE INTERNAL POLE

At the opposite end of our continuum is internal, individual, religious experience. While such experience is quickly given expression, unlike the external pole, the experience itself rather than the expression provides the basis, authority, or imperative for moral action.

Certainly one classic example of internal authority can be found in Buddhism, particularly the Mahayana Buddhism that developed in India but flowered in the Far East. Although one can find in Buddhism the external pole discussed above, particularly in the traditional notions of the precepts *(sila)* or rules laid down for monks and laypersons alike, at the higher levels of Buddhist practice and Buddhist attainment, externalized rules give way to enlightenment experience *(bodhi)* as the basis for all behavior.

In the Hinayana Buddhism of early Indian Buddhism, and subsequently in the Theravada Buddhism of Sri Lanka and Southeast Asia, the moral dimension or imperative arising out of the enlightenment experience is referred to as love *(metta)* for all beings. This love, together with other factors, is closely related to enlightenment and is thus thought of as the moral dimension of the enlightened life.

Mahayana Buddhsim makes the point even more dramatically. Mahayana espouses the *bodhisattva* (literally, "*bodhi* being") path and ideal as one of its central contributions to Buddhist thought and practice. This ideal or model for the religious life indicates that inherent in the enlightened wisdom *(prajna)* attained by *bodhisattvas* (and/or *buddhas*) is also compassion *(karuna)* as a basis upon which *bodhisattva*-action takes place for the benefit of all beings. To put it another way, enlightening experience or insight (wisdom) happens in the realization of an absolute nondual experience called "emptiness" *(sunyata)*. In such experience one has plunged "beneath" the self as a subject receiving a world of objects; one has "emptied" both self and world. Such experience, by its very nature, is absolutely selfless and leads necessarily to a selfless compassion as a basis for living a life in relation to others. Moral action in this case is not determined by obedience to exernalized expressions or rules; rather, it is determined by wisdom/compassion (that is, enlightenment) experience. Wisdom/compassion experience is, in short, the moral imperative for Mahayana Buddhism.

Another classic example can be found in the letters of Paul in the New Testament, particularly in the book of Romans. Paul speaks of an internal law of God, or the Spirit, or of Christ—a law of the "heart" rather than a written law of the (Jewish) tradition. This internal law is, he says, "written on the heart" and meant to be lived rather than merely heard or seen. In Romans 2:12–29, for example, he says that a real Jew is not one merely by external ways (for example, by the sign of circumcision), but "he is a Jew who is one inwardly; real circumcision is a matter of the heart, spiritual and not literal."

Paul calls Christians to discover (or rediscover) an internal, experiential "law"; a law of the spirit, or indwelling God-in-Christ. This law is no doubt related to Paul's insistence elsewhere on the importance both of the indwelling love of Christ as well as a faith by which one is saved. He seems to be pointing to the absolute centrality of a particular quality or kind of experience not only by which one is saved but by which the basis or imperative for all one's actions is established.

Jesus points to this same internal imperative when, in chapter 7 of Mark, he dramatically overturns all the Jewish dietary laws on the grounds that the external things (here, food) are not defiling and defiled but the internal intentions of actions. In verses 20–23 he says, "What comes out of a man is what defiles him. For from within, out of the heart of man, come evil thoughts, fornication, theft, murder, adultery, coveting, wickedness, deceit, licentiousness, envy, slander, pride, and foolishness." The implications are clear. Good or bad actions are grounded in the heart, or in particular qualities and characteristics of human experience, rather than in any particular tradition.

This internal role is less obviously present in primal traditions. Even there, however, it can perhaps be seen in the shaman as a particular type of religious functionary. The shaman is a kind of religious virtuoso who communicates directly with the sacred realm of gods or spirits in self-authenticating experience as especially manifested in dreams and visions. To the extent that such experience may become the basis for new insights, revelations, symbolic expressons, and modes of action in the world, it might be called yet another example of the internal pole.

The Oglala Sioux shaman, Black Elk, as reported in John Neihardt's *Black Elk Speaks*,[3] exemplified the internal command. His unique experiences in dream and vision became the authoritative ground and imperative for understanding what the tribe ought to do in the face of increasing pressures from Americans settling the West in the late nineteenth century. Such experiences, first personally and then shared with a community, can alter traditions, change religious expressions, and provide new bases for moral action.

In a very different context, autonomous human reason might also be seen as an example of the internal pole. Reasoning certainly could be considered a mode of human experience, and reasoning has certainly been understood by many (especially in the modern world) to be a basis, ground, or authority upon which moral decisions are made and moral actions taken. Whether this reason is religious or not is, of course, another issue. However, by the definition of religion offered in chapter 1, there is no reason why it could not be considered so; the context would determine the case. When truly autonomous reason (not dependent on others) operates in a religious context, the moral imperative is an internal one and not found in a tradition of (externalized) expressions.

The two poles we have just discussed exist, of course, at opposite ends of a continuum. Most of the religious life (and religion itself) is not lived at one or the other end of this but rather somewhere in the zones between. Wherever it is lived, however, the moral imperative can be defined as that which gives authority to or makes demands for particular kinds of moral action, and it is to that action that we now turn.

MORAL ACTION

The moral imperative, as we have discussed it above, does not necessarily satisfy the question about the actual content of any moral action. This is particularly true the closer one moves toward the internal pole, since qualities or characteristics of experience, rather than specified modes of action, are at stake there. At the experiential or internal end of the spectrum, the issue of specific moral actions (as well as thoughts or feelings) is left open and relative; that is, specific actions are in themselves not good or bad; they are good or bad depending on whether they express or are based in the moral imperative or not. The external pole is just the opposite. It tends to have already determined and expressed the specific actions constituted as moral; the moral imperative and moral action are, in those cases, very closely related.

A good example of this difference can be found in the issue of killing as a moral or immoral action. If, for example, one lives by the authority or imperative of the traditional expression, "Thou shalt not kill," then the imperative and the specific action designated as moral (or immoral) are one and the same; presumably one would not kill if one lived by that moral imperative. On the other hand, however, if one lives by a sense of justice as the moral imperative, the action is not specified; to kill or not to kill is dependent on whether justice is served or not, and the moral action is not necessarily determined by the moral imperative.

In both cases, moral action is motivated by the imperative, whether the imperative is external or internal.

We are therefore considering "moral action" (including moral thoughts and feelings) to be any action that arises on the basis of some moral imperative. Moral action is not abstract; it is specific action in life and can be considered as "first order" activity. Ethical action, to be considered later, is one step removed because it is reflective thought about morality and is hence a "second order" process.

Examples of moral action abound throughout the religions of humanity. Several examples will help clarify moral action as it arises from a moral imperative.

Taoism of China is often understood through the sacred writing called the Tao Te Ching. This book, representing a mystical form of Taoism, dates from approximately the sixth century B.C.E. In this text we find the following rather mysterious verse which, upon close inspection, says something important about both a moral imperative and moral action.

Thirty spokes
Share one hub.
Adapt the nothing [empty space] therein to the purposes in hand, and you will have the use of the cart. Knead clay in order to make a vessel. Adapt the nothing therein to the purpose in hand, and you will have the use of the vessel. Cut out doors and windows in order to make a room. Adapt the nothing therein to the purpose in hand, and you will have the use of the room. Thus what we gain is something, yet it is by virtue of Nothing that this can be put to use.[4]

In the context of the Tao Te Ching this passage points out that only by losing our life can we find it, or, to put it another way, only by emptying ourselves of our self can we truly (authentically) function in the world as human beings. By emptying or "becoming still" we come into harmony with the way *(Tao)* of all life and can thereby truly accomplish something. Only by awakening to the "no-thingness" or empty spaces in life can we have the true use or function of our lives.

Although an extended discussion of this idea would take us far afield, the point for our purposes is that, for the Tao Te Ching, only by becoming empty like the *Tao* can genuine action in the world take place. This emptying or "nothing" is thus the moral imperative upon which any action to be called moral can be based. Such action, the text makes clear, is always "noncontending action" or, more literally, "no-action" *(wu-wei)*. In the realm of moral action in short, nothing-action, or nothing-based action, is the something that is the use or functioning of nothing, and this action is always referred to or described as a noncontending action.

Bowed down then preserved;
Bent then straight;

Hollow then full;
Worn then new;
A little then benefited;
A lot then perplexed.
Therefore the sage embraces the One *(Tao)*
  and is a model for the empire.
He does not consider himself right,
  and so is illustrious;
He does not brag, and so has merit;
He does not boast, and so endures.
It is because he does not contend that
  no one in the empire contends with him.
The way the ancients had it, "Bowed
  down then preserved," is no empty
  saying.[5]

Highest good is like water. Because water excels in benefiting the myriad creatures without contending with them and settles where none would like to be, it comes close to the way.... It is because it does not contend that it is never at fault.[6]

The paradigm of this kind of moral action is the martial art called judo. Although the word judo is Japanese, and the art is often associated with Japan, both have historical roots in China. In fact, the word *do* is the Japanese pronunciation of *tao,* and the word judo means the "way of flowing with." Judo represents a noncontending action that "flows with" the energy and structure already there. Like water, it is strong action seeking a victory, but it does so by following the natural structures and intrinsic harmonies of the situation. Like the sage described above, it is action that benefits and preserves. It is, by definition, good (or moral) action.

As with most understandings of moral action that are based on experiential or internal imperatives, particular actions are not prescribed by the Tao Te Ching since the right action in one situation may be the wrong action in another. The important thing is to be noncontentious and in harmony with *Tao* in all situations; then one's actions will automatically be good. Where the moral imperative is more externalized, however, moral action is prescribed in moral codes, rules, or law. In these cases, great particularity and detailed specificity define moral actions.

An obvious example of this latter kind of moral action, based in externalized expressions, is the Ten Commandments found in both the Jewish and the Christian traditions. As summarized out of chapter 20 in Exodus, they are (as spoken by God):

You shall have no other gods before me.
You shall not make for yourselves a graven image....

You shall not take the name of the Lord your God in vain. . . .
Remember the sabbath day, to keep it holy. . . .
Honor your father and your mother. . . .
You shall not kill. . . .
You shall not commit adultery. . . .
You shall not steal. . . .
You shall not bear false witness against your neighbor. . . .
You shall not covet . . . anything that is your neighbor's.

Here and elsewhere in the Bible, specific commandments are given indicating what humans ought to do. Although some of these are open to interpretation regarding precisely what the appropriate action might be (for example, "You shall have no other gods before me"), others (for example, "You shall not kill") leave little room for such interpretation.

It should be noted that what we are calling moral action can well include mental actions as well. The Ten Commandments, for example, include the commandment against coveting. To covet or have desire for something that does not rightfully belong to one is clearly an immoral action here. Moral action thus extends to particular states of mind.

Another issue concerning the nature of moral action is also exemplified in the Ten Commandments. The first four commandments all indicate how people should relate to God and not just how they should relate to each other. This fact suggests two things about moral action in general, and about this particular formulation of moral action specifically.

In the first place, it reminds us that moral action, defined as ideals concerning what one ought to do or how one ought to be, is understood in this book as a religious expression. That is to say, it reminds us that morality as a religious expression must necessarily be grounded in religious faith or religious affirmation as we have defined it.

In the second place, it points to the fact that the line separating ritual action from moral action may be, in some cases, difficult or impossible to draw. In most religions, in fact, ritual action in the primary mode of religious expression or response, and moral action (now thought of as one's relationship to others) is a secondary mode. The "vertical" relationship to the holy often takes precedence over the "horizontal" relationship to others.

If, for example, one were to consider the Shinto religion of Japan in terms of moral action, one could start by looking at ritual. As a religion Shinto is, in large part, a ritual practice. One would have to look within ritual to find the moral imperative (for example, *harae* or ritual purity), and from ritual what we recognize as distinctive moral action arises (for example, etiquette and purity in one's relationships to others).

Another example can be observed in Hinduism, especially seen historically. The Hindu notion of *dharma* (duty) is the Hindu understanding of moral action. *Dharma,* however, not only indicates both ritual duty and general behavioral duty, but is historically based in notions of ritual obligations and duties. The notion of *dharma* is historically grounded in the elaborate ritual sacrifices of the ancient Vedic period in Hinduism. The primary understanding of what one ought to do was closely related to ritual action; only by extension and by historical development did the term come to mean all forms of duty.[7]

To return to the Ten Commandments, it is instructive to realize that the first four deal with how people ought to behave in their relationship to God, a relationship that has explicit connections with ritual action. The religious implication is clear: a right relationship to others must be grounded in a right relationship to God.

As prescriptions for moral action, however, the Ten Commandments are still rather general and open to interpretation. Other types of moral codes prescribe highly specific kinds of action as one can see, for example, in Islam. Although ritual action is important in Islam, the central religious expression is the Qur'an, understood as a revelation from Allah through his prophet Mohammed. This scripture prescribes both general and very specific actions that govern not only the right relationship to Allah and to others, but highly specific modes of action in the daily process of living. Thus we read, for example, an injunction against friendship with nonbelievers (including Jews and Christians): "O ye who believe! Take not the Jews and Christians for friends. They are friends one to another. He among you who taketh them for friends is one of them. Lo! Allah guideth not wrongdoing folk."[8] Similarly, other specific actions are denied: "O ye who believe! Strong drink and games of chance and idols and divining arrows are only an infamy of Satan's handiwork. Leave it aside in order that we may succeed."[9]

Here and elsewhere in the religions of humankind one can find the external pole of the moral imperative functioning and the prescriptions for moral action highly specified by the tradition. As in Islam, obedience becomes the watchword since the commandments have been given and it is the believer's duty to obey. On the other hand, where moral action is seen to arise out of internal experience (as in the case of the Tao Te Ching above), the watchword might be called faithfulness since to be full of faith is precisely to be experientially "turned over to" whatver the object of that faith might be. In such cases, moral action is less a question of obedience to externalized commandments than faithfulness to an internalized moral imperative.

ETHICS

Morality, as understood above, must be considered a central and important religious expression, one which—as a religious expression—has priority and primacy over ethics. Morality represents direct involvement in experiencing and expressing in one's life both a religious moral

imperative and religious moral action. Moral discourse and moral decision making "is a decidedly practical lanaguage."[10] That is, it is directly
related to establishing moral principles and "practicing" (living) the
moral life.

Ethics, on the other hand, refers largely to a process of systematic,
self-conscious, reflective analysis, interpretation, and thinking about
moral imperatives and actions. Again, Aiken suggests that in ethical
discourse (as distinct from moral discourse) critical questions about the
principles enunciated in moral discourse are raised—questions, for example, concerning the meaning, validity, and ramifications of this or
that morality. In what might be an overstatement to make the case he
says, "Few people have the time or inclination to engage in this (ethical)
discussion. Hence, it is generally limited to academic studies in ethics."[11]

If by "academic" we can mean systematic, rationally reflective, cognitive thought and interpretation, then Aiken's statement may well satisfy
us here. The main point, however, is that ethics is more theoretical and
less practical than morality, even though its ultimate concern or purpose may be similar (that is, a concern to determine how people ought
to act).

If ethics is a process of thinking and interpretation, then in some
sense even the morality we have already discussed is a kind of "ethic,"
especially as found in the religious expressions of a tradition. The ethi-
cist James Smurl, in his book on religious ethics, refers to this kind of
ethic as a "first instance" ethics where religious experience has already
been expressed (and thus "interpreted") in moral terms. He says, for
example: "Well-lived lives cast in well-told stories are the first instance
examples of religious ethics. Thus, we can identify the simplest roots of
religious ethics as memorable experiences made more memorable still
by their sensitive interpreters."[12] Precise examples, he suggests, are the
distinctions *hagaddeh/halakha* in Judaism, and *kerygma/didache* in Christianity. In the former, *hagaddeh* expresses the human condition as an
"exodus experience" seeking freedom while *halakha* refers to the teachings about appropriate modes of behavior that follow from *hagaddeh*. In
the latter, *kerygma* refers to the central meaning (experience) of the
Christ-message while *didache* is the teaching that follows from it.[13]

More often, however, ethics is a "second instance" or "second order"
enterprise, that is, a reflecting on moral principles and moral expressions already established in order to further interpret, understand, or
draw implications for particular situations.

The primary place one observes ethical discussion going on is within
the theological (or philosophical) traditions of particular religions. Ethics therefore tends to be limited to those kinds of religions that have
such theological traditions (most obviously, but not exclusively, the so-
called "world religions"), particularly Christianity, Judaism, Islam, Hinduism, Buddhism, and Confucianism. A particularly good example of

theological ethics from within a specific tradition can be found in contemporary Roman Catholicism. The "liberation theologies" of Central and South American Catholicism are theologies with a very central concern for moral implications, that is, how we ought to behave in situations of social repression and poverty. In recent years, the North Americn Catholic Bishops as well have practiced theological ethics in their major pronouncements on the moral implications of abortion, nuclear holocaust, and poverty. These pronouncements (as "letters" to their churches), and the processes that led to them, are exercises in theological ethics by which the implications of a Christian morality are reflected on within this or that specific situation calling for moral action.

Another important place where ethics as a religious expression takes place is in individual (or collective) moral decision making. Although such decision making may not be a formal kind of ethics, it is ethics insofar as it does not merely take moral action as a given but feels constrained to consider reflectively what the best course of action might be. As long as such reflection takes place within or on the basis of what we have defined in chapter 1 as religion, it is an instance of religious ethics.

There are, of course, innumerable examples of such ethical decision making. A rather simple one (a simple example but not a simple decision) might be found in a woman with an unwanted pregnancy facing a decision about abortion. Assuming she is religious but is not merely going to pursue a particular action because it is prescribed in an already-established system of morality (for example, the Catholic Church's prohibition against abortion), and assuming she is not going to rely on some other authority or mechanism by which a course of action is prescribed (for example, the advice of a friend or the flip of a coin), she faces a personal decision of an ethical nature. This decision might raise such fundamental questions as the rights of women to control their own bodies, the rights of the unborn, the nature of the moral imperative by which she lives and of the holy or transcendent reality to which it is connected, the ramifications of her actions for her family, and so forth. All such reflection could be considered an informal ethics, and presumably it would lead to some particular decision about a moral action (to abort or not).

Still a third place where one finds ethics being done is within the academic (more narrowly conceived) context. Whether such ethics could themselves be called religious is a large question that will not be pursued here. Suffice it to say that ethical thinking and thinking about ethics does, indeed, take place in institutions of higher learning around the world. Whether in philosophy departments, religion departments, or—as is now often the case—in medical or business schools, such enterprises often relate (explicitly or otherwise) to religion. Where they do not converse, or where the ethical thinking or thinking about ethics is not itself religiously grounded, then we have a secular or nonreligious ethics. On the other hand, where it is in some sense religiously grounded (see chapter 1), it is an instance of religious ethics. However, even "third instance" ethics, as an academic description of the ethics and morality of various religions, can serve a useful religious purpose; that is, such study can sensitize people to the moral dimension of religion and perhaps thereby sensitize people to their own moral life.

NOTES

1. John Neihardt, *Black Elk Speaks* (New York: Pocket Books, 1972), p. 2.
2. Chinua Achebe, *Things Fall Apart* (New York: Fawcett Crest, 1959).
3. See footnote 1.
4. D. C. Lau, trans., *Lao Tzu: Tao Te Ching* (Baltimore, Md.: Penguin Books, 1963), p. 67.
5. Ibid., p. 79.
6. Ibid., p. 64.
7. See Thomas J. Hopkins, *The Hindu Religious Tradition* (Belmont, Ca.: Dickenson Publishing Company, 1971), pp. 73–75.
8. M. M. Pickthall, trans., *The Meaning of the Glorious Koran* (New York, N.Y.: New American Library, n.d.), p. 101.
9. Ibid., pp. 104f.
10. As quoted in James Smurl, *Religious Ethics: A Systems Approach* (Englewood Cliffs, N.J.: Prentice-Hall, 1972), p. 91.
11. Ibid., p. 92.
12. Ibid., p. 91.
13. Ibid.

QUESTIONS FOR STUDY AND DISCUSSION

1. In order to highlight and clarify the various elements of morality and ethics, discuss the nature of and distinctions between

 a.   morality and ethics.
 b.   moral imperative and moral action.
 c.   external and internal poles.

2. In order to determine if any particular action is moral and religious, analyze some particular action of your own in terms of the nature of the moral imperative upon which it is based and the connection of that moral imperative to anything you might consider ultimate, sacred, or holy.

3. Compare and contrast in open discussion the moral imperative of any two religions or any two branches of a single religion.

PROJECTS

1. Study some particular religion and search out its moral imperative(s), its expression of moral actions, and (if there be any) its ethical

expressions. (This may be done through reading about a religion, reading some religious texts, and/or on-site interviewing or discussing.)

2. Try an experiment in ethical reflection. In the process, reflect on the moral imperative that might provide the basis for an action; reflect on the holy or sacred to which its related; reflect on the right thing to do given the above; and reflect on the implication or ramifications of your action.

3. In a series of interviews, find out what at least five different people feel is "moral action" with regard to the following issues: abortion, feeding the poor, providing sanctuary to illegal aliens, civil disobedience. In each case, try to find out if and how each person understands such action as "religious."

SUGGESTED READINGS

Beauchamp, Tom, and James Childress. *Principles of Biomedical Ethics*. 2d ed. New York: Oxford University Press, 1983.

Brendt, Richard B. *Ethical Theory*. Englewood Cliffs, N.J.: Prentice-Hall, 1959.

Ladd, John. *The Structure of a Moral Code: A Philosophical Analysis of Ethical Discourse Applied to the Ethics of the Navaho Indians*. Cambridge: Harvard University Press, 1957.

Little, David, and Sumner B. Twiss. *Comparative Religious Ethics*. San Francisco: Harper & Row, 1978.

Niebuhr, H. Richard. *Christ and Culture*. New York: Harper & Brothers, 1951.

Outka, Gene, and John P. Reeder, eds. *Religion and Morality: A Collection of Essays*. Garden City, N.Y.: Anchor Press, 1973.

Smurl, James. *Religious Ethics: A Systems Approach*. Englewood Cliffs, N.J.: Prentice-Hall, 1972.

Troeltsch, Ernst. *The Social Teaching of the Christian Church*, trans. Olive Wyon. New York: Harper, 1960.

Wallwork, Ernest. "Morality, Religion, and Kohlberg's Theory." In Brenda Munsey, ed. *Moral Development, Moral Education, and Kohlberg*. Birmingham, Ala.: Religious Education Press, 1980.

CHAPTER 9

Individual and Community

In every religion, unrestricted values find expression in both individual and communal ways. From the private prayers of a solitary individual to the idea that one's nation or society is itself a religious community, individual and communal expressions in religion are universal. So important and so interrelated are they that it seems useful to discuss them together: the individual is never totally devoid of community, and every community is finally made up of individuals. Individual and communal expressions in religion may be said to form a single continuum along which one might place specific religious phenomena. The activities and institution of Christian churches, for example, clearly represent communal religious expressions. The solitary religious activities of a particular Christian person, such as private meditation, giving money to the church, or helping one's neighbor clearly represent more individual expressions.

In most cases, of course, religious phenomena or expressions are simultaneously individual and communal, and the continuum only helps establish a tendency or emphasis. The community of the church, for example, is nothing without the individual activities of its members; the individual Christian actions imply a community and tradition called Christianity.

Whether individual or communal, of course, all religious expressions are grounded in individual experience. That experience itself, whether referred to as unrestricted values, faith, experience of the sacred, or religious experience, is generally influenced by community and tradition. In this sense, for example, the unrestricted values of a religion are mediated and passed on through the communal tradition in a process of what sociologist Peter Berger calls "collective memory."[1]

What this suggests is that the very basis of religion itself is inevitably both individual and communal. We can certainly assume, therefore, that the expressions of religion are going to include both individual and communal ones.

INDIVIDUAL EXPRESSIONS

PERSONAL RELIGION

"Religion is a personal and private thing" is a comment often made with intense feeling. There is indeed considerable merit in asserting that religion is personal or individual. Religion that is vital and alive is necessarily personal. A person who, in "the dark night of the soul," has experienced the presence of the holy in a very personal way can scarcely communicate the experience to others. Another person, whether alone or in a group, who participates in a ritual and who feels its saving, healing power is personally renewed. One for whom the scripture is an authority for belief and practice knows the personal tug of a sacred text. Or one who acts according to religiously inspired moral codes and does so without external, communal coercion expresses a personal religious morality. Collective customs and traditions may be followed, but religion involves more than automatic behavior or rote memory. Genuine religion involves personal experience and individual convictions which find expression in both individual and communal ways.

Although all religious experience is necessarily personal, our interest here in the expressions of that experience that operate at the individual end of the continuum mentioned above. To put it another way, personal experience can quickly become communally expressed (as we shall see below), but we are primarily interested, in this section, with religion as an individual and noncommunal expression. Here are some first-hand experiences told by way of example.[2]

1. A January blizzard was rapidly emptying New York's Fifth Avenue of its usual crowds. At midnight, sky scrapers were being vacated by janitors. A combination of bitter cold, snow-covered streets, and the late hour gave an eerie isolation to the nation's largest city. An old, bent cleaning woman, obviously weary from work, hobbled up the steps and into St. Patrick's Cathedral.

   As unobtrusively as possible I slipped into the huge Gothic church to observe the scrubwoman. She entered, crossed herself, lit a candle and lowered herself onto a kneeling bench between the pews. Her lips moved; her gnarled fingers passed over her rosary. After a few minutes she stood, more erect, it seemed, than before, slipped to the aisle, made a sign of the cross, and with quickened step almost hurried out the heavy wooden front door and back into the night. My glance caught the look of peace—or was it hope?—in her eyes. There seemed to be a satisfaction that transcended the tired furrows in her face.

2. At sunrise on a July morning I thought every Hindu in India must be making a pilgrimage to the river Ganges. The poor beggars, the

rich merchants, mothers pulling children along, trinket-sellers hawking their wares, boatmen soliciting passengers—all competed for space to walk and shout. Several stone steps below the street, along the river's edge, the crowd was no less congested but the mood was different. Hundreds were bathing; yet, with miraculous techniques, they were laundering the clothes they were wearing in the process. The moment a person gave up a spot at the water's edge another person stepped in to occupy it.

In the midst of the bathing, washing, and chanting, just above the ripples of the surface of the river, sat a yogi on a small plat-form. With one leg folded on his lap and the other behind his neck, with his left hand closing his left nostril and his right hand pointing upward, he sat motionless. He ignored the tumultous crowds around him and remained in absolute rigid and silent meditation. Despite the grotesque posture his face seemed relaxed. He was pursuing self-realization, a goal for many yogis.

3. It was my first night sleeping in the Chotokuin Buddhist temple in Kyoto. I was suddenly awakened by the sound of a deep gong followed by the tinkling of a bell. Soon a soft chant came from the next room. The sound penetrated easily through the rice paper walls. I quietly pulled myself up from my mat, dressed, and en-tered the rear of the assembly hall where one lone monk had begun his morning chant. He did not see me enter; or at least he paid no attention. His gutteral, monotoned chant rose in crescen-do, descended, and rose again. I sat silently, legs aching as I imitat-ed his lotus position. My stomach protested the early morning ne-glect. For an hour the near-hypnotic chanting continued until, without warning, the monk stopped. He touched the gong and bell, rose to his feet, bowed deeply to the statue of the Buddha before him, effortlessly slipped his feet into his sandals and, as he shuffled past me, graciously bowed and then vanished.

These vignettes are not unique; they are representative of individual expression in religion. They are not, however, totally individual or per-sonal. Reflect, a moment, on each illustration. The experience and expression in each case is individual, yet each occurs within or is related to a particular religious community.

The scrubwoman's orientation is clearly Roman Catholic. The per-sonal meaning gained from her midnight prayers is grounded in the communal, collective symbols preserved by Catholic Christianity, and her individual expression of devotion is thoroughly typical within that specific tradition. The yogi, performing his ritualized meditation, is en-gaged in a solitary act even though surrounded by hundreds of others. His personal spiritual discipline, however would surely be understood as part of his communal Hindu way of life. As an individual holy man, he plays his symbolic part in a religio-social structure. The Buddhist monk's morning chant is also part of the community expectation and made possible by the structured life of his temple community. Therefore, what appears to be and is individual, is usually related to a community as well.

THE RELIGIOUS VIRTUOSI

Another very different type of individual expression in religion can be seen in what Peter Berger has called the "religious virtuoso."[3] This is the individual whose experience and expression is so self-authenticating, unique, and definitive that renewal, reform, or change in the direction of religion takes place. Jesus comes to mind as a perfect example. While Jesus grew up in a Jewish community, something happened within his experience that was so definitive, important, and unique for him, that his expressions became relatively individual and unique. Many of these expressions were, of course, consistent with Jewish tradition and not particularly unique; others, however, were quite unique and seemed to call for religious reformation or revolution—at least that is how they were viewed by the people who became his followers. One example is in the ritual of the Passover which Jesus was celebrating with his disciples just before his death. Here, he shifted the emphasis from a Jewish Passover meal to the Last Supper of Christianity. Such changes in central religious expressions brought on by religious virtuosi are, at least in their origin, highly individual expressions.

The great founders, reformers, prophets, shamen, and seers of all religions belong in this category, as do individual visionaries that seem not connected to any particular religion referred to as such. While all are at some point communal, the focus is on individual religious "genius" expressed in unique and individual ways. The historical Buddha, Gautama Siddhartha, was such a person. While he grew up and was influenced by a general Hindu view of things, the enlightenment realization or insight he is said to have achieved was so unique, and his teachings or expressions of this so distinctive, that an entirely new religion grew up in response.

The Oglala Sioux shaman Black Elk, as reported in John Neihardt's book *Black Elk Speaks*,[4] is another example of the religious virtuoso, although perhaps not as dramatic an example as Jesus or Buddha. His shamanic visions, while clearly influenced by the religious symbols and communal traditions of the Oglala Sioux, were unique to him. The expressions of these visions in ritual, sacred story, and art became uniquely individual expressions that were then received by his people and made communal.

Examples of such religious virtuosi who seem to stand outside any particular religion are more difficult to identify simply because the word "religion" is less obviously present. The great artists or thinkers of all traditions, for example, play something of this part, whether or not they are clearly identified with any religion. Pablo Picasso, an avowed atheist, was nonetheless religious by our definition of religion, and his artistic expressions are the individual expressions of a religious virtuoso. Great poets and novelists can similarly be pointed to as expressing in their work a deep sensitivity to unrestricted values and a unique expression in their individual art.

An important subtype of the religious virtuoso is any individual whose experience is sufficiently self-authenticating to feel "called" to act definitively as a religious person. Individual people "called" into religious vocations or offices might be one example. From tribal priests and sorcerers to Jewish rabbis, or from ancient Taoist sages to Islamic ministers, the religious vocation serves as both an individual and communal expression.

The Jewish prophets are an excellent case in point. Time and again scripture indicates their sense of dramatic calling and their definitive, even direct, experience of God. Surely, too, we can see their unique and individual expressions based in this self-authenticating experience that allowed them to criticize the tradition and question its authority.

We need not go so far away in time and space, however, to find examples of this subtype. Anyone who truly discovers or rediscovers a faith *for themselves* and acts definitively and individually on that basis qualifies as an example. Such people may well live within religious community, but their faith and its expression is deeply and clearly their own.

INDIVIDUAL "RELIGIONS"

Still a third major type of individual religious expression can be found, perhaps more easily, outside any specific religious tradition and aside from the religious virtuoso. Moreover, this type may be thought of as more typical of the modern world than of traditional or ancient cultures and societies.

This type is comprised of individuals who experience deep values and sacred experience in and through modes of life and human expression that do not belong to any particular religious tradition, or are not in any obvious way easily identified as "religious." One particular example, especially within American life, is the private relationship of the individual to nature. Many people, if pressed, might well say that religious experience takes place for them within the beauty or grandeur of nature rather than within some particular religious community, symbol system, or institutional expression. How that experience is given expression may be as uniquely individual as the experience itself.

A particularly graphic example of this individual "religion" in relationship to nature can be found in the book *Pilgrim at Tinker Creek* by Annie Dillard.[5] The editor's descriptive subtitle to the book is "a mystical excursion into the natural world," and that is indeed one way to describe this autobiographical novel. The book indicates one person's deep "seeing" into the miracle of nature and life and the transformation of her life by that "seeing." It is an account of one person's experience of absolute unity with life—a deep and "religious" experience—and the book itself becomes the primary individual expression for us as the reader. No matter that the author uses some traditional religious expressions within the book; this is her unique and individual experience with nature, and her unique and individual expression.

Another important example of this individual "religion" can be found in and through participation in the arts. Insofar as profound aesthetic experience is closely akin to profound religious experience, individuals may well find religious experience and expression in and through the arts. Great art and literature carries something of the "unrestricted" about it, regardless of the presence of explicit religious themes. Great music, for example, can move people spiritually as well as emotionally.

If such involvement is deep and continuing in a person's life, a center of value and meaning by which life seems worthwhile, then art and aesthetic experience are functioning religiously for such persons, and art becomes their religion. Their response, of course, may have communal characteristics, but religiously speaking their expression will be quite individual—all the way from giving money to the arts to participating in the arts themselves.

These three types of individual expression in religion by no means exhaust the possibilities. They do, however, suggest some of the major ways in which religion and unrestricted values find expression on the individual end of the continuum.

COMMUNITY EXPRESSIONS

The sociologist of religion, Emile Durkheim, wrote that "in all of history we do not find a single religion without a church."[6] He meant, of course, that religion always finds expression in some form of community. That community, he explained, may be a local church or synagogue, a monastery, the society related to a mosque or temple, a cult community, or some informal organization. The community sometimes includes an entire people such as is meant in the terms Jewish community, Christendom, Hindu society, or the Islamic world. Sometimes there is a hierarchy such as in Roman Catholicism; sometimes there are priests, clergy, monks, or gurus who give official guidance to the community. In any case, Durkheim declared, "Wherever we observe the religious life, we find that it has a definite group as its foundation . . . for religious faith has its origin in society."[7] Durkheim then modified his position somewhat by adding that "society is a synthesis of human consciousness."[8] Yet he remained uncompromising in the insistence that religious origins as well as religious expressions are communal. In fact, he held that everything religious is nothing more or less than society divinized.

Sociologists and anthropologists in recent years have been less absolutistic and reductionistic in their emphasis on the social character of religion. Anthropologist Bronislaw Malinowski, for example, argues that while religion is manifested in societal action, strong religious moments also come in times of solitude when individuals are not involved in a crowd. Sociologist of religion Robert Bellah adds that religious thought and action may be seen in individual personalities as well as in groups.[9]

We must insist, however, that the variety of data available to the student of religion points to the community as a major arena in which religion is lived and expressed. Any discussion of community, however, is ambiguous without some clarification of the meaning of the word "community." Community can refer to the total society in which people share a common language, customs, life styles, and a sense of common peoplehood. In a more restricted way, community can refer to a limited number of persons whose association with one another is close, who experience a "common-unity," who share basic convictions and express those convictions in corporate and individual ways. Religious communities are of both kinds. The total society may be a religious community; the small voluntary association may also be a religious community. The latter is what we usually have in mind when we refer to "the religious community." It is important to remember, however, that the term applies to both situations.

So important is community in religion (as well as in all of human life), that Roger Schmidt, author of *Exploring Religion,* makes the following statement:

While an experience of holiness can take place independent of a believing community, the holy community has been, metaphorically speaking, the delivery room in which transcendent religious experiences occur, their genuineness is corroborated, their implications for living are put into practice, and their possibilities for growth are nurtured.[10]

This statement underlines what we have said above about the importance of tradition as collective memory, but it adds the importance of community in "socializing" religious experience so that it not only "belongs" but also is extended appropriately into one's life in terms of right actions and appropriate responses within a human community.

RELIGIOUS COMMUNITY AS SOCIETY AND NATION

In primal societies there is little, if any, difference between secular and sacred. Most if not all social activities are religious in nature and are based on an assumption that everything is sacred. The entire society exists in a climate of belief that the people are part of a divine cosmic order. Everything that is done is religious, and religion permeates all of society. Robert Bellah addresses this phenomenon when he says:

The individual and his society are seen as merged in a natural-divine cosmos. Traditional social structures and social practices are considered to be grounded in the divinely instituted cosmic order, and there is little tension between religious demand and social conformity. Indeed, social conformity is at every point reinforced with religious sanction.[11]

Judaism is one example of this intimate tie between religion and the sense of a social and cultural peoplehood. In ancient Israel, for example, the society was religious and the religion was the core of the society. Moses, Abraham, and other legendary persons were central in religious history and in social/cultural history as well. Religion and society were completely intertwined. When Jews began to live outside their original geographical bounds they carried this sensitivity with them. To this day, even nonobservant Jews consider themselves Jews because of a cultural and social heritage linking all Jews; more observant Jews feel connected, even across national identities, by a common sense of religious community.

The Jewish identification of society, culture, and religion is best exemplified in the contemporary state of Israel. A visitor to Jerusalem, for example, will be amazed at the transformation of that city every Friday. As late afternoon approaches, the noise of automobile and bus traffic gradually begins to cease. Before sundown an eerie silence hangs over the city. The Sabbath has begun. By the time darkness has settled around the white stones of the oriental-looking city, every business will be closed. Through the windows of almost every home can be seen candlelit tables. The silence is scarcely broken by those walking to the Western Wall to pray, or to a synagogue for Torah reading.

A similar observation can be made about Middle Eastern nations where Islam is a dominant religion. The onion-shaped domes of Muslim mosques are prominent in towns and cities, as are tall slender towers called minarets. The haunting call to prayer five times daily permeates every home, school, and business. The universal observance of Friday as a holy day, and the month-long fast of Ramadan, give more evidence of social, cultural, and religious unity. Throughout the Middle East, as well as in Pakistan, India, and Africa where one finds sizeble Muslim populations, the interrelationship of religion and society is present. Nowhere is the relationship closer than in present-day Iran where every aspect of the social order is religiously dominated.

Even India—a territory broad in space, diverse in languages and customs, and peopled with over seven hundred million—is in many ways a unified Hindu society or community. In full recognition that religions such as Sikkhism and Jainism have broken from the traditional Hinduism, there are common Hindu elements throughout India. There is sufficient commonality for us to speak appropriately of Hindu society as a religious community.

So too in Japan. Shinto, traditionally considered the state religion, is rooted in indigenous mythology. While Buddhism was imported and new religions abound, there is a commonly affirmed tradition linking Shinto and Japanese society. Even though people may support a Buddhist temple and expect the priest to officiate at funeral occasions, most of them still feel attached to traditional Shinto rites at times of marriage. Newly elected governmental officials, soon after election, inevitably go to the major Shinto shrine at Ise to pay their respects to the gods and to seek a blessing from the gods for a political career. Many businessmen also maintain a small Inari shrine, part of the Shinto tradition, somewhere on their business premises. It is difficult to distinguish between religion and society in Japan. Japan, as both a society and a culture, is thus in some sense a religious community.

If the entire community and religion are identical, or nearly so, as the above examples indicate, then what about the United States? Is it a religious community? After all, "in God we trust" is printed on the paper money and stamped on coins, the phrase "under God" is part of the official pledge of allegiance to the flag, the Christian holy day (Sunday) is also the national day of rest, and legal oaths are taken with one hand on the Bible. While the United States Constitution, through its first amendment, is intended to place restraints on the power of church and state over one another—thus guaranteeing religious freedom—the relationship of the total society to the Christian and Jewish tradition remains close in many ways. To the degree that this is true, religion and the social community in America are one and the same; America is a religious community.

This identity of religion with national community is even more obvious if one sees American religion not as Christianity but as a "civil religion." Civil religion, Robert Bellah declares, includes those "common elements of religious orientation that the great majority of Americans share."[12] Bellah presents a case for the unity of the American community and civil religion by quoting from presidential inaugural speeches and official documents. Characteristically these public utterances declare American dependence on transcendent values, just as public holidays like Memorial Day, the Fourth of July, and Thanksgiving are high holy days for the republic. The "saints" of this religion are persons like George Washington, Thomas Jefferson, and Martin Luther King, Jr., whom we revere as having special wisdom and power. Sacred places are tombs of presidents or even the rotunda of the nation's capitol building. Martyrs include every brave young person killed in military service to the country. These and other possible illustrations at least lend credibility to the claim that the whole of American public life and the symbols representing the values of the United States are religious.

RELIGIOUS COMMUNITY WITHIN SOCIETIES

More often, however, "religious community" has indicated particular groupings of people within a given nation or society. These groups are composed of people who are bound together by common convictions about ultimate or transcendent values. They affirm similar experiences of the holy. The sacred stories told in their midst are internalized as being "our" story. ("Remember how God led us out of bondage in Egypt," or "Jesus is our Lord and Savior.") Rituals, whether associated with cycles of nature, holy days, rites of passage, or times of crisis, are meaningful symbolic acts revealing a transcendent reality with power for the community. Such communities are often bound by a common body of writings held to be sacred scripture. Compatible beliefs are held among its members. Additional social factors such as similar ethnic background, language, economic or social status, and educational level help to bind the people together into a community.

Regardless of the specific factors that bring a group of people together and mold it into a community, that community seeks to preserve as well as renew whatever is religiously significant for the group. Whether we speak of "the church," the "chosen people," a Hindu *ashram,* a cultic commune, or monasticism, religious communities represent people coming together in "common-unity" to live out their faith. Just as Christians insist that the church is more than the church building, a similar assertion is made in all religious communities, for every religious community is that unity of persons in which every aspect of religiousness is expressed, and at least for the most devoutly loyal, it is through the community that religion is most fully expressed.

Moreover, local religious communities are usually not isolated groups having little connection with other groups. Often a local group is connected with a larger unit, referred to in Christianity as a denomination. In Christianity, for example, there are Baptists, United Methodists, United Presbyterians, Roman Catholics, Lutherans, or Episcopalians. Similarly, Jewish congregations are Orthodox, Conservative or Reform; each belongs to a larger sectarian division and community which is, in turn, part of the world Jewish community. Muslims, Hindus, and Buddhists also usually identify with one small community which is part of a sect and, in turn, a branch of the larger whole.

In spite of the universality of religious communities, striking differences, even differences within the same denomination or sect, make generalizations about religious communities difficult. Is there anything all religious communities have in common? Consider two common purposes. First, they seek to preserve the tradition, striving to keep it alive and vital for persons, and preserving it for succeeding generations. The community, wherever it is found, will therefore be conservative, seeking to "conserve" and preserve tradition and experience by retelling sacred stories, celebrating rituals, teaching and interpreting scriptures, and instructing in matters of belief and morals. Throughout its expression of religion in each of these ways, it will promote commitment from participants.

Second, the community seeks to enhance the religious fulfillment of persons, attempting new ways of experiencing the holy, telling old stories in new ways, expanding the horizons of belief, making relevant moral codes, creating new art forms, interpreting scripture for the present age, and even striving for authentic, new symbols to express beliefs. In these creative ways the community seeks to be a guide and inspiration for individual spiritual growth.

Community expressions of religion, then, both conserve the tradition and provide creative ways of renewing that tradition. Take a look, for instance, at the weekly newsletter of almost any collegiate Roman Catholic congregation. Such newsletters clearly illustrate the varied expressions within a community.

Careful examination of such newsletters exposes the traditional or conservative expressions. There will be various rituals, and masses daily during the week as well as on Saturday evening, Sunday mornings, and Sunday evening. Times are announced for confessions, baptisms, and marriage—all expressions within a religious community. The story of the birth of Jesus is to be told through carols and Eucharist liturgy. Books and classes are provided for exploration and presentation of Christian beliefs. Moral decisions and action involving human rights, sexuality, and abortion are encouraged. A clothing collection for the poor is to be held as a way of expressing moral convictions. In all these expressions the community is seeking to preserve and make alive the Christian tradition.

In addition, creative expressions are announced that seek to renew the faith and express it in a fresh way. Continued search for God, self, and the church is encouraged through study. Counseling is provided to assist in personal growth. Creative expression is suggested in the announcement about a rehearsal for the mass experimenting with folk music. Christmas music shows expression of the arts. Spaghetti suppers, coffee hours, and parties provide social expressions within a religious context.

The illustration of religious expressions within a campus community only hints at the full range of symbolic expressions and responses to that which is believed to be of unrestricted value. A study of other groups such as churches and synagogues will show a variety of emphases. We can only conclude that religious communities, both large and small, provide an important—even necessary—religious expression.

SUMMARY

Individuals express their religion in prayer, in the testimony of a virtuoso, or in literature and the arts. Yet we most often find individual religion to be related to some kind of community. An image of a long continuum with an individual emphasis on one end and the community on the other helps us see the many possible emphases along that continuum. Sometimes persons of profound spiritual depth sense that their experience and expressions conflict with community. These persons may withdraw from a community, or a religious group may refuse any identification with the individual. For the most part, however, the dynamic of religious expressions suggests a symbiotic relationship between an individual and some community. When a religious community is most alive, it creates a "tie that binds" individuals into something that transcends each of them alone; something that is larger than all of them together; something that even has, of itself, an element of transcendence and sacrality about it.

NOTES

1. Peter Berger, *The Heretical Imperative: Contemporary Possibilities of Religious Affirmation* (Garden City, N.Y.: Doubleday, 1980), p. 45.
2. Each of the vignettes that follow has been reconstructed from the experience of T. William Hall, one of the authors of this book.
3. Berger, p. 31.
4. John Neihardt, *Black Elk Speaks* (New York: Pocket Books, 1972).
5. Annie Dillard, *Pilgrim At Tinker Creek* (New York: Bantam Books, 1975).
6. As quoted by J. Milton Yinger, *Religion, Society, and the Individual: An Introduction to the Sociology of Religion* (New York: Macmillan, 1957), p. 345.
7. Yinger, p. 346.
8. Yinger, p. 348.
9. See Bronislaw Malinowski, *Magic, Science, and Religion, and Other Essays* (Boston: Beacon Press, 1948) and Robert Bellah, *Beyond Belief: Essays on Religion in a Post-Traditional World* (New York: Harper & Row, 1970), p. 12.
10. Roger Schmidt, *Exploring Religion* (Belmont, Calif.: Wadsworth, 1980), p. 255.
11. Bellah, p. 31.
12. Bellah, p. 171.

QUESTIONS FOR STUDY AND DISCUSSION

1. To what extent does a society create individuals and to what extent do individuals create society?

2. Discuss your own religion, or that of someone you know well, in terms of the degree to which it is your individual experience and expression, and/or the experience and expression of a community.

3. Compare the religious community you know best with a community known by a friend. How do your groups differ in (a) religious

expression, (b) organizational structure, and (c) relationship to the larger society?

4. What are some aspects of religion that seem appropriate primarily for individuals? What aspects seem appropriate primarily for groups?

PROJECTS

1. Organize a dialogue or debate among at least six students. Instruct half of the group to argue that religion is primarily individual. Instruct the other half to take the side that religion is primarily communal. Persons from each side should speak alternately. When the presentations have been made, have other class members identify the most persuasive arguments. Discussion will probably be difficult to conclude.

2. Over a period of one week jot down all the things you do that are intentionally religious. During the same period read carefully a daily newspaper noting activities reported about individuals that you judge to be religious. Check those items that, in some way, are related to a religious community.

SUGGESTED READINGS

Allport, Gordon W. *The Individual and His Religion: A Psychological Interpretation.* New York: Macmillan, 1961.

Bellah, Robert N. *Beyond Belief: Essays on Religion in a Post-Traditional World.* New York: Harper & Row, 1970.

Bellah, Robert N., and Phillip E. Hammond. *Varieties of Civil Religion.* San Francisco: Harper & Row, 1980.

Berger, Peter. *The Sacred Canopy: Elements of a Sociological Theory of Religion.* Garden City, N.Y.: Doubleday, 1980.

_____. *The Heretical Imperative: Contemporary Possibilities of Religious Affirmation.* Garden City, N.Y.: Doubleday, 1980.

Gilkey, Langdon. *Society and the Sacred: Toward a Theology of Culture in Decline.* New York: Crossroad, 1981.

Mann, Richard D. *The Light of Consciousness: Explorations in Transpersonal Psychology.* Albany, N.Y.: State University of New York Press, 1984.

Maslow, Abraham H. *Religious, Values, and Peak Experiences.* Columbus, Ohio: State University Press, 1964.

Yinger, J. Milton. *Religion, Society, and the Individual: An Introduction to the Sociology of Religion.* New York: Macmillan, 1957.

Part III

LOOKING BACK, LOOKING AHEAD

CHAPTER 10

Religions: Paths and Accents

To this point in our study of religion we have neither systematically nor explicitly discussed any particular religion or, indeed, just what "a religion" is. We have focused instead on what constitutes religion in general, first by way of defining "religion" as an object of study and second by looking at a variety of generic types of expression. "Religion" has not been defined by the religions, although the vast bulk of religious data are found in the religions.

Now, however, it is time to say emphatically that no one actually lives religiously "in general" or "generically." People's faith, as well as their expressions of it, most often have a very specific, "brand-name" content. Religion, as actually lived out in people's lives, is also lived out in a specific context of culture, language, society, history, and tradition.

Focusing on the general and generic has been useful, of course, because it has allowed us to make generalizations that cut across all religion, to understand how religion functions in human existence, and to realize that religion may appear in places we might not expect. At this point, however, we wish to indicate the nature and importance of particular religions.

RELIGIONS AS SYMBOL SYSTEMS

Although we have not studied any particular religions in this book, we have used the religions as primary examples of the general structures and patterns of religious expression. It should now be clear that the religions not only have a specific content but that their content differs in spite of the common patterns and expressions. Christian and Buddhist morality, for example, may share certain common structures and religious intentions; yet it would be a serious mistake to conclude that the actual content of Christian morality and Buddhist morality is the same. Similarly, while the mythologies of all religions share certain common features, each religion tells its own sacred stories.

Religions are, in fact, distinguished from each other by the unique character of their expressions, their unrestricted values, and the whole cultural, social, and historical context within which they are lived. A religion might be defined, therefore, as *a particular set or system of interrelated, interlocking, mutually dependent symbolic expressions that point to common and shared unrestricted values or faith.* These "symbol systems" are lived out by particular people in particular contexts of community, tradition, history, and culture.

The larger and more complex the particular religion, of course, the less tightly systematic and interlocking it is, and the more difficult it is to identify wholly shared expressions and shared values. Religions as complex as Christianity or Hinduism, for example, become difficult to deal with in terms of expressions shared across the whole religion. The office of the Pope is a Christian institutional expression of importance only to Roman Catholics. The god Vishnu, in Hinduism, is the supreme expression of the holy only to the Vaishnavites, that is, the Vishnu sect(s) of Hinduism. In Christianity some traditions focus on the Christ of faith as their central expression; others focus on the Jesus of history. Moreover, the Christianity of the Zulu Zionists in South Africa, the Japanese of the nineteenth century, Russian Orthodoxy, contemporary Unitarian Universalists, or Central American Voodoo cults is diverse in the extreme. Such widely divergent types of Christianity seriously qualify the idea that Christianity is one symbol system.

In spite of these difficulties, religions are distinct from one another and constitute self-contained systems insofar as they share, at one level or another and in one sense or another, common expressions and values. Christians share scripture, a particular history, an idea of the church, as well as certain beliefs, rituals, morality, and art. Perhaps, at bottom, there is a central, shared expression in Jesus as Christ. Perhaps this expression reveals a common, unrestricted value, that is, God's incarnate love. To the extent that there are these shared expressions and value, as well as a people willing to call themselves "Christians," we can identify a particular symbol system passed down through history as a religious tradition called Christianity.

This theme of unity and diversity within any given religion can be pursued in a variety of ways. Diversity is clearly expressed, for example, by the sectarian divisions within complex religions. Buddhism is not only divided into three major subdivisions (Theravada, Mahayana, and Vajrayana), but Mahayana is, in turn, divided into widely divergent sectarian groupings. This diversity carries with it diverse expressions and values to the point that it seems we have different religions within one religion! All these groups, however, want in some way or another to claim they are Buddhists and to claim certain shared expressions such as the historical Buddha and his teaching. All Buddhists, for example, are united in being able to say, "I take refuge in the Buddha, I take refuge in the Dharma (teaching, truth), I take refuge in the Sangha (monastic community)." Of course, they may interpret these in extremely diverse ways, but nonetheless a unity, of sorts, is established thereby.

Less complex religions are easier to see as interlocking, mutually dependent symbol systems. This is especially true of religions that have not traveled to diverse cultures or faced and survived major historical disruptions. It is also truer of religions in which membership is governed more by heredity than voluntary acceptance. However complex Judaism is, for example, even as it has traveled to other cultures, it is more easily identified as a unified system because of the strong sense of a shared peoplehood, a shared history, and a shared sacred homeland.

A clear example of a less diverse religion, yet one living on in the modern world, is Shinto. The symbolic expressions and unrestricted values of Shinto more nearly constitute a coherent and wholly shared system than probably any other of the major world religions. There are many reasons for this, one of which is the deep identity of Shinto with the Japanese culture itself and the relative stability and continuity of Japanese society over the centuries.

Other examples of symbolic unity are even more obvious. The smaller and less complex the religion the clearer will be its shared and systematic unity. A new religious cult in America, for example, will have that clarity. A tribal religious system in traditional black Africa would manifest a more easily identifiable system of expressions and a single unrestricted value. Religions of antiquity such as Norse religion, Egyptian religion, Greek religion, Confucianism, and Zoroastrianism would also tend to have this more systematic and shared unity. None of these religions is "simple," but all have less diversity within them than some of the larger world religions mentioned above.

A very different way to consider religious symbol systems, or religions, is to consider whole cultures, or major aspects of cultures, as religious, especially when they are not already considered religious in some more obvious sense. Certainly our definition of religion in chapter 1 allows us to view culture this way. The theologian Paul Tillich, in fact, says, "Religion is the substance of culture, and culture the form of religion."[1] If culture expresses a people's unrestricted valuing or fundamental orientation in reality, then it is a religious datum.

In this sense American culture and tradition can be considered a religion in and of itself. As a matter of fact, one branch of the study of American religion has devoted itself to investigating what it calls American "civil religion." This civil religion has its own unique expressions that are influenced by Christianity or Judaism but not defined thereby. Its mythology is the sacred story of its founding; its rituals are its national holidays and special national events; its art is the secular literature, music, and visual arts; its ethic is one of freedom and justice; its holy is the ideal of a free and just society; its scripture is the Constitution and Bill of Rights.

Such civil religions exist elsewhere, especially where national identity and ideology is strong, and cultural tradition is cohesive and clear. From Soviet communism to American democracy, and from Japanese nationalism to French nationalism, such civil religions can be found. Some are more influenced by or identified with particular religions than others, but in each case the national ideology and cultural expression constitutes its own distinctive, religious symbol system.

Particular aspects of a culture could be looked at in the same way. The artistic traditions of one culture, or the sport and play of another could be religious data and constitute particular symbol systems. These and many other examples point out the rich possibilities that exist for finding "religions" where we might least expect them. Certainly "religions" should not be merely defined by the world religions, nor should they be merely defined by the more obviously and self-consciously religious systems. The student of religion has a responsibility to discover religion functioning in other places as well, and whole cultures, or aspects thereof, are only one place to start.

A final word remains to be said on the importance of historical and cultural contexts in religious symbol systems. Religions or symbol systems never exist in a vacuum of time, society, and culture. The historical and cultural context within which a religion exists stands in an important dialectical relationship to a religion: religions influence the times and cultures they live in, and those times and cultures influence religions. American Christianity, for example, has clearly influenced both American history and American culture. The fact that we must call it "American" Christianity shows that the influence has worked the other way as well. The same can be said for almost all religions; certainly it is true of all the world religions living today. The symbol systems called religions are not only highly particular in their content, therefore, but greatly influenced by their historical, cultural setting.

RELIGIONS AS PATHS AND TRADITIONS

Several chapters have mentioned the transformative power of religion in the lives of both individuals and groups. Religions function in people's lives to help move them forward—both away from essential problems that may face them and toward essential ideals they envision. Religions function as essential means by which this process takes place.[2] To put it another way, religions function as "paths" or "ways" by which people journey through life in a religious manner. Religions help provide a fundamental orientation within reality and a certain direction to life that religious people find necessary. Religions help provide paths, signposts, and mechanisms by which people know where they have been, where and who they are, and where they are going. As part of this process religions provide human beings an access to transcendent reality—an access and reality that help infuse life with transformative power and meaning. Religious symbol systems not only provide "windows" into the realm of the spirit but allow the light of that realm to "enlighten" this mundane life and transform it.

The character of the path and the direction it leads are as diverse as the variety of religions. While some interpreters of the religions feel that "all roads lead to Rome," or that all religions are seeking the same thing, this truth is not obvious. In some cases, for example, the path and the goal may be an individual matter; in other cases the means and end may be highly communal. The paths are as diverse as the differing content of expressions discussed above; the goals are as diverse as the kinds of unrestricted values that motivate people's religious lives. The only generalization possible is that all paths are made up of symbolic expressions, and all goals have to do with continuing to live in a meaningful and sacred world of one sort of another.

Very closely related is the fact that religions also function as specific traditions. The word "tradition" not only suggests a particular symbol system within which people live and are transformed, but it also indicates that this system and path has often been passed on and sustained through time, although not in unchanging form. Tradition represents the power of particular symbol systems to mediate, keep alive, and renew those values and modes of experience necessary for a "living" religion. A "living" religion, however, is in perpetual change. Individual experiences and symbolic expressions are in dialectical relationship. Each helps shape, modify, and keep alive the other.[3] New experiences may demand reinterpretation of belief systems, new rituals, or revised moral codes. Cultural changes such as liberation movements, economic upheaval, or artistic developments may provide new symbols of meaning. Thus traditions can and most often do change. Even institutional structures provide radical changes, as happened in sixteenth-century Europe with the Protestant Reformation or with the Second Vatican Council in the 1960s.

On the other hand, religious traditions sometimes appear to be changeless. It is interesting to reflect on the question: "Why do some traditions seem to be static, that is, appear to remain unchanged over many years?" The most immediate answer is that the particular symbol system expresses for the people their unrestricted values and helps them in their journey in life toward their highest goals. Thus no change seems needed. There may be, however, more subtle reasons for apparent stability in some traditions. It may be, for example, that a conservative posture is inevitable for many people. That is, the desire to preserve values of the past—especially unrestricted values—provides a secure basis for living in a troubled world. Or it may be that a specific religious tradition has developed a priestly class of people who hold primary authority in their own hands and are unwilling to relinquish that power, a process that would happen inevitably with change. These authorities might claim that truth never changes; hence religious expressions of the past must remain unchanged to be in harmony with eternal and unchanging truth. Again, we might conjecture that a community resists change and the instability that comes with uncertainty of the new. But whatever the reasons, a human search for continuity of meaning seems to work against rapid change within any tradition.

The tension, then, between change and stasis in a religious tradition will probably characterize each tradition, leading toward some stability amid changes. Without this process, we can expect that a tradition will, in time, die. It will die when the symbol system is no longer an expression of the people's deepest experiences and their unrestricted values.

ACCENTS IN THE RELIGIONS

As indicated above, religions have certain common features and yet diversity as well. Still another way to describe both unity and diversity in the religions is through the idea of "accents," that is, emphases and tendencies that can be found both within religions and among them. Each religion, or even a major subdivision within a religion, shows certain accented characteristics. To look at these accents not only helps to grasp something about the religion, but it provides interesting clues to distinctive types of religiousness that cut across or are found within several religions.

Before discussing the accents of any particular religion it is important to indicate the complexity and difficulty in making these kinds of generalizations about a religion. Larger and more complex religions—for example, most of the so-called "world religions"—evidence tremendous diversity within them—even to the point of causing one to wonder if such diverse phenomena could belong to the same religion! One pervasive set of accents found in many such religions, for example, is found in the distinction between the "elite" or "normative" element in a religion, and the popular or folk element. An awareness of this distinction makes it possible for us to recognize two kinds of religiousness within the same religion. These two different accents may be complementary but are clearly different.

Buddhism provides a clear example. One scholar has discussed the Buddhism of contemporary Burma as divided into three distinct and different forms of religiosity: the *nibbanic* Buddhism of the religious elite, which centers on monastic practices leading to *nirvanic* realization; the *kammatic* Buddhism of the laity, which centers on meritorious actions *(karma)* leading to benefits in this life and the next; and *apotropaic* Buddhism, which centers on magical practices to avert danger *(apotropa-*

ic) and is practiced by the uneducated masses.[4] So diverse are these strands that it is difficult to generalize about Burmese Buddhism, much less Buddhism as a whole!

Similar comments could be made about almost any religion that resides in a complex society or spreads across a variety of cultures. Such comments would not be limited to the elite/popular distinction made above, but could be multiplied in terms of other distinctive polarities and accents.

One set of distinctive accents found both within and among the great world religions is the mystical and nonmystical type of religiosity. Mysticism is that form of religion tending to experience the holy deeply within the human/natural world, while nonmystical forms tend to discover the holy primarily outside or beyond this world. Most of the world religions give evidence of both kinds of religiosity within them. Thus the Sufi sect of Islam, or Hasidism within Judaism, represent mysticism. In the Western religions, mysticism is the "hidden" and minority strand, while nonmysticism dominates. In the Eastern religions the reverse tends to be true.[5]

A less obvious and more recently discovered kind of accent revolves around male and female types of religiosity. Especially within the primal, tribal religions there are differences between the religious practices and expressions of men and women. Some are even kept secret from the opposite gender! Even within religions such as Orthodox Judaism the religious practices of the men are quite different from those of the women. A shift from male/female to "feminine" and "masculine" opens up even larger possible distinctions. The Western religions, for example, seem dominated by images of masculinity, both in the deity and in the hierarchy of priestly offices. The Eastern religions, particularly Hinduism, much more clearly affirm the feminine principle as part of divine reality.

Another set of accents can be introduced by mentioning theologian Paul Tillich's distinction between ontological and moral types of faith.[6] He suggests that all faith entails both a sense of the presence of the holy within the world (ontological faith) and a sense of the holy as making a demand on the human to become what it ought to be (moral faith). Beyond this, however, Tillich indicates that various religions, or major branches thereof, reveal a tendency to emphasize one or the other of these characteristics. Thus some religions are more sacramental or mystical by emphasizing the presence of the holy. Others, for example Judaism or Confucianism, emphasize the religious law and/or the ethical dimensions of religion.

Rather closely related is another major polarity, the distinction between understandings of the holy as supernatural or beyond the natural, and understandings of the holy as encompassed by the natural. Monotheistic or polytheistic religions emphasize the former while mystical, humanistic, and pantheistic religions tend toward the latter. Although exceptions can easily be found, one could also say that the Eastern religions tend toward the "natural" while Western religions accent the supernatural.

If we keep our focus on the world religions, yet another set of accents is the distinction between religions of revelation and religions of self-discovery. Again, although there are important qualifications, one can refer to the Western religions as religions of revelation in which the central expressions of the religion are revealed in definitive, once-for-all events: Jahweh reveals himself through the law and commandments to ancient Israel, God reveals himself by the incarnation in Christ, and Allah speaks through his prophet Muhammad. These revelations determine the unique and authoritative centers of these religions and clearly mark them off from other religions. Each religion feels that its particular revelation is the unique and "final" truth.

The Eastern religions, on the other hand, tend to be religions of discovery. The sacred texts of almost all of them indicate human processes of self- and world-discovery as the means by which sacred truths are found and expressed. Major portions of Hinduism, as well as most of Buddhism, Taoism, and Confucianism reflect this tendency. The Buddha told his disciples at the end of his life, for example, "to work out their own salvation—Buddhas can only point the way." The Buddha's truths are meant to be rediscovered afresh by every Buddhist; they are not the revealed truths of a divinity.

Confucianism is similar in that the teachings of Confucius are not divinely revealed; they are the "discoveries" of Confucius and his followers who, through education and moral discipline, arrived at them and sought to spread them for others to follow. The classical Taoist tradition is similar in emphasizing the importance for each person to experience the unity with and truth of Tao.

Another accent found in the religions is that of world rejection and world affirmation. Closely related is the distinction between ultimate fulfillment or "salvation" beyond this world or within it. World-rejecting religions tend to find that this world, this body, or this life are only momentary "prisons" for the spirit or soul. Ultimate reality may play a part in this world, but both it and ultimate human fulfillment are somehow beyond this world. Therefore, Hinduism speaks of *moksha* or release from this world of birth and death, and of the release of spiritualized self *(purusa)* from the confines of nature and matter *(prakriti)*. Similarly, early Theravada Buddhism tended to emphasize nirvana as a release from *samsara,* the vicious circle of suffering.

The Western religions, especially Christianity and Islam, also have strong elements of world rejection. Visions of fulfillment in paradise, or at the end of time when all is to be drawn up into the life of God, are cases in point. The Zoroastrian paradigm, which predates and probably influenced the Western religions, sees history and this world as a temporary battleground between the forces of evil and the forces of good. In the end, time and the world itself will cease in the "final resurrection" or "judgment day" when all is brought back to its original home in the life of God. Christianity and Islam both carry such ideas with them.

World-affirming religions, on the other hand, stress the presence of the holy in this world and the fulfillment of human existence within this life. Mahayana Buddhism, for example, emphasizes nirvana as an awakening experience within *samsara*—in fact, an enlightening experience which then sees that this *samsaric* life is, itself, nirvana. In the ideal of the *bodhisattva*, Mahayana stresses that enlightenment, together with the compassion it engenders, takes place within this life and is meant to be lived out in it. This very body/mind is a buddha-in-the-making, a *bodhisattva;* this very world/life is the arena of salvation.

In affirming a particular human community Judaism also tends to be world affirming. The messianic age may yet be coming, but it will come into this world and life to fulfill it. In the meantime the people of Israel, the "chosen people," are God's people and in covenant with him. Life is affirmed and fulfilled by being in right relationship to God.

Christianity has within it a strong world-affirming accent as well. Christians preach that "God so loved the world that he gave his only begotten Son." A truly incarnational theme would seem to dictate the idea that God now "dwells among us" and thereby affirms us and the world as the primary sphere of divine activity. In this view, the kingdom of God is not beyond history but within our own hearts, within a loving community, or within the social order itself.

Although other accents could be described, space does not allow us to extend this discussion. One final set of accents, therefore, will close this section and chapter.

As one looks out over the religions of humanity one cannot help but perceive a pattern in notions of the holy. The object of unrestricted values or faith, expressed in various images or ideas of the holy, seems to appear in three relatively distinct types which relate to (1) the natural world, (2) the psychological world, and (3) the sociological world. Insofar as this is the case, specific religions, or branches thereof, can be seen as accenting one or the other emphasis.

1 Religions accenting the natural world are religions that see the sacred as intimately connected with nature—whether nature as the nonhuman world of earth or nature as the whole cosmos. Such religions stress that the very being of the world is a creative act of the divine, and the divine or holy is to be found in and through the workings of nature/cosmos itself. The Genesis story of creation is certainly one example.

God is the creator and preserver of the natural (as well the human) world, and, as the book of Job so dramatically shows, God is the underlying power of that natural world itself. Many polytheistic and pantheistic religions, from Native American religion to Shinto, also accent this affirmation of the sacred as manifest in nature. The gods of nature are, around the world, the most populous group of all. They represent the human experience of the natural world as the revelation or manifestation of unseen, creative powers.

2. The psychological accent is very different. Here, the holy is experienced and expressed as a function of particular modes of consciousness. The "larger life" that the holy represents is not "out there" but within our own mind. Generally speaking this accent is to be found in mystical traditions emphasizing direct experience prior to naming, or unitive experience (via yogas or "yoking" techniques) with the holy. The yogic traditions of Hinduism, Buddhism, and Taoism are all examples. In the latter, for example, Tao is a state of the mind by which one is absolutely at one with the way things naturally are. In Buddhism the word *buddha* means one who is "awakened," and *nirvana* is this awakened existence.

As we have indicated above, the Western religions have this mystical element as well, even though it does not represent the dominant view or normative tradition. In the New Testament, for example, Paul speaks of having a "mind in Christ," or of the "law of the heart" as the true law. In doing so, he is emphasizing the centrality of a specific state of mind; one must be "dead to sin and alive to Christ" experientially and in this very moment! One must make God's love present in one's own life, which is to say one's own mind and experience. The radical message of the incarnation is to shift from the God of nature to the indwelling God-in Christ.

3. The sociological accent finds the holy within community, or the experience of "common-unity." The "larger life" of sacred reality is found in the collectivity of human existence, in the sense that human community is something more than merely the sum of the parts. From the sense of a sacred nation to the sense of a sacred peoplehood, this important accent can be found in many religions. It dominates where the communal expression of religion discussed in chapter 9 takes center stage, for example, in Judaism, certain forms of Protestant Christianity, and Confucianism.

The world religions are not the only place to find the community accent. The Oglala Sioux shaman, Black Elk, expresses this accent when he speaks of the "sacred hoop of the nation," the fertile and sacred peoplehood that has been broken and scattered.[7] Similarly, religions that stress the veneration of ancestral spirits also reflect this accent. The community in this case includes the spirits of the dead; together, the living and the dead form a seamless whole which is, itself, a sacred reality.

SUMMARY

There are, of course, many ways to speak of the religions of humanity—both in general and specifically. Our purpose here has been to remind you that religion is always lived out in particular symbol systems which, in turn, function religiously in people's lives to transform life in meaningful ways and to constitute traditions that carry both expressions and experience down through time and community.

Beyond that, however, we have provided specific information about religions by means of discussing a variety of accents, or particular types of religiousness as discovered within and among the religions. Our discussion in this case has made primary use of the so-called world religions, although we have tried to suggest that all other religions might reflect one or another of these accents as well.

As we look back over our study in this book, we hope you understand the importance of particular religions, both their variety and unique particularity as well as their common patterns or accents. Religions are where religion is lived.

NOTES

1. Paul Tillich, *Theology of Culture* ed. Robert C. Kimball (New York: Oxford University Press, 1959), p. 42.
2. See the transformative model explained in chapter 6.
3. See Peter Berger, *The Heretical Imperative: Contemporary Possibilities of Religious Affirmation* (Garden City, N.Y.: Anchor PressDoubleday, 1979), pp. 42–50.
4. Melford Spiro, *Buddhism and Society:* A Great Tradition and its Burmese Vicissitudes (New York: Harper & Row, 1970).
5. For a relatively full discussion of this issue within and among the world religions, see Berger, chapter 6.
6. Paul Tillich, *The Dynamics of Faith*, ed. Ruth Nanda Ashen (New York: Harper & Row, 1956), chapter 4.
7. See John Neihardt, *Black Elk Speaks* (New York: Pocket Books, 1972).

CHAPTER 11

Methodological Reflections

Religion is as old as ancient mythologies and primitive rituals; it is as old as the human expression of meaning. The study of religion, however, is a new human activity, especially the kind of scholarship practiced in colleges and universities in the second half of the twentieth century. The study of religion has the task of describing, understanding, and evaluating the expressions of religion in all of its forms, to the end that students may gain knowledge, be liberated from ignorance, and develop an appreciation for the phenomenon being studied. Religion itself, however, is more than research and thinking about something; it involves convictions, feelings, and dedicated action. It is this difference between religion as a lived phenomenon and the study of religion that leads to the problem of method in religious studies.

THE HISTORY AND PROBLEM OF METHOD

How shall we study religion in such a way that religion itself will be thoroughly understood and not distorted? How shall we do it so that the scholar may be free from the kind of religious involvement and commitment that make critical evaluation of religion difficult, if not impossible? In short, if we are on the "inside" of a religion we may not be able to be scholarly critics because of our personal devotion. Yet if we are on the "outside" we may not be able to understand the intimate power and dynamics of religious faith and practice because of our distance from it. A brief sketch of the history of religious studies may help focus this problem.

General scholarship within the religious communities is not new. The rabbis who wrote the Talmud, along with the early Christian fathers in the same period, were the intellectuals of their day. Later, medieval theologians and philosophers spent their whole lives writing and teaching within a particular religious tradition. All such theologizing within specific traditions is "scholarly" as well as religious.

Yet the study of religion as an autonomous discipline, what we now call "the academic study of religion," had its beginnings only in the nineteenth century. The historian of religions Max Müller characterized this new concern when he wrote that the purpose of the study of religion is "to find out what religion is, what foundation it has ... and what follows from its historical growth." Müller believed the task of studying many religions to be extremely important for he added, "He who knows one religion knows none."[1] Other European scholars in the nineteenth century who are still famous for their contributions to scholarship in religion include Auguste Comte, Ludwig Feuerbach, Ernest Renan, Julius Wellhausen, William James, and James G. Frazer.

During the nineteenth century, European and American church-related colleges of the Protestant and Roman Catholic traditions offered courses in religion, yet they paid little attention to the scholars just named. The courses taught, often required of all students, were apologetic and served the purpose of indoctrinating the students into the Christian tradition. During the same period the large and well-known American private universities like Yale, Harvard, Columbia, Princeton, and Chicago did little to further the academic study of religion in a direct way. Often studies in religion were left to the classics, history, anthropology, sociology, or philosophy departments.

Beginning in the middle of the nineteenth century and continuing for one hundred years, the major nondenominational theological seminaries carried on the task of scholarship in religion in the American context. The seminaries were able to keep two purposes alive and in creative tension—that of training professional clergy and that of educating scholar-teachers in religion. Whereas the conservative or fundamentalist seminaries limited areas of inquiry so that their doctrines might remain undisturbed, the major theological seminaries were the academic religious establishment in America.

The academic religious establishment, however, changed immediately after World War II when new departments of religion were developed in state colleges and universities as well as in private universities. Krister Stendahl, while Dean of the Harvard University Divinity School, said that the center for the academic study of religion is moving away from the seminaries to the departments of religion. In a major address delivered at Princeton University in 1968 he declared, "It has ... reached a point where the question whether a religion department has a proper place within the college and graduate faculty of arts and sciences can be considered resolved in the affirmative, for state universities no less than for private schools."[2]

Such a shift in the location of the academic study of religion had a profound effect on the nature of religious studies. Departments of religion in secular colleges and universities sought for new curricular models distinct from those developed in the theological seminaries. In the new curricula, courses were changed: "Old Testament" was replaced with "History and Religion of Israel"; "Christian Theology" became "Western Religious Thought." New courses were introduced in the major traditions—Buddhism, Hinduism, and Islam along with Judaism and Christianity. In every case, the "new" secular study of religion in America now connected with similar developments in Europe.

With the study of religion finding a new home in secular institutions, both public and private, the context became academic, not religious. Whereas at one time it was assumed in church-related institutions that there was only one true religion and that this was Christianity (sometimes even the sponsoring denomination), the new assumption was quite different—in fact the opposite. The new approach gave no preference to any particular religious claim to truth. Rather, all religions were to be studied without fear or favor. Objectivity was the key word.

If in our time we return to the older position, then the teaching of religion will be but a form of evangelism. Open inquiry, which is expected in the college or university, will be impossible. If, however, we take the secularized approach, we may distort religion and represent it as little else than "a curious museum within which to study the aberrations of the human spirit."[3] Rather than capitulate to either extreme position, we are now seeking methods of inquiry that will permit religion to be studied fairly and appreciatively as well as critically. These methods must be among those with approved credentials in the scholarly community. At the same time, the methods must not distort the data of religion being examined.

"INSIDE" VERSUS "OUTSIDE"

Thinking through the inside and outside approaches to the study of religion may help in dealing with appropriate methods of inquiry. Being on the inside means that the person who is studying a particular religion is a member of that community. As an insider, this student is committed to the unrestricted value being examined. The scriptures, rituals, artistic expressions, and beliefs of that group are embraced by the student. He or she thinks, feels, and acts out of commitment to that particular religious faith. Such a person knows one religion intimately. The obvious danger is that being on the inside of a religion with personal involvement and commitment may distort the capacity to be a critical scholar.

An outsider is a student of religion whose primary identification is that of a scholar who uses secular methods of inquiry created by the academic community. This person believes that religion is worth studying, yet he or she is not necessarily a member of one of the historical religious communities; such a person stands aloof in an attempt to be "objective" and dispassionate in scholarship. Scholarly methodology now recognizes, however, that complete objectivity is impossible. We all harbor assumptions and biases that inevitably affect the results of our study.

Moreover, the danger of the position of being completely outside is that the data being studied can easily be reduced to fit methodological categories. A scholar is then in danger of asserting that religion is "nothing but" that which the method can readily explain. Reductionism thus follows, with religion being reduced to secular norms. Religion faces the risk of being "explained away" from this point of view.

We appear, then, to be caught in a dilemma where extremes are unacceptable. If we know religion from the inside we may lose the possibility of critical judgement so essential to scholarly pursuits. If we are a complete outsider we can be rigorous and objective; yet by being an outsider we run the risk of distorting the very stuff of religion by studying it merely as a quaint, but dead, phenomenon.

The perspective of the sociology of knowledge may provide some aid in dealing with the dilemma. A major sociological assumption is that all systems of belief grow out of and are sustained within a specific community. Moreover, a community is a group of people who have developed a commonly understood symbol system and who know the same things because they share a common body of assumptions about what it is to know. Moreover, they share a common mythos; they understand a common group of stories about their origin, about what is important, about how people should interrelate, and about correct roles for men, women, government officials, priests, physicians, and scholars. The community of people has its sacred places and times; its shared beliefs; its similar ways of expressing emotion.

From this sociological point of view people on the inside of a specific religious community share an understanding of their religion without having to resort to objective inquiry. When, for example, the Jewish congregation gathers on a Sabbath evening for worship, they share pageantry. The Shema is said: "Hear O Isreal, the Lord our God, the Lord is One." The Torah is brought out from the ark and read; the cantor sings; prayers are said. And those who participate in the worship, if they do so out of deliberate desire rather than some external coercion, have an intuitive sense of what it all means. They seem to know—at least vaguely—the meaning and truth of Judaism because they are within the community. The same kind of social dynamics are at work in a Christian community, a community of Zen monks, or any other group that shares a common mythos and symbol system.

It would appear, therefore, that one way to "know" religion would be from within a specific community of people: to use its language, to join in its worship, to embrace its myths and stories as one's own, to meditate on its scriptures, to celebrate through its rituals—in short, to be an insider rather than an outsider. H. Richard Niebuhr had something like this in mind when he wrote approvingly of "inner history" in opposition to "outer history" as conveying the truth of the Christian revelation to people.[4]

The student of religion is in great difficulty, however, if he or she accepts uncritically the view that being on the inside is a necessary condition for knowledge of religion. The academic community insists that the insider's claim must be qualified by some type of critical reflection. People in the academic environment will probably argue that while a religious tradition may hide some of its knowledge from the outsider, the outsider has access to all the data. The outsider, for example, may make such a thorough study that she or he can convincingly argue on behalf of a religious tradition, or play the role of a priest or rabbi in a dramatic production with power and pursuasiveness. The claim might even be made that a person who is outside the community may have certain insights hidden from the insider.

If we continue to turn this problem of inside and outside over in our minds, it seems reasonable to say that the scholar who is not a person of traditional religious faith is also an insider in a way analogous to the religious insider. The scholar is part of a community, a community of people who are committed to the study of religion. This is a community that desires to understand, appreciate, and evaluate religion whenever and wherever it is found. The philosopher Michael Polanyi is instructive when he insists that for there to be any kind of knowledge—secular as well as religious—there must be a community of people who possess the same assumptions, use a common language, and participate in the same tradition. This "social-knowledge" principle is equally true for the scientific community as for the religious community. Scientists share a common empirical method of inquiry; they utilize the same criteria for the verification of assertions; they can continue their search for "truth" because they share the same general understanding of what it is to know.[5]

Such observations drawn from the sociology of knowledge seem to be changing the polarity of inside versus outside. From this perspective there are no outsiders; there are only insiders in different communities. To be more specific, within the community of scholars of religion we share a common vocabulary and an assumption that religions have played an important role in human cultures. We exhibit common practices such as classroom dialogue, disciplined reading, examinations, and professional conferences. If this enterprise of the study of religion is entered into with a sense of deliberate dedication to a task believed to be significantly valuable, then it is analogous to a religious community. The scholar is inside a particular, committed community which is not totally dissimilar in structure and function from a religious community.

To make the matter even more complicated, the scholar of religion who is inside the community of scholars dedicated to the study of religion may also be an insider in a particular traditional religion such as

Judaism or Roman Catholic Christianity. As a committed member of two communities—that of the scholar and that of a traditional religious faith—he or she may find that the two communities enrich each other. The scholar's work, for example, may enhance religious life as it suggests new insights and aids in the deepening of religious faith. At the same time, the experience of being devoutly religious may give valuable data and suggest unique interpretations to the scholar's work.

On the other hand, these two aspects may clash seriously. The commitment, for example, to the God of the Bible may conflict with the commitment to philosophical scholarship that has led the person into serious doubts about biblical theism. Or again, the process of demythologization, so characteristic of many scholars' work, may make participating in Jewish or Christian rituals seem a hollow sham. Conversely, the powerful tug of the mystery of the transcendent felt in traditional rituals, and the coherent meaning offered by the worshiping and believing community, may persuade the scholar to abandon the study of religion. Whenever these conflicts come—and they arise for most of us—we seek ways to adjudicate the conflict. Otherwise we must give up being inside a traditional religion or give up being inside the community of scholars who study religion.

The approach that appears to offer promise of overcoming unnecessary conflict between authentic religiousness and the scholarly study of religion—the latter of which may be critical of religion, just as religion may stand in judgment against the absoluteness of any particular scholarly ideology—would appear to be located on the boundary between the two inside stances. This boundary position is, on the one hand, empathetic to a particular religion or religious expression, seeking to understand it on its own terms. On the other hand, it seeks to reflect critically on the data of religion from within the framework of the scholarly enterprise. Sometimes one will actually be an insider in the religion being studied. Sometimes we will imagine ourselves being inside that community of faith. As scholars we will always be inside an inquiring community such as that of a sociologist or historian or philosopher investigating religion. At all times we will seek to remain at the boundary, in creative tension between two inside positions.

Approaches to Religious Understanding Inside Religion

A student who is not a Buddhist, a Native American, or an African Dinka need not fully embrace one of those traditions in order to become something of an insider. Yet every effort needs to be made to think and feel as they do. Techniques would include immersion into the culture surrounding the religion. Reading texts "through their eyes" should be attempted. Seeking the meanings expressed in their poetry and art would be helpful. Participating in their ritual acts—as foreign as they may feel—would give hints of the transforming power present in the ritual. Thinking, feeling, and acting as if we lived totally within a religious community not our own would surely let us stand within part of the circle of lived religion.

If we are a participating member of a religion being studied, being on the inside is no problem. That experience will provide the opportunity for existentially knowing the inside of a culture and religion. The practicing Roman Catholic, for example, will have a "feel" for the rich liturgical tradition, the warm affection for the Bishop of Rome, and the satisfaction of a sacramental life. One who is mystically inclined will have little difficulty understanding the expression of ecstasy from mystics within the varied traditions. Whether functioning "as if" one were on the inside, or actually living on the inside, the student of religion can do scholarly work.

Approaches to Religious Understanding Inside the Scholarly Community

If being on the inside of religion provides a distinctively intimate knowledge, the student of religion also has at his or her disposal ways of gaining, organizing, and testing knowledge that will be useful in understanding and interpreting religion from a scholarly perspective. The scholar, by definition, is one who uses all the intellectual tools available in the task of understanding the phenomena under investigation. Yet in utilizing the available methods, the scholar is often in danger of falling into the fallacy of reductionism. That is, the data, in this case religion, may be reduced to fit into a single mode of inquiry and/or be explained away in terms of scientific world view.

In the perspective being developed here, however, we would seek to avoid such reductionism. What, then, are some of the methods open to the student of religion? The natural sciences provide a method that has grown in importance in this century, yet they have only limited use in the study of religion in that the nature of most religious data are such that they do not lend themselves to the scientific method. Only in the areas of religion where an assertion is made about some empirical fact is the method of the sciences appropriate for testing such assertions. If, for example, the theory of the creation of the world is meant to be a literal statement, then the scientific method is a proper one for testing the truth of the proposition. But just as the method of studying physics is not the most useful approach for interpreting poetry, and mathematics is not the best academic discipline for studying human emotions, the sciences are of only limited value in the study of religion.

The methods of the social sciences, especially sociology, cultural anthropology, and psychology, are often used in religious studies. Sociology is the rigorous study of society with a concern for the origin and nature of society, as well as an inquiry into the forms and functions of human groups. Since sociologists seek information about all aspects of social living and wish to understand the way groups function, they will be concerned with religious communities. Questions, then, about religion as a social phenomena can and should be studied using the various sociological tools.

Cultural anthropology, while it draws upon biology, sociology, and geography, is the scholarly discipline that studies human beings within specific cultural contexts. With vast amounts of data having been gathered from every known civilization, cultural anthropologists are interested in understanding people and their life styles, physical anatomy, language, and religious systems. We can surely expect that the cultural anthropologist whose specialization is South Asia will deal in depth with Hindu religion and culture. Such an academic approach is clearly relevant to the study of religion.

Another social science, psychology, provides methods that may be used for religious studies. Yet psychology is not a single area of inquiry with one method; it is a vast field with many schools of thought and an equally diverse group of methods of study. But whether psychology is concerned with a study of the psyche or the behavior patterns of rats, the approach of the various psychologies provides the scholarly community with important tools for the study of religion—both of religious experience and of religious behavior.

The social sciences, as illustrated by the fields of sociology, cultural anthropology, and psychology, provide specific methods for the study of religion. Scholars who use those methods will, in fact, be inside the scholarly community even as they seek to be empathetic to the data coming from inside another community, the religious community.

The historical method is clearly another method useful in religious studies. Whether this method is conceived of as a chronological ordering or a specific interpretation of events, history does provide methods for the study of religion. Since the study of religion needs data, and history or historical research helps find data, it is a necessary aspect of studying religion.

The rational mode of inquiry known as philosophy has long been applied to religious inquiry. Ancient Greek philosophers were both critics and supporters of religion. Classical philosophers through the centuries have been concerned with questions of metaphysics, epistemology, and axiology, and thus they were inescapably involved with religious questions. Also, philosophy of religion became a discipline in which systems of religious belief were clarified, defended, and criticized. Later philosophers who have been influenced by scientific principles of verification, however, have been less interested in religious questions. Nevertheless, philosophy remains a discipline closely related to religious studies. When questions of meaning, value, and truth are being asked, then philosophical methods are essential to the student of religion.

Another method that is of special interest to students of religion is called phenomenology. This branch of philosophy, utilized by people like Gerardus van der Leeuw, Joachim Wach, and Mircea Eliade, seeks to set aside all preconceptions about what is "real" or "true" and lets what is being studied speak for itself on the basis of its own experience and "truth." Eliade, in writing about the method, states, "A religious phenomenon will only be recognized as such if it is grasped at its own level, that is to say if it is studied as something religious."[6]

Recent scholars in the field of religion have developed newer methods of inquiry and interpretation. For example, comparative mythologists such as Joseph Campbell and David Miller have shown the interrelationship between ancient mythologies and archetypal images in the psyche, and through their constructive theories they have given a distinctive mode of religious inquiry and interpretation. Moreover, Stanley Romaine Hopper, Nathan Scott, and Amos Wilder have shown the relevance of literary criticism to the task of understanding religious meaning.

A sketch of the academic disciplines clearly indicates, then, that there are many different methods of investigation. There is no a priori basis for repudiating any method. Rather, we propose that any method is useful if, in using it, the student can maintain the "boundary" stance, that is, a stance that does not reduce religion to fit into limited methodological categories. On the other hand, any method that provides tools for inquiry and illuminates what is in religion, while avoiding distorting and reducing the data to its own categories, is surely useful as a method of study. The particular method to be chosen will depend on the data to be studied and the purpose of investigation.

A RESOLUTION OF THE PROBLEM OF METHOD

Thus far we have attempted to identify several aspects of the problem of method in the study of religion. First, we sketched the history of the field of study, placing the current study of religion in a secular and academic environment. Second, we tried to show the dilemma facing the student of religion: If we are simply on the inside of a religious tradition, it is difficult to gain a critical and comprehensive view of religion because we are too involved. If we are simply detached as an objective scholar, we may ignore the limits in objectivity and fail to grasp the essentials of religiousness because our intellectual tools too easily reduce religion to the limited scope of the particular method.

As a tentative solution to the second problem, we proposed that the student of religion is inevitably an insider in the scholarly community. The issue, then, is not one of being simply inside or outside. Rather, the scholar can function in the area where the inside of religion and inside of the scholarly world overlap, at the boundary of both. The danger is that we may fall off the thin edge into one camp or the other, negating the possibility of scholarship in religion.

Third, we sketched various methods of inquiry that are available within the academic community. We proposed that all of these methods are useful. The particular method used at any one time will depend on the specific data under consideration and the purpose of the investigation.

We are now nearing a solution to the problem of method. Moreover, this solution has profound implications for a question we have thus far avoided: Is there one "true" religion, and do all questions within religion have one "true" answer? It is to the solution of the dual problem—the problem of method and the problem of religious truth—that we now turn.

If religious expressions are varied, as this book asserts and illustrates, then we have a tremendous variety of data to examine as students of religion. Moreover, if there are many methods of inquiry, as suggested by the different academic disciplines, we have a rich variety of methods available for our study. There seems to be no self-evident reason for claiming that one religious expression is more universally representative or valid than others. Nor does there appear to be any reason to hold that one scholarly method is always superior to all others. We seem to have many expressions, many issues, and many methods.

If we are to be serious students of religion, avoiding every kind of closed-mindedness and dogmatism, two demands will be made on us: First, we must be open in our observation and inquiry to all data in the various religions. We must listen, observe, read, look, and let those data present themselves to us in their full power and on their own terms. Second, we may select whatever mode of inquiry is appropriate to our specific task and to the data being examined. We must be prepared to encourage others to use alternate methods, expecting their description and interpretation to be influenced by their method. With a plurality of data and with a variety of purposes for study, it seems to follow that we will use a plurality of methods.

If an adequate method is really a plurality of methods within the scholarly "boundary" position, then we will be freed from the haunting question often placed to us: But what is the truth of religion or in religion? The focus of attention and the purpose of our inquiry will not be to find a single universal truth. Our goal, rather, will be to search for adequate understanding, broader visions of religious meaning, significant interpretations, more humane solutions to burning issues confronting religious people, and intelligibility.

The implications of the epistemological pluralism being developed here do not necessarily lead to mere relativism. That is, we are not proposing that one idea, one method, one way of interpreting the data is just as good as another. Rather, we are asserting that all insights and conclusions are relative to the data being examined and the method of inquiry as well as the thoroughness of the study.

The approach proposed here demands empathetic research and, at the same time, rigorous scholarship in one or more secular methods. Such a posture leads to responsible scholarship and to confidence in the results of the study. For example, as scholars we can be convinced that our own work is adequate in that we have been faithful to the data as well as to the demands of precise study. We can speak confidently about the human meaning and ultimate values conveyed in myth, story, scripture, or art. We will be able to understand the pathos and pain of people who can find no resolution to questions of religious belief, and we can also rejoice with those who are confident in their answers. But we may have to settle for truths (with a small "t") rather than any absolute Truth. Such a conclusion, rather than discouraging the student of religion, may serve as a motivation for further study so that answers, partially found, may be clarified, and ambiguities may become less clouded. Finally, we may discover, if slowly and painfully, what we cognitively and conatively affirm as unrestricted value.

NOTES

1. Quoted in Jean Jacques Waardenburg, *Classical Approaches to the Study of Religion: Aims, Methods, and Theories of Research* (The Hague: Mouton, 1973), p. 14.
2. Given at Princeton University in 1968 at a conference honoring Professor George Thomas. Later printed as "Biblical Studies in the University," in Paul Ramsey and John F. Wilson, eds., *The Study of Religion in Colleges and Universities* (Princeton, N.J.: Princeton University Press, 1970), p. 23.
3. Robert N. Bellah, "Religion in the University: Changing Consciousness, Changing Structures," in Claude Welch, *Religion in the Undergraduate Curriculum: An Analysis and Interpretation.* (Washington, D.C.: Association of American Colleges, 1972), p. 14.
4. See H. Richard Niebuhr, *The Meaning of Revelation* (New York: Macmillan, 1941).
5. Michael Polanyi, *Science, Faith, and Society* (Chicago: University of Chicago Press, 1964), chap. 2.
6. Mircea Eliade, *Patterns in Comparative Religion*, trans Rosemary Sheed. (New York: World, Meridan Books, 1972), p. xiii.

CHAPTER 12

The Future of Religion

In the concluding chapter of this book we turn to the question of the future of religion. What will the future hold for religion? In what forms will religion appear and what claims will it make? Will religion be a significant force within the life of the future or a relatively trivial presence? We readily admit that questions such as these cannot be answered with any certainty. The future is not yet; it is open and subject to the accidents and vagaries that have assaulted human intention and consciousness throughout history. This inevitable uncertainty makes the status of assertion about the future risky at best. Nevertheless, the imaginative anticipation and critical speculation needed to respond to the question of the future of religion are both legitimate and important to our academic field.

For the student in the field of relgious studies the question of the future of religion combines a legitimate concern for the prospective nature of data with important critical reflection on the appropriate strategies for their study. Through such intellectual curiosity attention is focused on the historical, social, and cultural forces of transformation, growth, and decay that affect the data of a field as well as their interpretation. By asking such questions as, "What might be said about the prevalence, locus, focus, and plausibility of religious beliefs in the future?" or "Will the acceptance and practice of religious rituals expand or contract in the future and why might this be the case?" we introduce a new perspective to the field that sensitizes a student to present trends and tendencies affecting the expression of religion. Using his or her imagination, a student is asked to extrapolate from the present a scenario of the future, giving account of the projected changes and the agents of change. While this project is both imaginative and speculative in nature, a field of study will disregard such intellectual curiosity as its own peril. In sensitizing a student to the possibilities of the future, a field of study guards against the risk of becoming static, insensitive to changes occurring in the present, and complacent with its own definitions and perspectives. Thus we conclude that questions about the future of religion are both legitimate and important.

A JOURNEY OUT OF THE PRESENT

Whatever forms the future of religion may take, they will appear within the human dynamic of a dialectical self-world creation as focused through the experience of unrestricted value. The human environment (the world) influences self-definition, and the self continuously projects an interpretation of the world. When this mutual cocreation is focused by the experience of the unrestricted in value, religion may be said to condition or affect the future. The future of religion will appear within the metaphorical journey of human creativity as it moves from what has been (the past) through the possible (the present) to what will be (the future). Let us clarify this metaphoric journey, which suggests intentional travel to a new location, by considering how the terms world, individual, community, and unrestricted value might function within it. This clarification will provide the first step in answer to our question of the future of religion.

THE WORLD

Every animal has an environment, but only the human animal has the capacity for using language or symbol to transform its environment into a world—an intelligible whole of space and time. The world is at once a given, a limit, a condition of human experience that demands interpretation and, at the same time, appears as the product of interpretation. It is at once an objective reality and an interpretation of reality; a destiny and a context of opportunity for those who so interpret it. Throughout history, humankind has lived in different "worlds" or interpreted "the world" differently. For example, the world of Christendom was not the world of the Aztec, and neither is the contemporary world of modern science and technology. While different worlds can and have coexisted, one contemporary world is reaching out in threat and promise to affect all others. Those of us who live in Europe and North America, or in one of the highly developed technological countries of the globe, are coming to recognize that the understanding and actions of this world, generated by a minority of the earths population, have such impact upon the global environment that the future of humankind itself will be directly affected, if not terminated, by its journey. Thus we will consider the question of the future of religion in the context of this world. We will identify and discuss this world in terms of four of its major characteristics.

First, our world is significantly informed by technology and the scientific theories that ground it. For example, the technologies of transporation and communication have made the world appear smaller and instantly present. When the globe can be circled by a spacecraft in a matter of hours, no location on it is "too far" away. When the sights and sounds of a battlefield on the other side of the globe can be brought by satellite transmission into your living room in a matter of minutes, the notion of "neighboring" takes on an entirely new meaning. The technologies of production and distribution have brought new meanings to the notions of global resources, labor, and markets. It is no longer solely the millionaire world traveler who drives a Japanese car, eats beef from Argentina, wears shoes from Italy, or buys a coat made in Taiwan. Products made by workers using resources from all over the globe are staples in the everyday life of the average U.S. citizen. The technologies of medicine and modern warfare have introduced to human experience hopes and fears that would appear unintelligible, miraculous, or demonic in other worlds. The capacity to transplant a limb or a heart is now accepted as one more opportunity within the everyday world. So, too, is the terrible capacity to devastate the entire planet through nuclear holocaust. Such is the world that we experience as obvious and take for granted as a condition of the future. The future of religion will be affected by and must influence this world of science and technology.

Second, under the impact of the scientific perspective and its multiple technologies, our world appears more diverse and less homogenous, more complex and less simple, than the worlds previously identified by historical record. With travel and communication comes a sharing of symbols, cultures, and their particular traditions. On any day in the streets of New York City one can meet people from all over the world. These people bring with them their religious preferences, economic persuasions, political commitments, and sexual orientations. Buddhists and Hindus, Socialists and Marxists, can be heard in conversation on the subway or in a hotel lobby. The world has come to our shores; it is in our streets and on our television. With its arrival has come a new sense of the nature of local customs and traditions. What before was "one" is now in our world "one among many." What before was relatively certain and unchallenged is now risked in the face of living alternatives. The pluralism and relativity of symbol systems—religious, political, economic—has become personal experience for many people in our world. This experience has its effects. It displaces innocence. Plausibility structures that once functioned invisibly to provide a sense of certainty now come under pressure; modes for the transmission of particular traditions find themselves in a new and challenging environment. It should therefore come as no surprise if being religious takes on new forms in a future arising from this world.

Third, our world, influenced as it is by technology, science, pluralism, and relativity, exhibits no explicit religious tutelage or control in its basic institutions—legal, political, economic, or educational. Rather, there appears a separation between the institutionalization of the experience of unrestricted value and of the order and process of the everyday, common, or secular world. The means by which such a separation has appeared has been called the process of secularization. This process is not necessarily antireligious, but it has relegated the religious to the status of one more element within the world in need of legitimation. In the present, religion no longer functions as the self-evident legitimation of the world. Religious experience and expression are certainly not excluded from this secular world, but they must now compete for plausibility and acceptance both among the plurality of religious expressions and with the secular expressions of value and fact. The future religion within such a world is not obvious. It is not that religion is threatened by a hostile environment so much as one that ignores it or treats its expressions as being of marginal importance to the conduct of daily affairs.

Fourth, the constellation of the forces of technology, science, pluralism, relativity, and the process of secularization has produced a world that emphasizes human decision, choice, and the intentional modification of the self-world dialectic. Humanity has always been and is now restricted by its environment, its destiny, and the limits of the world. Humanity's present experience of the world, however, is one of the continuing collapse of formerly recognized restrictions and the repeated opening of new vistas. Whether it be the new frontiers of space, the possibility of fifth-generation "thinking" computers, or the creation of life in a test tube and genetic engineering, the momentum of the world is one that emphasizes human achievement and the conquering of what was earlier perceived as destiny, necessity, or inevitability. The role of human decision, both individual and communal, is prominent in defining any future arising from this world. Religion in the future must respond to a world that has historicized destiny and judged it to be maleable in the hands of the human.

THE INDIVIDUAL

In considering the question of the future of religion as a journey out of the present, it is important to note the role of the individual or self who must choose to actualize him or herself within the world. It is the individual human being who must integrate the self-world relationship. It follows, as a corollary on our discussion of "the world," that the individual must synthesize, in an act of existential self-definition, the fundamental forces informing his or her world. The individual must either integrate into his or her self-understanding the presence of scientific technology, secularization, pluralism, relativity, and the emphasis on human decision, or risk a marginalized existence on the borders of the world. Either the individual will successfully incorporate these forces into a centered self or face the breakdown of the self, the paralysis of action, and the functional loss of the self-world relationship. The future of religion must face this challenge.

The first feature of the experience of self in our world is that of the loss of certainty and an increase of doubt and anxiety. This is not to say that uncertainty, doubt or anxiety are not characteristic of other worlds. Rather, it is to focus emphasis on the consequence of the process of secularization, pluralism, and relativity for contemporary human consciousness. Inexorably the individual is drawn to experience a plethora of competing interpretations of the world which she or he inhabits. For example, not only is there an economic perspective but there are capitalist and socialist theories, or steady-state and growth strategies. Not only is there a religious perspective but there is the reality of competing religious traditions and subtraditions within them. In some worlds the very distinction between the economic and the religious would be unthinkable. In the contemporary Western world not only are the distinctions relevant, but further differentiation within the perspectives makes competition and decision inevitable. The process of secularization renders inappropriate any attempt to resolve the problems of competition and uncertainty by elevating any one perspective or tradition to a position of unquestioned authority. All divine, absolute, or unrestricted perspectives are relativized by the process of secularization, including those of the secular itself. To be an individual in our world is to inherit the gift and the curse of the loss of certainty and the presence of doubt and anxiety. Each individual will carry forward this experience into the future. The religious expressions of the future will incorporate this legacy.

The second feature of the self in our world is an increased emphasis on individual experience and the ability to make choices. Individual experience and decision have been and are important elements in all worlds. In the contemporary world, however, they receive more emphasis as a result of the particular cluster of influences surrounding us. While individuals may participate as members in communities of interpretation, the relativization of tradition resulting from the process of secularization forces individuals to decide in the face of competing alternatives. It is not that subjectivism rules, or that traditional authority has no weight, but rather that any legitimation must appeal to a base in individual experience. While arguing from personal experience alone is inadequate, all adequate argumentation will involve a matching of personal experience. That Mom or Dad have experienced it is not enough. Appeals to the virtuosi or the name of tradition are insufficient. Finally, it is the individual's experience that must confirm or criticize the traditional and the novel, the communal and the idiosyncratic. The process of secularization and the reality of pluralism and relativity exhibit with stark clarity the contemporary logic of demand and risk that requires the individual to define him or herself with respect to personal experience. It is this experience that defines the future for the individual in our world. It is this experience that will qualify the future expression of religion.

THE COMMUNITY

The future of religion is inextricably involved with the future of communities that nurture and sustain the human—the family, the school, the work force, health care, religious communities, the state, and the nation. Through communities language is shared, self-consciousness is shaped, conscience is legitimized, and human life is lived. Communities both reflect and participate in the process of dynamic self-world interpretation. They are subject to the forces at work in the world and may respond to these forces in a variety of ways. In our world, communities must respond to the forces of secularization, pluralism, relativity, and the pervasive presence of scientific technology. How they respond will directly affect the course of the human journey out of the present and into the future.

Consider three types of responses that might be made by contemporary communities. These responses represent models or paradigms that may or may not be acutalized by particular historical communities. Ideally, communities may oppose the forces informing the world, embrace these same forces, or critically appropriate some while rejecting others. Communities standing in opposition to contemporary forces represent the first ideal type. These communities tend to be traditional (orthodox) or revolutionary, depending on the nature of their response. The traditional community opposes the forces of the present, those that would change the past, in the name of conservation or preservation. The modern is viewed as a dilution or corruption of the older, purer, more original, and appropriate order. The forces of change are those of decay and destruction. They must be opposed or rejected. The revolutionary community radically opposes the forces of the present on the grounds that they inappropriately restrict or inhibit the appearance of the ideal of humanity. In the name of a future ideal, which is nowhere found in the present order, they would cut the present to its roots and introduce the new order.

Religious communities, as societies or within societies, have reflected this type in both its traditional and revolutionary modes at different periods of history. This option remains open today to those communities prepared to accept the consequences for their members and message. Every type of response affects the self-understanding of its members and their interpretation of the world. This response has theological implications; it limits the ways in which the unrestricted may be appropriately symbolized. A simple opposition produces a mentality that "ghettoizes" the members of the community as well as its beliefs

and practices, thus making it difficult to sustain and recruit membership. Such a response represents the religious as opposed to the forces
of the world, thus creating a either/or alternative. The future of religion will be influenced by this response of opposition.

A second type of community response is that of affiliation. Identifying with the force of modernity, a community "goes native" and strives
to become a chief exemplar of one or more of the major forces of the
present. Within this type, the norms or standards of the present provide the legitimation of the real and the true, the good and the worthwhile. The message of the community response of affiliation is that
dislocation and anomie are the fruits of those who do not embrace the
forces of the present. Flights of fancy and the frights of the ghetto are
the alternatives of the alienated and disaffected. In our world, the response of affiliation requires a community to embrace the process of
secularization, to recognize and affirm pluralism, relativity, and the ex-
pansive presence of scientific technology. The individual members of
the community seek a shared or collective identity committed to the
assimilation and the enhancement of these forces.

Religious communities, as societies or within societies, have embraced
the option of affiliation at various points in history. This option remains
open to the future of religion for those communities who are prepared
to risk the loss of their prophetic or iconoclastic role in return for a
more prominent cultic posture as a legitimizing force in the world. As
with the first type, this response of affiliation has theological consequences that directly affect the way in which the sacred or the unrestricted in value may be expressed.

The third type of community response identifies a posture of both
critical opposition and informed affiliation with the forces of the
present. This response both rejects and yet embraces and reappropri-
ates elements of the dominant characteristics of the modern world. In
this type of response the community is neither primarily traditional or
revolutionary, nor cultic exemplar, but is identified by its self-consciously assumed experimental and experiential disposition. The importance
of tradition is recognized and affirmed, but it is placed within a framework of dialogue or conversation between and among traditions. The
reality of pluralism and the relativity of tradition appears neither as a
blessing nor a curse, but rather as opportunity for choice or decision.
The importance of the process of secularization, of science and its technological ramifications, are recognized as significant perspectives of
thought and action but not as the absolute criteria of knowledge, reality, and value. The experimental and experiential type of community
response is one that assumes an open future and takes responsibility for
a considered review of the alternatives experienced by its members.

Religious communities can identify with this third type on the conditions that their traditions are recognized as relative, their assertions and

actions are understood to be born in risk, and their corporate futures are pledged to follow the directions and choices of their memberships. The experimental nature of the community is exhibited in its commitment to a dialogue among its members and with the forces of the world, to the end of informed participation in the necessary experiment of self- and world-definition.

UNRESTRICTED VALUE

Given the definition of religion with which we have worked in this book, the question of the future of religion will necessarily involve the possibility and actuality of the human experience of, appropriate expression of, and response to that which is perceived to be of unrestricted value. In the present, expressions of the unrestricted in value must contend with the particular forces of the secular world. Thus the issues of pluralism and religious expression, or the processes of secularization and religious expression, become terms in which one possesses and answers the question of the future of religion. Consider the following examples.

In the religions of Judaism, Christianity, and Islam, the unrestricted in value has traditionally been expressed in terms of a supernaturalistic monotheism. The process of secularization, informed by the perspective of science and the ethos of technology, is at best neutral, if not hostile, to such a scheme for interpreting cosmic reality, the human condition, or the appropriate destiny of humankind. The functional "naturalism" inherent in the process of secularization distracts from the obviousness, the self-evident plausibility, of religious experiences expressing beliefs, rituals, or sacred scripture from a supernaturalistic perspective. The same is true for religious traditions, such as Hinduism or Buddhism, that focus on a mystical experience transcending the distinctions, multiplicity, and relationships of secular experience. The legitimation of the supernaturalistic or mystical interpretations of experience of reality is not supported by the forces characteristic of the contemporary world.

This is not to say that people in the future will not experience the unrestricted in value from the perspectives of the supernatural and the mystical. It is to say, however, that such experience and expression must contest with alternative interpretations of the world and will thus lose their sense of obviousness and certainty. How religions respond to this contestation will provide one answer to the question of the future of religion.

We have used specific religious traditions as examples of this point. However, you will find that it holds true for the experience of civil religions as well as noninstitutionalized religious experience and expression. The myths of a community's founding or its manifest destiny may similarly invoke the supernatural or the mystical, as is the case in the United States and Japan. Thus the contest will reverberate through the most inclusive institutions of government and law. This is another element in the answer to the question of the future of religion.

A second example of how the experience and expression of the unrestricted in value is affected by the present world appears in the jostling of religious traditions among themselves in a pluralistic environment. As the world is further defined by interdependence and interlaced by communication systems, the divergence of religious expression becomes an unavoidable fact encountered in personal and communal experience. Differences in religious expressions and the cognitive dissonance produced by their interaction becomes an experiential and not just theoretical reality. How does one adjust to this reality or adjudicate the disparity of claims? Response to this question will in part provide an answer to the question of the future of religion.

We began this section by asserting that the future of religion will appear within the metaphorical journey of human creativity as it moves from what has been, through what is possible, to what will be. To clarify the notion of journey out of the present, we discussed its basic constituents—world, individual, community, and unrestricted value. Having thus set the context for the question of the future of religion, we are now prepared to sketch our response.

IMAGINING THE FUTURE OF RELIGION

What follows in this section is an imaginative projection; it is an informed speculation about what might be as drawn from hints, spun from trends and tendencies, and boldly cast forward as an interpretive net attempting to snare an always elusive future. Building upon the preceding section and some additional assumptions to be noted at the outset, we will envision the future of religion and the possible role it suggests for the field of religious studies.

No claims are made for this vision other than that it has been helpful to us in attempting to gain imaginative access to an otherwise inaccessible future. It is not the only scenario that could be projected. If you find it wrongheaded, or are offended by its limitations, we encourage you to project some helpful scenarios of your own.

BASIC ASSUMPTIONS

Our vision of the future of religion assumes that the threat of the world does not eliminate its promise. That is to say, we proceed as if the possibility of global holocaust or nuclear genocide will be avoided. The future of religion and that of humankind are so linked that a termination of the human is also the termination of religion.

Our vision of the future of religion assumes that the major forces characterizing the world at present will continue into the future. The presence of technology and the understanding of science will continue to grow and fundamentally inform the world of the future. The process of secularization, the reality of pluralism, and the experience of the relativity of cultural traditions will affect the self-definition of more and more people on the globe. The order of influence of this "world" will expand.

Our vision of the future of religion assumes that the human experience of the unrestricted in value will continue, and that its symbolic expression will increase in variety. Increased diversity will characterize religion in the future. While the modes of expression through story, ritual, belief, scripture, morality, art, and literature may remain unchanged, their content will change. While particular religious traditions will perpetuate themselves, new traditions will join the conversations of the future and old traditions will change.

Our vision of the future sees the vitality of religion rising in a continual dialogue of conversation, and in competition or contestation. The energy and focus of this dialogue and contestation will be varied for individuals and communities. Individuals and communities will not only discourse with the powers of the world, but with and among themselves. Religious traditions will control and influence by the power of persuasion. Individuals will consent and commit on the basis of personal experience and reflection.

Our vision of the future sees the role of the field of religion as an important element in the many dialogues and contestations characterizing the new time. The study of religion will focus its critical attention on the experience of the human condition. This experience will be investigated phenomenologically, historically, psychologically, sociologically, and philosophically through textual, laboratory, and field studies so that the widest range of data and methods are brought to the dialogue. Comparative studies will flourish in a context that encourages the individual student toward an analytic, experimental, and experiential search for truth.

A DIALOGUE

Our vision of the future of religion emphasizes the concept of dialogue—an open conversation in which the parties are willing to consider alternatives to and modification of their positions. Dialogue involves a mutual exchange that may range from sharing information to engaging in argumentation. It may produce significant change or yield little modification in the positions of the conversational partners. Every instance of dialogue involves the interaction of symbols in expression and response. This concept of dialogue is the key to our scenario of the future of religion.

In our vision of the future, the term *dialogue* functions both metaphorically and literally. Metaphorically it can be said that a religious tradition (for example, Christianity) is in dialogue with the forces of secularization if the members of this tradition are seriously considering the implications of these forces for their own religious self-understandings and response to the world. In this metaphorical usage the emphasis is upon the openness to study; to learn or "listen to" the implicit claims brought by the symbolic expressions of science and the realities of technology to the interpretation of the human condition, and to make an appropriate response. Clearly the forces of secularization or a tradition do not literally speak. However, if one views tradition as a generalization over a human membership, and views the perspective of scientific technology as the product of human imagination, thought, and action, then the possibility of our metaphorical use of dialogue manifests itself.

Metaphorical dialogue is important to our vision of the future, but so is literal dialogue. In this case it means actual conversations between and among people of various traditions, within a tradition itself, and of different religious persuasions. The forms of these dialogues may be official, as in the case of an ecumenical council, or unofficial, as in the case of the discussion among coworkers or friends. Dialogue can occur within an institutional religious setting, in a living room, or in a classroom. We claim that dialogue, metaphorically and literally, provides the keystone for understanding the future of religion. Dialogue will increase in number and intensity in the future. In our scenario dialogue will be the chief characteristic of the future of religion.

In making this assertion about dialogue we are well aware that in the future some religious individuals and groups will reject the option of dialogue. It is not our claim that everyone will pursue this option. There will always be people and communities whose contact with the forces of modernity and other religious persuasions will cause a fanatical rejection, making dialogue impossible. Today, this defensive reaction is particularly understandable from groups in developing countries. The strangeness or novelty of "the modern," and the magnitude of religious pluralism, provides for a potentially shocking experience. In addition, one must account for different degrees of literacy and flexibility of response within symbol systems. There is a sense in which dialogue demands a level of familiarity requiring time; it cannot be rushed. Thus individuals and communities will find themselves at different stages with respect to readiness for dialogue. Our point, however, is that the forces of the future, unless thrust into a context of global crisis or tragedy that reintroduces the inflexible and the fanatical as more plausible alternatives, lead inevitably toward the logic of dialogue.

The impetus for the dialogues of the future will be found both within the religious traditions themselves and in the world. The world as a secular context appears to the perspective of religions as lacking a degree of legitimation which only religious expression can bring to its institutions and its sense of destiny. While one may not reject the functions and values of the institutions of the world, human beings have sought and will seek for a deeper, more religious understanding of the world. Where function is elevated to the exclusive interpretation of the world—and we can expect some individuals to attempt such exclusive elevation—response to such "reductionist" or exclusive evaluations, will be understood as logical from the perspective of religion. Where the persistent experience of the human continues to pose such existential questions as, "What is the ultimate destiny of humankind? or, "Is life finally meaningful in the face of evil, suffering, and the tragedies of this world?" institutional postures inherently incapable of addressing these issues will be understood as themselves part of the question and therefore in need of more adequate interpretation.

As religious communities attempt to mount persuasive challenges to criticize and augment the self-interpretation of the forces of the world, they will find themselves engaged in at least three different types of dialogues. The first type will involve communities with the individual members of their own traditions; the second type will involve the members of other religious traditions; and the third type will involve representatives of the world's institutions. Let us consider each of these types of dialogue and assess how they give form to religion in the future.

The experience of the relativity of all cultural traditions, which the process of secularization and the reality of pluralism have brought to the inhabitants of the modern world, has forced upon individuals not only a loss of certainty but a demand for discussion and choice within traditions that is unparalleled in previous worlds. In this situation the individual members of religious communities become fundamentally responsible for the state of the tradition in transmission. It drives the individual to reflect upon his or her personal experience in conversation with those originating experiences, or paradigm experiences, that the tradition seeks to represent. To take this demand seriously is to let loose within traditional communities forces of potential change or transformation. Traditional authority, if not consensual or persuasive, inevitably comes under challenge. The mode of the experimental and the role of the experiential are elevated within this type of dialogue. They will have a fundamental effect on the symbolic expression of the communities, their liturgy and ritual, their beliefs and moral codes, the whole spectrum of representative expression.

Does such a dialogue weaken or strengthen religion in the future? Response to this question will vary depending upon your perspective. If one views the strength of religion in terms of the ability of a traditional religious community to command compliance, to the point of a unifed assimilation of members to the party position, then the fact of dialogue of this first type must be understood as a step toward anarchy and an inevitable weakening of religion. Such a dialogue, if encouraged or allowed to continue, would be heretical or subversive, producing a dissolution of truth and value. The opposite view would understand such dialogue as a major opportunity for a reawakening or a rebirth of tradition in a mode more sensitive to personal experience and confession. What appears as anarchy from the first point of view is here regarded as critical reaffirmation and growth. Within this first type of dialogue, how one answers the question of whether religion will grow stronger or weaker in the future will depend upon the particular perspective one brings to the issue of the authority of a tradition.

In our vision, any activity leading people to a novel expression or critical reaffirmation of religious symbols adds to the general vitality of religion. While hierarchical traditional authority will be challenged, noetic traditional authority (that confirmed in the experience of members) will be championed. In this type of dialogue it is not necessary that either perspective overcome the other for change as growth to appear. We see the tension between the perspectives in this dialogue producing a dynamic for significant religious expression in the future.

The second type of dialogue occurs between and among the religious traditions themselves. The contemporary experience of the relativity of human traditions, religious and secular alike, does not impugn the worth or importance of the traditional. Rather, it confirms a central tenet of religious experience: to attempt to express the unrestricted in value within the restrictions of human symbolic expression is to acknowledge the necessity for a continual iconoclastic or prophetic tension with respect to one's own religious tradition as well as others. As individuals experience the "shrinking" of the globe and the actualities of pluralism, the momentum toward questioning the claims and counterclaims of particular religious traditions accelerates. While this situation might seem to present an almost impossible cacophany of competing voices, overwhelming to the sensitive ear, the logic of dialogue suggests that the individual will "hear" only those "voices" that she or he is capable of discriminating and identifying. The responsibility of an individual in this second type of dialogue will vary according to the individual's capacity to differentiate the voices calling for a response.

The study of religion, whether formal or informal, whether organized within an academic curriculum or pursued on one's own, has the effect of increasing both the range and the quality of an individual's responsibility. While studies can provide information, develop skills of interrogation, suggest strategies of interpretation, and thus expand the range of dialogue, they cannot make the response in dialogue. Religion remains confessional; a person or people symbolically express their personal perception of the unrestricted in value. The study of religion creates for its students an appreciation of the expanded range of voices and, at the same time, introduces a demand for a richer response. Religious studies increase an individual's responsibility by sensitizing him or her for dialogue. Education abets dialogue. It challenges narrowness and ignorance by introducing the discomfort of the novel and demanding a dialogue of growth. In our vision, the study of religion will strengthen the vitality of religion in the future by engaging people in sensitive and critical dialogue of the second type.

The third type of dialogue involves individuals and communities with representatives of the forces of the secular world. Those who would speak for the opportunities of scientific technology in shaping the future of the human, or in directing the destiny of the planet, require a response from religious communities and individuals. While such responses may take the forms of simple opposition or affiliation, our vision sees religiously mature persons entering the dialogue through the perspective of experimentation and experience. While the process of secularization has relativized the religious traditions, it has also stripped the spokespeople of science, technology, politics, and economics of their mantle of infallibility. The future is humbling in the sense that "the answer" has fled before the face of experience in search of innocence and naivete. Humility, however, brings the possibility of constructive and imaginative dialogue among students of the human condition. The sciences, natural and social, have presented a picture of the human that would have been unintelligible to those religious virtuosi of the past who inspired and gave form to much religious expression of our time. Does this mean that religious expression is an anachronistic or antiquarian voice not worthy of an active role in dialogue with the modern images of the human? Not at all! Our vision of the future sees a dialogue between the knowledge of the sciences and the wisdom embodied in the symbolic expressions of religion. As human experience is consulted as a guide for directing the future, the repositories of past experience (tradition) are found to harbor helpful hints and insights in such areas as ecology, depth psychology, cosmology, and epistemology. Similarly, as this dialogue finds the language of modern science unlocking new perspective on religious expression, the vitality of religion will be enhanced through the mutual cocreation of knowledge and understanding.

Once again, our vision projects an important role for the field of religious studies in promoting dialogues of this third type. In the colleges and universities of the future the study of religion will be understood from an increasingly interdisciplinary perspective. Scholars identified as professors of religion will themselves be in an expanded dialogue, not only with their colleagues in the humanities but with those who inhabit the laboratories of the natural sciences and those whose laboratories are the public institutions. The human condition will be recognized as a central target of significant opportunity for cooperative exploration. The data considered and produced by such studies will themselves fuel the dialogue of the members of the contemporary society.

Our vision of the future of religion has focused on the prominent presence of dialogue and has not explored in any detail forces in the world that would inhibit its development. This is not because we do not anticipate such a negative presence. Fear, pride, prejudice, arrogance, greed, and insensitivity have plagued the human condition since the dawn of historical record. We do not imagine that they will miraculously disappear from the future. Indeed, they will stalk the possibility of dialogue at every turn and make menacingly real the threat of the contemporary world. The promise of the present, however, has not yet capitulated to these forces and thus demands that a narrative of hope inform our imaginings of the future. Our scenario projects this hope through the vehicle of dialogue, but stops short of seeing the results of these varied conversations. Such results are for the future generations to confirm with their studies or by their imposed absence.

SUMMARY

In this chapter we have attempted to respond to the question of the future of religion. We acknowledged that while such a question could at best be approached through imaginative anticipation and critical speculation, it was, nevertheless, legitimate and important because it sensitized the student to trends and tendencies in the present expression of religion and forced critical self-reflection upon the field of study itself. We created a scenario of the future of religion by imagining it as a metaphorical journey of human creativity out of the present described in terms of its constituents—world, individual, community, and unrestricted value. In the context of this journey we expressed our scenario through the vehicle of dialogue and the possibilities it opens to humankind. These opportunities sketched forms of religious vitality and the role that religious may play in the evolution of these forms.

Our vision of the future of religion is but one attempt at imaginative anticipation and critical speculation. It is our hope that as you conclude the study of this text you will yourself attempt to develop a scenario of the future of religion and your role within it as a student of the field of religion. We began our study with an invitation. It is fitting that we conclude it by inviting you to participate in its future.

Index